Is there a single formula that builds irresistible success? A single formula that gives you many times the success power you ever had before? Napoleon Hill's great new book shows you that there is such a formula, what it is, why it works so well—and exactly how to use it for your own great break-through to wealth of every kind. "Know your own mind, live your own life," says Napoleon Hill. He shows you how, in being yourself, you find your best self. He gives you secrets of personal influence that can pyramid your powers far beyond anything you ever thought could be.

GROW RICH!
WITH PEACE
OF MIND

by Napoleon Hill

FAWCETT CREST • NEW YORK

Foreword

I began to plan this book in the closing years of the nineteenth century. It has thus been nearly seventy years in preparation. During those years I have witnessed more vital changes in the affairs of men than had taken place in all the previous years of the history of civilization. I have seen the advent of the automobile, the airplane, radio, television, atomic power, the age of space. I have seen electric power spread across the country, industry rise to levels of production beyond nineteenth-century dreams, science and technology enjoy an almost explosive development.

I have seen old nations disappear, new nations arise, jungles give way to paved roads, cities burgeon where sleepy villages once stood. And I have seen people adapt themselves to all these changes and go right on being people, just as they have been for uncounted thousands of years.

You will find this book takes cognizance of the changing world. In speaking of people, however, I speak of the forces which always have moved people and always will. We still see that without sufficient money our lives are mean and hemmed in, so we want success in earning money. And along with money-success we want to be free of fears, nervous tensions, self-induced illness, worries, unhappiness. That is, in addition to money-success we seek peace of mind to make our lives complete. While this book may help you win great wealth, it can help you win peace of mind in abounding measure.

As you will see, when we speak of peace of mind we speak of more than *peace* as a restful state. Peace of mind is at the same time restful and dynamic, or, we might say, a restful base upon which your life-dynamism stands. It has been called the wealth without which you cannot really be wealthy. It manifests itself in many ways:

> It is freedom from negative forces which may take possession of the mind, and from any such negative attitudes as worry and inferiority.
> It is freedom from any feeling of want.
> It is freedom from self-induced mental and physical ailments of the kind which chronically degrade life.

It is freedom from all fears, especially the seven basic fears we shall expose in all their ugliness.

It is freedom from the common human weakness of seeking something for nothing.

It is possession of the joy of work and accomplishment.

It is the habit of being one's self and doing one's own thinking.

It is the habit of checking one's attitudes toward life and toward one's fellow men, and always adjusting these attitudes for the better.

It is the habit of *helping others to help themselves!*

It is freedom from anxiety over what may happen to you after you die.

It is the habit of going the extra mile in all human relationships.

It is the habit of thinking in terms of what you wish to do, instead of thinking of the obstacles which may get in your way.

It is the habit of laughing at the petty misfortunes which may overtake you.

It is the habit of giving before trying to get.

Peace of mind covers a surprisingly broad field, doesn't it? In every way you use it, it helps you win money-success— and more. Peace of mind helps you live your life on your own terms, in values of your own choosing, so that every day your life grows richer and greater.

This volume is written by a man who has found peace of mind the hard way, by trial and error. Its purpose is to help others find their own peace of mind, along with money-success, by a shorter and less costly route. If some of the episodes seem ultra-personal, please remember that it is the seemingly small events of a man's life which make up the greater portion of his experiences.

In my own personal experiences you may see your own. Notice how small experiences conceal both success and failure. They are the first testing ground in which you are given the opportunity to prove that *you* are the master of your fate, *you* are the captain of your soul.

I realize that nobody wishes to take medicine prescribed by a doctor who does not take it himself when seeking the benefits he proclaims. The "medicine" given herein is the "medicine" proved by its marvelous effect upon myself and thousands of others.

Thanks to circumstances I have had the aid of more than five hundred of the most successful men in America. These men allowed me to go behind the curtains of their private lives and see for myself both their good qualities and their weaknesses; their successes and their failures; how they enjoyed or did not enjoy using their money; how this factor related itself to their possession or nonpossession of peace of mind.

It was with the Science of Personal Achievement, built on my interviews and research, that I have helped thousands of men and women whip poverty, wipe out the effects of a negatively conditioned childhood, solve problems, rise above circumstances which held them back.

Let me say I did this many years after I myself had risen above a heritage of five evils—you may know some or all of them—

Poverty	Illiteracy
Ignorance	Hopelessness
Fear	

As a youngster I was often hungry. There was a time when I ate bark I scraped off birch trees. Until I reached my teens I continued to be hungry.

I am still hungry! Not for physical food, but for mental food; food for a searching mind which still seeks to know more about why some men succeed and some fail, some have inward peace and some have inward conflict. But I have left my childhood handicaps far behind.

There came a time when one of the world's richest men, Andrew Carnegie, backed me in a plan to find the secrets of money-success and life-success. I have been an adviser to three United States Presidents, William Howard Taft, Woodrow Wilson, and Franklin D. Roosevelt, and I helped the first President of the Philippines to attain freedom for his people.

There was a period in which I courted fame. I craved for it, prayed for it and worked endlessly to achieve it. At long last my mail came from all over the world, sackfuls, more than I ever could read, let alone answer. Promoters looking for my co-operation came by the score, merchants offered me all kinds of credit and many offered to buy my endorsement of their wares.

My tastes now are different. It was when I found that if I wanted any sleep I could not have a telephone registered in my name that I began to appreciate peace of mind.

Yet while I courted fame I never stopped writing. Book followed book in my effort to tell the world what I had learned about success, about the value of a positive state of mind, about human relations. Here is a list of the books I have written—*The Law of Success* (8 volumes); *Think and Grow Rich; How to Sell Your Way Through Life; The Master-Key to Riches; How to Raise Your Own Salary; Mental Dynamite* (16 volumes); *Science of Personal Achievement;* and a seventeen-lesson course now being taught in home study and local class groups in the U.S. and many other countries.

The passing years have helped me judge the value of these books and gauge their effect upon their readers. They have helped hundreds of thousands, perhaps millions, to build lives of happiness and success. I have been interested, all this while, in finding out which of the many items of advice have turned out to be most useful and of most universal application. I have checked carefully to see which anecdotes and types of anecdotes have provided the upward turning point at which a man finds himself and *goes*.

This book represents, in part, a careful choice of items which have stood the test of time. In reading these items you will know that they in particular have something which takes hold in the mind and builds the power of the mind to will the best and find it.

Also you will find much that is new. The world changes—not in principle, but in certain aspects which bring different kinds of opportunities to the seeking man. More money-making opportunities have arisen in the United States during the past two decades than existed in all of our previous history, and still they swarm thick and fast. You will acquire a vast vision for these opportunities as you read this book.

You will find, if you have read my previous works, that this one has a new and different objective, emphasizing values which money alone cannot buy. All of my books show in many ways that there is more to life than making money. This book proves the point far more fully than I was able to prove it years ago—and shows, too, that peace of mind in itself is a mighty force in helping you make money.

I have said this book has been nearly seventy years in the planning. Quite true, but until recently I did not know it. I believe we all are guided by invisible sources of inspiration, and recently there came to me inspiration from a strange and very real source, revealing how much of my life has been spent in preparing to write these pages, urging me to uncover my typewriter and get to work.

The man who speaks to you is in his eighties. His life remains full and hearty. His possessions—of which he surely has enough—have not taken away the thrill of accomplishment. The book is the first step of accomplishment; the best of the accomplishment comes in knowing that this book will bring wealth and happiness to those who read and think.

I am ready now to write more clearly and maturely than ever was possible to me before. Join me and we will go on a fascinating journey together . . . a journey towards riches . . . a journey toward the fulfillment of your dearest dreams . . . a journey toward a Supreme Secret which gives you mastery of life itself.

Contents

1

Know Your Own Mind, Live Your Own Life

You have a great potential for success, but first you must know your own mind and live your own life—then you will find and enjoy that mighty potential. Become acquainted with your inner self and you can win what you want within a time limit of your own choosing. Certain special techniques help you win the goals of your dearest dreams, and every one of these techniques is easily within your power.

SOMEWHERE along the path of life, every *successful* man finds out how to live his own life as he wishes to live it.

The younger you are when you discover this mighty power, the more likely you are to live successfully and happily. Yet even in later years, many make the great change—from letting others make them what they are, to making sure that they make their lives to their own liking.

The Creator gave man the prerogative of power over his own mind. It must have been the Creator's purpose to encourage man to live his own life, think his own thoughts, find his own goals and achieve them. Simply by exercising this profound prerogative you can bring abundance into your life, and with it know the greatest wealth of all, peace of mind, without which there can be no real happiness.

You live in a world filled with outside influences which impinge upon you. You are influenced by other people's acts and wishes, by law and custom, by your duties and your responsibilities. Everything you do has some effect upon others, as do their actions upon you. And yet you must find out how to live your own life, use your own mind, go on toward the dream *you* wish to make real and solid. *Know thyself,* said the ancient Greek philosophers, and this remains key advice for the man who would be in all ways wealthy. Without knowing yourself and being yourself, you cannot truly use the one Great Secret which gives you power to mold your future and make life carry you the way you want to go.

9

Let us then take off on our trip to Happy Valley!

Do not think of me as a back-seat driver. Rather, you are at the wheel and I merely call your attention to a trustworthy road map whereon the main highway is marked beyond question. On your journey to riches and peace of mind, the road grows smoother and straighter as you travel.

Never believe you don't have what it takes. Probably you are reading under an electric light. You know that Thomas A. Edison gave the first practical electric light to the world. But did you know that Edison was thrown out of school in the early grades after his teacher decided he had an "addled" mind and could not take schooling?

This then was the impact of another person's opinion upon Thomas Edison—to let him know with the voice of authority that he didn't have what it takes to absorb even a primary education! Where would he have been if he had allowed this directive to take charge of his thinking?

Fortunately for him and fortunately for the world, Edison decided to live his own life. Through early adversity, Edison discovered something he might never have learned through formal schooling. He learned, first, that he had a mind he could control and direct toward any desired end. Then he learned he could use the technical training of other men and successfully direct scientific research even though he himself never had been schooled in any of the sciences. When he took full possession of that "addled" mind it produced not only the incandescent lamp but also one great discovery after another.

A boy finds a friend and finds himself. I too was nearly doomed by a false label of unworthiness. I was then nine years old. My mother had died a year before, and I lived with relatives. To them and to my own father I was a problem child who never would accomplish anything save, perhaps, what a life of crime can accomplish.

I was doing my best to live up to my reputation as the successor of Jesse James. I even had a six-shooter which I had learned to handle like an expert. Then a certain woman came upon the scene and she changed my life. That woman was my stepmother.

Long before she arrived I had been thoroughly conditioned by my relatives to hate her. I found this very easy to do. She arrived, and my father brought her to our house where the relatives had gathered to meet her. He introduced her all around. At length he found me, where I stood in a corner doing my very best to look tough.

"And here," said my father, "is your stepson, Napoleon, beyond doubt the meanest boy in Wise County. We don't expect much good from him. I wouldn't be surprised if he starts throwing rocks at you by tomorrow morning."

At that moment, I believe my life hung in the balance.

It was a wise and wonderful woman who placed her hand under my stubborn chin and raised my head so that she could look me squarely in the eyes. She said only a few words, but they lifted me onto an entirely new level.

Turning to my father, my stepmother said: "You are wrong about this boy. He is not the meanest boy in Wise County or anywhere else. He is a very alert and intelligent boy, and all he needs is some worthy objective toward which to direct his very good mind."

That was the first time in my life that anyone had said anything good about me. I straightened up, threw out my chest and grinned. Then and there I sensed that "that woman" who had come to take my mother's place—as my relatives referred to her—was one of those rare people who can help others find the best that is in them.

That was the end of my six-shooter days. Increasingly finding myself as I grew older, I discovered my talent for writing. My stepmother helped me master the typewriter. With the aid of the typewriter I became a writer for newspapers. Through that experience I qualified to interview successful men, and thus I came to sit down with Andrew Carnegie. Out of that interview—which ran on through the better part of three days and nights—came my commitment to search out the secret of successful achievement, not merely as a matter of words, but as a pattern of definite action in the lives of men who have achieved great wealth. Out of this grew the organization of the Science of Personal Achievement which has reverberated around the world, bringing prosperity and peace of mind to millions of men and women.

Great artists also live their own lives, or they could not be great. One of the great opera stars of all time, Madame Schumann-Heink, as a young girl went to a music teacher to have her voice tested. He listened a few minutes, then said brusquely: "That's enough! Go back to your sewing machine. You may become a first-class seamstress. A singer, no!"

Remember, that was the voice of authority speaking. The girl could have been forgiven for deciding then and there that she would never sing again. Yet she had and kept possession of her own mind. She became all the more determined that she would learn to sing and to sing well. This she did, and the world became richer. So it has been with many another case in which great personal talent might have been lost forever if the possessor of that talent had not felt it even when the "experts" said it was not there.

Adversity? It's a tonic, not a stumbling block! Every adversity carries the seed of an equal or greater benefit. Very few march straight to success without going through periods of temporary failure and discouragement. Yet when you are in possession of your inner self there is no such thing as a knockout blow. You may be knocked down, but you can bounce right back. You may detour on rough roads, but you always can find your way back to the paved highway.

You may think this applies only to simple matters. Think, then, of the infinitely complex matter of winning the independence of a colonial territory—and not only that, but of focusing the many scattered influences which make sure you become the country's first President.

In 1910 I became the personal counselor of Manuel L. Quezon. I not only counseled him politically but, perhaps more importantly, I taught him the Science of Personal Achievement which then was quite new.

Señor Quezon was the first President of the Philippine Islands when they gained their freedom. In 1910, however, that time was far in the future. The goal of freeing his people possessed Quezon's mind, and he saw himself as the first President of the new nation. I assured him he could realize both ambitions, yet we knew that such great events do not come to pass overnight.

There is a well-recognized power in setting up a definite goal. Few, however, realize the power of setting a realistic time limit in which one intends to attain that goal. After having counseled Señor Quezon for some years, I induced him to set a definite time limit for freeing the Philippines and becoming the new nation's leader. I also prepared an affirmation which he repeated to himself daily. It closed with a statement of this nature: "I will allow no person's opinion, no influence to enter my mind which does not harmonize with my purpose." Both the time limit and the affirmation were of great help to Quezon in knowing his own mind and keeping his own direction in the face of the enormous difficulties which beset him.

Twenty-four years and six months from the day Quezon began to use the Science of Personal Achievement, he became the first President of the free Philippine Islands.

Coincidence? Coincidence despite a world war which intervened and many other factors which were not foreseeable? I do not think it was a coincidence, for I have seen this principle of Personal Achievement work for so many people in so many different situations that coincidence must be ruled out.

We shall touch upon the principle again. Right now I shall tell you about just one man, presently doing business in Chicago, who has used it with notable success.

W. Clement Stone was in high school when he discovered his own goals, his own direction in which the powers of his own mind would take him. Soon he was selling insurance at such a rate that he made more money than his teachers. Today his fortune is estimated at more than $160 million and it is increasing rapidly.

In 1939, however, he faced disaster. At that time he was the head of an agency, representing a big casualty company, which sold a special accident and health policy. One day the parent company "pulled the string" and terminated his contract with two weeks' notice.

Mr. Stone did not have large reserves. It was imperative to keep that contract going. He spent forty-five minutes in refreshing his contact with his inner self; then he decided that within those critical two weeks he would persuade the casualty company it was against their own best interest to terminate his contract. The company had very cogent reasons for ending the contract. Nevertheless, they did change their minds as he wished them to and Stone kept on marching toward his fortune.

He then decided that by 1956 he would own his own big health and accident insurance company. By 1956 he did.

He decided that by 1956 he would have $10 million dollars of his own. He did.

I heard recently that Mr. Stone has set up a lifetime goal of $600 million. I do not know his deadline date, but I have no doubt that on or before that date he will have the stated sum; and further, that he will use a good part of it as he always has used his money—to benefit mankind. The concept of $600 million may frighten a man who thinks small, but a man who knows the secrets of Personal Achievement merely says: *Why not?*

A little while ago I made a survey for the purpose of learning who were the ten men who had made the most outstanding application of the Science of Personal Achievement in the United States.

W. Clement Stone was third from the top of the list. The other two were Andrew Carnegie, the sponsor of my twenty years of research, and Thomas Alva Edison, the greatest inventor of all time.

I met Mr. Stone for the first time in 1953. It was then that I began to unravel the dramatic story of his rise to fame and fortune, starting in business for himself with only one hundred dollars in cash and a copy of my most popular book, *Think and Grow Rich.* I was so intrigued by the effective application Stone had made of my success philosophy that I accepted his offer to help him take the Science of Personal Achievement to his entire insurance personnel.

The task covered ten years during which I devoted all of my time to helping Mr. Stone indoctrinate his entire organization with my success philosophy. It was a tremendous job but it paid off in terms which proved conclusively that my twenty years of research under the direction of Andrew Carnegie had uncovered a miraculous formula for helping people to get from where they were to where they wished to be in life.

When I first began my association with Mr. Stone, many of his top executives frowned upon the alliance as being a waste of time. They had never heard of a success philosophy based upon what five hundred outstanding men had learned from a lifetime of experience through the trial and error method, and they were naturally suspicious of it.

Five years later these same executives met with Mr. Stone and myself in a business conference. To my great surprise Mr. Stone arose and addressed himself to the group. "Gentlemen," said he, "the Combined Insurance Company of America is now performing miracles." Then a long pause, after which he said—"The company was performing no miracles before Napoleon Hill came here."

When I began my association with Mr. Stone the annual premium income from policy holders was around $24 million, and Mr. Stone's personal fortune was estimated to be around $3 million. When the association was discontinued by mutual consent ten years later, the annual premium income of the company was around $84 million and Mr. Stone's personal fortune was estimated to be more than $160 million.

How much did I get from the association? you may wish to ask. The cash I received was negligible in comparison with that which Mr. Stone received, but I was not working for monetary reward; I was after something far greater than that which could have been gained by any amount of money, for I had proved during those ten years of association with Mr. Stone that the Science of Personal Achievement could perform miracles for those who embraced it and made intelligent application of it.

More important still, I had laid the foundation for the Napoleon Hill Academy, which is now organizing and conducting franchise schools for the teaching of the Science of Personal Achievement throughout the United States and eventually will reach throughout the free world. The far-flung significance of these schools may be brought into understandable focus by the fact that the Science of Personal Achievement has turned out to be a perfect antidote for communism; something I had not anticipated when I began the organization of the philosophy in 1908. Which reminds me that, truly, "man proposes but God disposes."

It may well be that the Science of Personal Achievement will become a strong factor in neutralizing the cancerous evil known as communism, which now threatens the liberty of all mankind.

The Science of Personal Achievement is already under option to a group of men who are having it translated into Spanish for the purpose of taking it to the people of all Spanish-speaking countries, starting with our Latin-American friends of the South. I plan eventually to have the philosophy translated into all the major languages of the world.

So, who is wise enough to say what I got from my ten years of association with W. Clement Stone, or wise enough to understand the hand of fate which brought the two of us together?

The dramatic story of Arnold Reed. Arnold Reed is another insurance executive whose life story and its relation to the Science of Personal Achievement parallels that of W. Clement Stone. In many respects his story, as it related to the success philosophy, is more dramatic than the Stone story.

Mr. Reed was a top-ranking life insurance salesman, with a record of sales production seldom equaled by anyone in this field. Mr. Reed's sales started at around one million dollars annually and pyramided upward far beyond this amount. He was associated with an insurance company headed by a man whom he regarded as his personal friend.

Unfortunately (or was it?) Arnold had not read carefully the fine print of his contract with the company, for he learned later that it contained a clause which deprived him of his renewal premium commissions, the one factor in the insurance salesman's work which gives him his greatest incentive to do a good job.

This discovery shocked Arnold so severely that he went home and went to bed, refusing to eat or to communicate with his friends. Doctors were called in to diagnose his ailment but not one of them could find anything wrong with him physically. It was not his body that was sick, it was his soul, for the shock he had experienced through the perfidy of his friend had cut the line of communication between him and the source of inspiration which had made him a great life insurance salesman; *that source which alone can make men truly great!*

Slowly but surely Arnold Reed was dying.

His ailment was one that no doctor could cure. The doctors who had attended him knew this and frankly admitted they could offer no hope. Then a miracle happened. A friend of Arnold's, who had long been a student of my success philosophy, visited Arnold and presented him with *Think and Grow Rich.* "Here is a book," he told Arnold, "which has worked wonders for me and I want you to read it."

Arnold took the book, threw it on the bed beside him and turned away without comment. Hours later he picked up the book, opened it and, lo! something in it caught his eye and he read it through. Then he read it again, and again, and on the third time around he felt the surge of a power which he readily recognized as one which could bring him out of the dungeon of despair into which he had fallen.

He got out of bed and began to write letters to his friends who knew of his record as a life insurance salesman, offering them an opportunity to join with him in organizing a life insurance company under the name of Great Commonwealth Life Insurance Company.

The friends responded quickly and generously. The amount of money needed was oversubscribed and much of it had to be returned to the senders. All of this took place at about the time I was beginning my alliance with W. Clement Stone.

Now, some twelve years later, the Great Commonwealth Life Insurance Company is one of the most successful in its field, with a gross premium income of over $9 million in 1966, and rapidly increasing toward the new goal which Arnold Reed has set at a billion dollars annually.

The company is operating in a major portion of the United States and it has a sales organization of over four hundred dedicated men and women who have tuned in and drawn upon that mysterious power that brought Arnold Reed out of the shadows of death; and they are doing a job that is without parallel in the insurance industry.

The Great Commonwealth Life Insurance Company conducts schools in many parts of the country in which new recruits to its sales force are trained. The first thing each trainee receives is a copy of *Think and Grow Rich* and a briefing on what this book has done for Arnold Reed and the company.

The last time I spoke to the sales organization of the Great Commonwealth, Arnold Reed marched onto the platform holding me by the arm. He held up a copy of *Think and Grow Rich* as he said, "My friends, if it had not been for this book and my dear friend here on my left, there would have been no Great Commonwealth Life Insurance Company and I would now be six feet under the ground."

It was the shortest and the most dramatic introduction I had ever experienced, and it filled me so deeply with emotion that I could hardly begin my speech.

Arnold Reed is a truly great leader of men, as evidenced by the phenomenal record he has established with Great Commonwealth. The main secret of his leadership is his belief in what he is doing and his sincerity in his relationship with his associates, two qualities without which no man may become a great leader at any level of life.

A success-conscious mind functions rapidly and effectively. In my hundreds of interviews with men who had made fortunes, I noticed how well their minds were focused on success. Some of these men were well educated. Some, for example Henry Ford, were notably uninformed in some areas of "school learning." It never was the formal education or the lack of it which gave these men the power to use their minds with such drive and effect, nor was it unusual intelligence. What was it, then, which impelled their minds to seize upon great goals, then winnow all the circumstances of life and make use of what could help them achieve their ambitions? It was *success consciousness.*

First you must know your own mind; then you find success consciousness. When Henry Ford mastered the art of making a good, inexpensive automobile, he still went on using his success consciousness. He had to make sure his cars were well distributed and their sale pushed in every part of the country. For this he needed capital. The bankers had capital to lend, but he did not want outside financial interests to take hold of his company.

Ford's truly efficient mind showed him the way to get the capital he needed even while he built up his distributing organization. First, he allotted his entire output of automobiles only to distributors who held the Ford franchise. Then he made it clear that each distributor must accept a fixed quota of cars, advancing in cash a percentage of the purchase price before the cars were delivered.

This plan made every distributor practically a partner in the Ford business, yet it did not affect Mr. Ford's control of the business. Again, without affecting his control, it provided him with the necessary operating capital. Moreover, it provided his dealers with a very definite incentive toward finding a buyer for every car—actually the same incentive they would have had if they had been operating their own independent businesses.

I have heard it said that this plan worked a hardship on some of the Ford distributors. Having known some dealers since before the Model T car, however, and having looked at today's record, I can say that most Ford dealers are noteworthy for their success.

Two bicycle mechanics, Orville and Wilbur Wright, gave the world its first successful airplane. What kept their minds clicking, caused them first to build the world's first wind tunnel, caused them to find a secret of wingtip control which nobody else had thought of? What caused them to surmount limitations of material and of power which still make that first flight look "impossible"? First they took control of their own minds and their own lives; then they were guided by the success consciousness which always follows.

Is today's world different? Only in some details. Take such a device as a memory core, a tiny magnetic gadget which operates by the thousands in many modern computers. The

Wright brothers did not know of such things, nor did Henry Ford or Andrew Carnegie or Thomas Edison. A young man named Merlyn Mickelson, in 1955, looked at the rapidly dawning computer age and saw what every age offers—a need and a way to fill it. He started to manufacture memory cores in his basement. His first investment in tools and supplies came to $7.21. His first employees were friends and neighboring housewives who "pitched in." Today, not yet forty, Mr. Mickelson still makes memory cores. He is President and 75 per cent owner of a $16-million-a-year company, and the company stock he holds is worth about $47 million.

Can success consciousness be instilled into a mind already filled with a record of failure? When you come to know your own mind and live your own life, you can wipe out a record of failure just as surely as you can erase the message on a tape recorder, leaving a wonderfully receptive tape—or mind—to receive new and better impressions.

Some people have been able to do this for themselves. Others need help. I well remember a man I helped to find himself. As you will see, I got him started and once he knew where he was going, he did the rest.

This was a dead-broke man just out of the Army. I believe he used the Army as a refuge, but eventually he was back in civilian clothes, looking for a job. The mere mention of "hard times" seemed to be enough to flatten him. He was shabby. He was hungry. He was willing to settle for crumbs if only he could get them.

He came to see me about finding work. At the outset he announced: "All I want is a place to sleep and enough to eat."

A place to sleep and enough to eat—in a world that throbs with riches!

Something prompted me to ask: "Why settle for a meal ticket? How would you like to become a millionaire?"

He looked at me with glassy eyes, swaying. "Please don't joke with me."

"I assure you I'm serious. Every man has some kind of assets, and every man can turn his assets into a million dollars or many millions if he uses them correctly."

He sighed. "What do you mean by assets? I have a nickel in my pocket."

"Bring your mind around to the positive side," I said, "and you have the most important asset you'll ever have. We'll work on that. Now let's take inventory of your skills. Sit down, we'll talk better. What did you do in the Army?"

He had been a cook. Before going into the Army he had been a Fuller Brush salesman. He was a good cook, I discovered, but obviously he had not been a good salesman. Still, he knew something about selling and in talking to him I discovered he still wanted to sell. At the outset, however, he had no belief he ever could become a good salesman. The memory of past failures inhibited him and I had to help him break those self-inflicted mental blocks and see, not what he had been, but what he could be.

We talked for some time and meanwhile my own mind was busily at work. My mind was not weakened by hunger and hopelessness. There had been a time when my mind had known as much despair as did his; but now I was filled with success consciousness.

Questing about, my uninhibited mind remembered that special new kinds of cookware were now being developed. A new kind of cookware of great benefit to the housewife—a man who could talk about cooking and even demonstrate—a man who could be made into a good salesman—and there we had the winning combination.

"Suppose you represented a company that makes a new kind of aluminum cookware," I said. "This cookware offers many advantages. It should be seen in action; then it will practically sell itself. Any housewife, for a small consideration—say, some free pots or pans for her own use—should be glad to invite her neighbors in for a home-cooked dinner. You cook that dinner with the special cookware, and after dinner you take orders for complete, matched sets. If twenty ladies are present, I'm sure you could induce half of them to purchase. Some of these would be eager to run similar dinner parties in their own homes. The business would become self-perpetuating."

"Sounds okay," my young soldier friend replied. "But where am I going to sleep meanwhile? And where am I going to eat? And where am I going to get a few clean shirts and a new suit? Not to mention the question of where I am going to get some money or credit to get started on?"

Such questions are typical of the mind which does not yet know itself, and so sums up all the obstacles rather than looking directly at the goal.

"Get yourself into the right frame of mind," I said, "and you will either find what you need or find a way to do without and still achieve your goal. When your mind can truly picture a desired goal, and feel success consciousness driving it toward that goal, you can win that goal. Let us put aside all other matters and investigate your state of mind."

Actually the young man was very close to having the desired positive state of mind. I waited till I was sure he had it, however. Then I said he was a good risk, and I gave him the use of our guest room, and his meals. I let him use my charge account at Marshall Field's so that he could be well dressed. I guaranteed his note for his first outfit of cookware.

During his first week he cleared nearly one hundred dollars in profit. The second week he doubled that amount. In a little while he began to train other men and women, whom he managed. Most of all, he instilled in them the success consciousness which now had full hold of his mind, and as they prospered, so did he.

At the end of four years, the young man who had been so hungry and broken-spirited, so very far from being a millionaire, was worth more than four million dollars. Moreover, his newly keen and efficient mind had perfected a home-demonstration selling plan which now nets millions of dollars annually to a large corps of salespeople.

When the bells of heaven ring with joy. When a man finds his own mind and fills it with successful consciousness, or when another man helps him do so, I fancy that the bells of heaven ring with joy. Here is one more soul who has broken the chains forged by his fearful imagination.

Now you can see why I chose to begin this book by revealing what it means to take possession of your own mind, live your own life, find your real self that has no limitations. When you do this you have an asset worth *whatever values you choose to make it worth*.

Think again of what is involved in creating an independent nation. Think of ancient India with its teeming millions, under British rule for generation after generation. Think of the Mahatma Gandhi, a man who had no money, controlled no army, did not own a house, did not even own a pair of pants. Yet he had an asset which was greater than all the might of the British Empire—the capacity to take possession of his own mind and direct it toward purposes of his own choosing. He chose to free India, and he lived to see the achievement of his purpose.

Thanks to the influence of Mahatma Gandhi, my Science

of Personal Achievement now has many millions of followers in India. Whether your goal is money, the well-being of others, or a combination of these—as well it may be—know that there is nothing beyond the power of a mind that knows itself and believes in its own capabilities.

The spiritual defenses within the castle of your mind. I have purposely used the word "defenses" in order to call your attention to its varying meanings. A mind that is "on the defensive" is not an open mind. It is more likely to be a frightened mind, full of excuses and evasions, and hardly capable of lifting its possessor's eyes to the far horizons of accomplishment. In speaking of spiritual defenses, then, I speak of nothing that is negative: rather I speak of certain areas within which one may withdraw and thus become more completely one's *self*.

Every successful person I have known has surrounded himself with these spiritual defenses in one way or another. I adopted the system, and have found it invaluable. Here is how it works.

Consider your mind to be laid out in the pattern of some medieval castles. At the center there is a tower, or "keep," which is impregnable as it can be made. Going outward from the keep you would come to a wall not so formidable; and again going outward you would come to another wall which serves as the first line of defense.

A person approaching the castle first would have to pass the outer wall. This wall of *spiritual* defense in your mind need not be very high. Anyone who has a legitimate excuse for entering your mind with his ideas can climb this wall. If he does not have a legitimate excuse, however, the wall discourages him. When you set up such a wall, others come to know it is there and you give yourself a valuable protection.

A person who passes the first line of defense now confronts the second line which you may set up on certain occasions and not on others. When your mind sets up this wall, nobody may climb it unless that person has something strongly in common with you, or something importantly beneficial to share with you at that moment.

The inmost castle of protection is the most important of all. It is small, barely big enough to surround you, but when your mind retreats within that keep it is removed from every outside influence. With me, only the Creator can penetrate my inmost spiritual castle. Find yours and you find a source of great strength. Here is where you can find your inmost thoughts, undisturbed by outside influences; and until you find this castle you never can know them. Here is where you can search all the values of a problem and find a solution which otherwise you might not see. Here, especially, is where your fully possessed mind reveals *what can be done*—and when you come out of your retreat you know that it will be done and that you will do it.

At first you may find it necessary to retreat physically from the world into a quiet room or perhaps to some place distant from your business and from people who know you. This often is a good idea even when you have practice in finding the most inmost privacy of your mind, because there are many physical circumstances which break into thought.

When you have several times retreated to your thick-walled keep, however, you will find you can enter it for a few seconds even in the midst of others who are talking all around you. I have seen many successful men do this, and thus illustrate some of the power to which they owe their success. It is a great renewer of the spirit, a kind of recharge of ability and self-confidence and abiding faith.

All that I have to say in this book is keyed to one Supreme Secret.

This Secret has been strongly sketched in throughout this chapter. You have seen it, and already it is beginning to penetrate your subconscious mind—which never forgets.

CHECKING ON CHAPTER 1:

Never believe you don't have what it takes
A man who succeeds in life must know where he is going, must fully possess his own mind and believe with full faith that *this is it*. Knowing this, he can shunt aside any outside influences which may attempt to discourage him. Even the "voice of authority" speaking to a child cannot prevail against a mind that knows itself. Even a child who is a potential criminal can be directed toward an honest and successful life when you show him his own vast potential for making good.

Adversity? It's a tonic, not a stumbling block
Life often brings hardship and discouragement, but a mind that knows itself becomes filled with success consciousness

that never is lost. You can help yourself by setting up a time limit within which you will achieve great goals. Even an unforeseeable world war did not prove a great enough obstacle to prevail against this mighty Personal Achievement technique.

A success-conscious mind functions rapidly and effectively
Once you fill your mind with your self-directed success consciousness, you achieve a level of mind efficiency which does not depend on formal education. Seeing your preferred goal ahead of you, you are magnificently able to find ways to get what you want. For a pioneer of the automobile age or a pioneer in the construction of modern computer parts, the principle which makes your mind work rapidly and effectively is always the same.

Can success consciousness be instilled into another's mind?
Even the most discouraged and beaten man can have all his success potential revived when another mind, full of success consciousness, evokes the same great power in his. Belief in success, not in obstacles to success, can spread from one mind to another until millions share the same great goal.

The spiritual defenses within the castle of your mind
Within your own mind you can set up three spiritual walls which are stronger than stone. Within these walls your mind can know itself and be itself—and still absorb all the good, constructive influences you wish to bring in. You will be proof against unwanted negative influences, time-wasting and the like. Within your innermost wall you will always have the means to renew your spirit, recharge your confidence and faith.

2

Close the Doors on Your Past

Whenever you meet a misfortune, put it into your past. Keep your mind upon future achievement, and you will find that mistakes of the past often work to fill the future with good fortune. Your wealth and your peace of mind are strongly connected with each other. Even at the lowest-level jobs, your success waits within your own mind. Add value to your work and you set in motion the forces that make the concepts of your mind turn into the realities of living.

WHEN I was still a poor youth in Wise County, Virginia, I invested twenty-five cents in a raffle ticket. The prize was a horse—and I won! A horse was of considerable value to a farming family in those days, and this one, all agreed, was a good horse. Filled with pride, I led him home. How fortunate I was!

Or was I? Having installed my horse carefully in the stable, I treated him to oats, corn and hay—all he could eat. That same night he broke out of the stable, went down to the river and drank his fill of water. As anyone who knows horses could have predicted, the poor bloated animal foundered and died. It cost me five dollars to have him hauled away and buried. So much for my good luck!

Yet who can tell the uses of the past? I was able in later years to look back upon that incident and see I *had* been fortunate. You see, I never again have been tempted to risk money in any kind of gambling. Surely I have saved the cost of many horses, let alone saved my peace of mind.

Now let me tell you of a more serious incident which cost a man's life, threatened my own life, prevented me from taking advantage of a great opportunity, seemed like an unmitigated disaster—and yet turned out to be for my boundless good and the good of others as well.

At that time I had completed the first draft of *The Science of Personal Achievement,* in eight volumes, and I needed a publisher. Mr. Don R. Mellett, publisher of the Canton, Ohio *Daily News,* became my partner and business manager. We induced Judge Elbert H. Gary, Chairman of the Board of the United States Steel Corporation, to supply the money necessary to print the first edition. Furthermore, Judge Gary agreed to purchase a complete set of the books for every key man employed in that vast corporation. The contract had not yet been signed, but I was on top of the world.

Now, Mr. Mellett had been using his newspaper as a means to expose a very unholy alliance between the bootleggers and the police force of his city. Three days before we were to meet Judge Gary, a member of the police force and a gangster shot and killed Don Mellett. Because I had been associated with him, the gang believed I too had had something to do with their exposure. I missed assassination by only a few hours.

For a year I had to hide. At length the murderers were caught, convicted and given lifetime sentences in prison. Meanwhile Judge Gary had died. All my plans were upset, I had had to waste much precious time while in hiding, and I had no publisher. I was right back where I had started—or rather, I was behind where I had been.

I made a new start and found a publisher for my writings. That is a story in itself, but it is not the point of *this* story.

I found out later that if Judge Gary had become my financial backer, and if *The Science of Personal Achievement* had been distributed within the United States Steel Corporation as had been planned, I would forever after have been looked upon as a tool of Big Business. *The Science of Personal Achievement* would have been greeted with suspicion, would have been turned down cold by many of those whom it now serves. Furthermore, I might have been inhibited against making statements I have made from time to time against Big Business when it forgets its real purpose, which is to build a better world for mankind.

Every adversity has within it the seed of an equivalent or a greater benefit. Can you remember that? Write it on a card. Carry the card in your pocket and read it daily! In that phrase lies the key to many a man's peace of mind. It is not the Supreme Secret to which I have referred but it lives on the same street. Set it firmly into your consciousness: *Every adversity has within it the seed of an equivalent or a greater benefit.*

Thus it is possible, and strongly advisable, to CLOSE THE DOORS TO YOUR PAST insofar as any regrets or bitterness or post-mortems are concerned. You are searching for wealth and peace of mind. Neither the way to wealth nor the way to peace of mind leads through the graveyard of unpleasant experiences long past.

When you have attained peace of mind, your mind will automatically reject every thought and every mental reaction which is not beneficial to your welfare. Meanwhile, help yourself attain this great command-of-mind and all it can do for you. Avoid all negative mental influences and especially avoid that shadow of mournful regret which can keep all the sunshine out of your life—and keep out other gold as well.

Time is the great magician. Close the door on ugly experiences, disappointments and frustrations! Then the great magician, Time, can transmute past sorrows and mistakes into present rewards, success and happiness.

Knut Hamsun, a Norwegian immigrant, failed at everything he tried in this country. In desperation he decided to write the story of his struggles. His book, which he called *Hunger,* won the Nobel Prize for literature. Hamsun's terrible experiences at length had made him a rich and famous man.

Harry S. Truman failed as a haberdasher. If, from then on, he had considered himself a failure, he certainly could not have entered upon the road to the presidency.

We have also the example of another man who took up storekeeping; but the store failed.

He took up engineering and also failed. The sheriff sold his surveying instruments to pay his debts.

He joined a group of soldiers in an Indian war and had the rank of captain. His record as a soldier was so poor that he was reduced to the rank of private and sent home.

He was passionately in love and engaged to be married. The girl died and left him in a terrible state of shock.

He took up law. He won few cases.

He went into politics, ran for office and was defeated.

Is it astonishing that Abraham Lincoln eventually became President? In a way it is and in a way it is not. He *might* have allowed his mind to drag failure and discouragement after him, as a prisoner drags his chains. After all, so many people do—and they are indeed prisoners of the past, never able to break free of the image of failure which, to them, means *me.*

He did not do this, however. The way in which he determinedly left failure behind him was no miracle—it is a grand privilege available to every human being. The man who became President had been tempered in the fires of life, or he could not have been what he was nor have done what he did.

You cannot see all of the great Plan of your life. You can make it full and rewarding, however, if you treat each sorrow and setback as a tempering toward greater and richer experiences to come.

Let me suggest:

Keep yourself aware of life's endless combinations of circumstances

Have you been disappointed in love? Your heart feels literally broken. You can see no joy in the world. You may wish to take an overdose of sleeping pills and end it all. Yet is it likely that nowhere in the world exists the woman (or man) who can take the place of the one you lost? A moment of thought within the citadel of your deepest mind will show you this is hardly possible.

So it happened with me, for after a dreadful disappointment of the heart I met a combination of circumstances which led at last to the perfect wife. There is a more poignant point to the story. When, after a violent lover's quarrel, my first sweetheart turned away from me, married another man, I thought the world had ended. Five years later the man she married committed suicide, unbalanced by the constant friction of living with the woman I had been so anxious to marry. Where would I have been with a terror of a woman who heckled me instead of helping me?

Every adversity has within it the seed of an equivalent or greater benefit.

Remember that even *a condition which the world calls HANDICAP you can call BENEFIT—and make it truly so.*

I have mentioned that Thomas A. Edison had little formal schooling. W. Clement Stone, the highly successful insurance man, was a high school dropout. So many men have succeeded despite the lack of "book learning" that, without in the least downgrading education, we may say the lack of it need not be a handicap. It depends on the man.

But what of Edison's deafness? Surely a very marginal ability to hear is a handicap. But again it depends on the man.

Edison as a boy had been a "candy butcher" on trains. Once a man lifted him and his entire load of candy onto a train by his ears—and that was the beginning of the end of his hearing. He could have dwelt all his life on this cruel and damaging experience. Like many another, he could have put his major energies into bewailing his fate; but he didn't.

When I visited him, he was dependent upon a hearing aid —a primitive thing by today's standards. When I was sure we understood each other's minds I asked him if he had not found his deafness a great handicap. He replied:

"To the contrary, deafness has been a great help to me. It has saved me from having to listen to a lot of worthless chatter and it has taught me to *hear from within.*"

Anyone who wants peace of mind should remember those last three words. By transmuting his affliction into a benefit,

Mr. Edison learned how to tune in on all the subtle power which waits within every mind. He felt, too, that he heard, from within, the voice of an Infinite Intelligence and received guidance from an infallible Source.

Every adversity has within it the seed of an equivalent or greater benefit.

When you speak of failure, you attract failure. When you speak of success, you attract success. I once made a survey of more than 30,000 men and women to ascertain their staying qualities in the face of failure and defeat.

For the majority of those people it took one—only *one*—setback to wed them to defeat.

Of those who kept on aspiring, another large percentage got started in various projects but quit even before meeting with defeat. The defeat came not from circumstances but from the built-in attitude of defeat which they carried from the past. Instead of closing the door on the past, they ran back through that door at every opportunity. Needless to say there were no Fords or Edisons in this group.

On the other hand, I am reminded of a man named Arthur Decio who built his career out of a family failure that had cost all of his father's savings. It was a business in mobile homes which never got going. Now the father handed it to the son, hopelessly. What could Decio, then in his twenties, do with the business? Most men would have liquidated it on the spot.

Starting in his garage next to the railroad tracks in Elkhart, Indiana, Mr. Decio first designed a small, easily transportable mobile home which research had shown him was needed. Later he applied General Motors methods in a business which never had known them before. He introduced frequent model changes. He built a network of dealers. He brought out four lines of mobile homes, each competing with the others. His company's sales in four years have increased 500 per cent, and Mr. Decio has made five million dollars out of the business that was about to fail.

Today's population includes a large proportion of young-marrieds and retired couples, both groups being prime customers for mobile homes. Of course Mr. Decio realizes this, for every age has its special ways.

The many failures who turned up in my survey of some years ago displayed a failure-quality which belongs to any age. Not only had these people failed, but *they kept on living with their failure.* They spoke of it in preference to other topics. They lived in the past tense, reliving the pain of what had been.

Those who had succeeded, however, spoke in the future tense. Their eyes were not upon their past—which often contained a good share of mistakes—but ever upon the future, upon their great objectives. This too was the invariable case with those five hundred and more vastly successful men whom I interviewed at the behest of Andrew Carnegie. On their way up they talked "the way up." Where failure had been laid behind, failure stayed behind—and notably it stayed out of their conversation.

Concerning success and failure, I have observed another trait which has much to do with peace of mind.

It is obvious that those who are filled with malice and envy do not have peace of mind; their malice and envy sour their lives. Failure so often hates the very sight of success. Speaking with successful men, I have noticed they speak in complimentary terms of other men who are succeeding. Their attitude is not one of envy, but of willingness to learn from others. The failure, on the other hand, goes out of his way to find some adverse criticism of the successful person. If he can't find anything doubtful about the way that person does business, then he will pick at some other area. His malice is evident, and so is the sad fact that he not only cannot command what money can buy, but also he cannot attain peace of mind.

Is there a definite connection between being wealthy and having peace of mind?   There is a connection, but it is not absolute. There certainly are poor people who have peace of mind: but they are far more rare than folklore would have us believe. You need not be a millionaire, but without sufficient money you are cut off from much in life that sustains the spirit. If you are continually worrying about where your next meal is to come from—when you'll be able to get your shoes repaired—how you are going to pay your dentist bill—how many more years your house can go without paint—you have no peace of mind. If your lack of funds forces you to live in a shabby neighborhood so that you constantly worry about the influence upon your children, you have no peace of mind. If you cannot occasionally buy and cherish something that is beautiful—if you cannot afford a vacation you really enjoy —if you cannot partake of a motion picture or a stage show which you know is very much worthwhile—your mind does not have the chance to satisfy itself. Money brings much good into your life and much that nobody should have to do without.

It is no surprise that there are many rich people who enjoy peace of mind. But there are many who do not. If the main purpose of a fortune is to make its possessor worry about keeping his fortune, peace of mind goes out the window.

One of the failures which have illuminated my knowledge and strengthened my soul came when I was quite wealthy. I simply became poor—quite poor. The circumstances are revealing.

Perhaps as a compensation for the dirt-poor days of my youth, I became enamored of big houses, big cars, lush acreage and similar symbols of wealth. Perhaps I was merely in line with my times, which seemed to demand that when a man had money, he had to display it. Today's millionaires are much less ostentatious.

At any rate, my books were selling well, I had made a name as a trainer of salesmen, other enterprises prospered—and so it seemed imperative that I must drive a Rolls-Royce. Soon I had a pair of Rolls-Royces. Soon after this, I cradled my cars in a big garage on a large estate in the Catskill Mountains, north of New York City. I saw that estate as a monument to my achievements.

The estate called for servants, for a maintenance staff, for foremen over the maintenance men. It called for lavish dinner parties, the expense of which would have made John D. Rockefeller groan. Once I gave out a general invitation to a barbecue dinner, expecting that perhaps a hundred people would show up. Over three thousand attended! The highway was tied up with a traffic jam for two miles each way, and the traffic patrolmen never did forgive me.

The clubhouse on the estate could sleep forty guests in comfort and was seldom without a full load. Once the overflow swept into my private quarters. I arrived home—hoping for some peace of mind—and found a stranger asleep in my bed. Moreover, he had appropriated the only pair of pajamas I had available.

Let us draw the curtain on the Hill estate. It went for a song shortly after the crash of '29. When I got over the initial shock, how relieved I felt! How peaceful, how newly powerful was the mind which had been overlaid with worry!

Three of my friends, whose combined assets were less than

the amount I lost when I lost my estate, did not have faith in the great principle that every adversity has within it the seed of an equivalent benefit. One jumped off a high building on Wall Street; one fired a bullet into his brain; and the third man was hauled out of the Hudson River six weeks after he had jumped in.

I made money again. Of course I did. The principles of the Science of Achievement saw to that. My lost estate had not lost with it my knowledge that any goal set up by a human mind can be achieved by that mind's possessor. Ever since, I have lived comfortably but without show. What good is money when it becomes a millstone?

Make sure your work and your money benefit someone besides yourself. One of the positive results that came after I had firmly closed the door on my experiences in the Catskill Mountains was this: I found time in which to write more books. These books have benefited me and they have benefited mankind—and so they have benefited me with more than money.

When Andrew Carnegie decided to use his great wealth to found free libraries, he greatly increased his peace of mind.

Henry Ford was pretty tough about giving away his money. When at length he learned it was possible to find people who deserved it and would use it well, I am sure he felt the same quiet satisfaction.

There is another important principle which insures that as your wealth grows, so will your peace of mind.

Do not hurt any other person in order that you may succeed. I am thankful I learned this early in life. When a man discovers himself and with it the ways in which he can earn big money, now and then he will see a way to put some extra weight on his side of the scales. Like the butcher's hand which is weighed along with the hamburger, it wouldn't be noticed. I could have added to my wealth by dishonest means on many an occasion, but I would have lost my peace of mind.

Among the men I interviewed after I accepted my commission from Andrew Carnegie were several who were little better than pirates of the business world. (In most cases I did not know this at the time.) Later events often showed how much they had given up when, in effect, they stole from others or ruthlessly ruined others in order to aggrandize themselves.

Some went to prison. Some stayed out of prison on legal technicalities, but who has peace of mind when no honest man will look him in the face?

Today is the day of the large service corporation, often with a tremendous office staff. A man in a factory is likely to be judged by the kind of work he puts out, but a man in an office can push himself upward with various tricks of personality, tricks of paperwork, tricks of getting the other fellow to assume responsibility for mistakes, and so forth. To step up the ladder by stepping on another man's face is to make a mockery of the money you earn. There is no peace of mind in this and often there is no health, no ability to be happy, no harmony at home. You can be left with the ability to buy what money can buy—and a degree of unhappiness rather more acute than a beggar's.

I have spoken to several men in my classes who confessed they had cut many corners of honesty and business morality. Now they wished to make a new start—but was it possible? When they attained the only true wealth, honestly earned wealth, would they not still be made miserable by the tensions of guilt?

I assured them they would not if only they closed the door on the past. Let them consider dishonesty a mistake, even a disaster—but a past disaster.

This is an important point with many ramifications. Not necessarily dishonesty, but also any other negative state of mind held in the past can be left in the past just as one leaves physical circumstances.

I showed these men that now they were finding a new *self*. The past *could not* matter.

The world is full of examples of men who learned from their own bad consciences, or even in prison, that *no* dishonesty *ever* pays. The lesson learned is the lesson learned, and for most men there is time enough and world enough to start again and build a glorious future.

For an exception, I give you Al Capone. During the Great Depression, this notorious gangster set up free soup kitchens at which he fed numbers of the unemployed. He was fond of calling attention to these soup kitchens as proof of the good he was doing his fellow man. Of course I speak of no such mockeries.

Rather let us think of men like O. Henry, who served a jail sentence for a crime. Surely it helped him at last to find himself, for it was afterward that he became known for his wonderful stories with all their deep understanding of human nature.

Close the door on your past and keep it closed. I have heard it said that you never really get over the death of a loved one. This is so in the sense that every circumstance of your life, every joy and every sorrow, has an effect in shaping you into what you are. But you have great control over the way it shapes you—never forget that!

I am not one of those who believe in doing away with the natural emotion of sorrow when death occurs. Tears and sorrow are provided by nature as a safety valve for the overflowing emotions. Yet most people wait too long to close the door on mourning; or they never close it. We say: "There is no use in worrying over something you can't control." Yet we worry over death for unconscionable periods of time, knowing all the while we cannot control it.

The physical body comes from the air and the soil and goes back to the sources from which it came. Perhaps the mental and spiritual portions and some mysterious essence of life also go back to sources we can sense but cannot discover. So be it! Carry along with you not the pain you knew when a loved one died, but rather the positive and sustaining memories. As life is a natural process, so death is also.

Do you think it is possible to have only one great love in your life, especially if that love was sealed in marriage? Human experience proves this is not so. While I believe firmly in marriage, I know that the word "marriage" is not always synonymous with the word "happiness." You have a right to happiness, and this is your life. When a marriage turns out to have been a mistake, when it can be broken but it is not broken, then the mistake is perpetuated and shadows all the rest of life. Sometimes the door of the past must be closed upon a marriage before either party to that marriage, or both, can find any kind of life-success.

A job that is past opens a new door to the future. Suppose you have lost your job through no fault of your own. Suppose, then, you nurse a great resentment and a festering hatred of your former employer who was so unjust to you. Meanwhile you are going around looking for another job— and something is saying *No* to any prospective future employer. What says *No*? The negative qualities of hatred and resentment which beam from your mind to his. He cannot tell just what it is, but he feels something disturbing about you and he doesn't want you in his office or his shop.

Put the temporary setback firmly behind you, however—go out with a determined will to get a better job than the one you lose—and anyone who interviews you will feel the positive qualities that mean *good man*. What if you are questioned about your former employer? Say nothing bad about him! What was bad must always stay in the past and never be allowed to hinder the future.

Jobs also seem to be favorite spots in which to grow grudges. Of course you have rights and it is no part of success or peace of mind to allow yourself to be stepped upon. Many little scratches in human relations, however, are nothing but that, just little scratches, and need not be reacted to as though they were deep wounds.

How BIG are you? It takes a big person to succeed. To begin with, it takes a big person to see what is big, and worth one's attention, rather than waste emotional energy on trifling matters. When you see how you damage yourself by bearing resentment and grudges, you can put small annoyances in the past as soon as they occur. At times it is advisable to talk things over, point out how another person wounds others, and start afresh with the air cleared. But a nursed grudge is a viper in the bosom. It is a treasured *negative*, and you not only let it take away your peace of mind, you also encourage the formation of ulcers and many other ailments which the mind can inflict upon the body. Close that door!

It is wonderful and gratifying to see how the habit of closing the door upon the past becomes one of the greatest of sustaining habits. It helps you take possession of your own mind and condition it for the attainment of any purpose you desire.

Go the extra mile. I have often been asked to give a man *something to do* that helps him leave resentment behind him; especially where his job and his career are concerned. The best possible action is this: go the extra mile.

Give more service and better service than you are paid for. Find out more about your job and the job above it than you absolutely have to know. Work in a way that makes your job do more than it is expected to do for the organization that employs you.

A young man was an estimator for a large printing firm. He didn't pay much attention to type faces, being content to let the customers go on using the type faces to which they were accustomed. This made his job easier—but, as I pointed out to him, it did nothing to qualify him as a man who really knows his job.

He studied type faces, arrangements of type on a page and other matters which lend effect and even artistry to broadsides and brochures. When his boss received compliments on "the beautiful jobs you turn out," the boss realized what this young man was doing for his firm's reputation. The young man is now an executive of the firm, where before he was scarcely noticed. The young man also has relieved himself of a feeling of bitterness which might, in the end, have resulted in making him an old man with a mean little salary and a mean little soul.

A saleswoman at a dry goods counter had decided that her salary and her small commissions paid her for going through the routine motions of selling what she found on the shelves, and that was that. One day a woman asked her so pleasantly and so positively to look for an item in the depths of the stockroom that she found herself looking; and when she discovered the item, she felt "bigger inside." Thereafter she made a point of suggesting items which were not visible and of putting through special orders even when they resulted in little benefit to herself.

Soon she had a regular clientele. Customers were willing to wait in order to have her serve them. Moreover, her knowledge of her business caused the buyer to rely upon her judgment. She is a buyer now, with a grand career opening before her. She says: "There are two factors that can make you successful; your job and yourself. You are always the most important factor."

Of course you don't have to feel mean and small and imposed upon before you go the extra mile!

A tonic in itself, the willingness to do more than you absolutely must is the hallmark of the big earner, the great leader, the happy and hearty person who day by day builds value into his life.

See yourself on the next step up the ladder, and the next step above that one, and many rewarding steps ahead, and the image takes hold firmly in your mind and gets you going. Should you meet a situation in which your extra efforts are not rewarded, your positive mind finds courage and resourcefulness and you leave the job that's wrong for you—push it back into your past—and find another in which the image becomes real. Where you start never matters so much as where you are going—and it is first within your own mind that you conceive greatly and begin to *go*.

Again the Supreme Secret has been mentioned in several ways. You may not yet be able to put it into words, but it works more and more strongly in your favor as you read successive chapters of this book.

CHECKING ON CHAPTER 2:

Every adversity has within it the seeds of an equivalent or a greater benefit
As you meet the circumstances of life they may seem adverse and damaging. Later you find that every so-called misfortune sows the seed of greater fortune to come. To help this mighty dynamic work its wonders in your life, close the door on your past. Carry along with you only what is pleasant and instructive. Leaving gloom and pain behind you, you can see the future and make it yours.

Keep yourself aware of life's endless combinations of circumstances
Do not believe that one experience of lost love or lost opportunity or other misfortune has ended your chances of winning what you thought you had lost. Some of the world's greatest men knew failure after failure as they grew toward their ultimate success. Even a handicap becomes a benefit when the man himself decides the way in which it will be a benefit to him.

When you speak of failure you attract failure; when you speak of success you attract success
The failure typically dwells upon his failure and drags it through his life like a prisoner dragging his chains. The failure also tends to be envious of those who succeed, and his envy and his malice rob him not only of wealth but also of peace of mind. Every age has its special advantages. An entire business may be labeled *failure* and yet come to life and make millions in the hands of a man who sees success and speaks only of success.

Is there a definite connection between wealth and peace of mind?
There is a strong connection, but it is not unbreakable. Suf-

ficient money is necessary to almost everyone who wishes to attain peace of mind, but wealth can steal happiness away from those who make it dishonestly or do not use it correctly. Use your work and your wealth to help others. Above all, make sure that as you climb the ladder of success you do not step upon anyone else. Cutting the corners of dishonesty sets up a feeling of guilt which can destroy happiness. Even so, one who has erred can put his error firmly in the past, close the door and go on to great accomplishment.

Go the extra mile

In work situations especially, grudges and a feeling of resentment play havoc with the mind's ability to conceive and achieve. Going the extra mile has a tonic effect in relieving the mind of built-in obstacles. Add to your work more than you are paid for. Always qualify yourself for the next step upward and the steps beyond. People who succeed are not people who hold grudges or who withhold their best work, but those who in every act and thought pave their way toward greater things.

3

The Basic Mental Attitude That Brings Wealth and Peace of Mind

A life of wealth enjoyed by a mind at peace comes most often to men who maintain a positive mental attitude. With definiteness of purpose you add great positive power to your own mental attitude, and you can use definite motives to sustain the actions which propel you toward your goal. At the same time you can set up spiritual guardians to keep your attitudes at a high "Yes" level, avoid conflicts of motive, tune-in on other positive minds.

THE computers which are beginning to manage our world are complicated devices. Most of them, however, have a very simple basic principle: they say *Yes* or *No*. They either open a kind of electrical gate or they keep it closed, and by multiplying this process they can assimilate and select all kinds of information.

The mind of man is far more wonderful than any machine. Within it, however, there seems to be a kind of Yes-No valve at the focal point of thinking. It is as though your awareness of a circumstance of life—sent to your brain by your sight, hearing and other senses—presents itself at the Yes-No point to be processed. A person who maintains a positive attitude will find every possible *Yes* in that circumstance and make it part of his life. A person who maintains a negative mental attitude will lean toward the *No* side, miss much that is good, live with much that is painful and damaging.

Nothing but a mental attitude? Nothing but a mental attitude, but it is right there that your success or your failure, your peace of mind or your nervous tension, your tendency toward good health or your tendency toward illness begins.

Fortunately it is possible for anyone to make the change from negativism to positivism, and thus basically condition his brain to bring all that is good in life. Moreover, there are certain "control levers" which the Creator makes available to us, and it is easy to see how successful people use these levers, once you know what they are.

I shall give you some here and some in other chapters so as to reinforce your memory. Now and then you will find repetition of names, facts and methods in this book, always with a view toward helping you remember.

Control your mental attitude with definiteness of purpose. Emerson said: "The world makes way for a man who knows where he is going."

Think what it means to know where you are going! Automatically you rid yourself of all kinds of fears and doubts which may have crept into the making-up-your-mind process. Your purpose is definite and—presto!—all the limitless forces of your mind focus upon that purpose and no other. Knowing your purpose, you cannot be led astray by circumstances or words which have nothing to do with your purpose. Where, before, a day's work may have contained a good deal of wasted motion, now your efforts are lined up so that each mental or physical motion helps every other motion.

You can see the connection with building wealth, for work done well is a basic wealth-builder. Now see the connection with peace of mind. A man who works wholeheartedly at his job is not concerned with such matters as finding fault with others, disturbing his conscience by cutting corners in his work, watching the clock and so forth. Nor will he be discouraged by any obstacles which may crop up; his positive and focused mental attitude keeps him in a prime position to handle problems and overcome them.

Is this a secret of "genius"? I have mentioned that many eminently successful men do not possess any greater intelligence than most other men possess. Yet their achievements are such that we may say that these men have "genius." Surely it is the positive mental attitude of these men which makes their brain-power, not greater, but more efficient and more available than most others'. When I spoke to such men as Henry Ford, Andrew Carnegie and Thomas A. Edison, I spoke with minds free of any fear or doubt that they could do anything they wished to do.

I know that Andrew Carnegie was well aware of the need for a positive mental attitude. Before he undertook to back me in my success, he really put me "on the spot" as to my mental attitude.

Looking at me shrewdly across his desk, that canny Scot said: "We've talked a long time and I have shown you the greatest opportunity a young man ever had to become famous, rich and useful. Now—if I choose you out of the two hundred and forty other applicants for this job—if I introduce you to the outstandingly successful men in America—if I help you get their collaboration in finding out the true philosophy of success—will you devote twenty years to the job, earning your own living as you go along? We have had sufficient discussion. I want your answer—yes or no."

I began to think of all the obstacles that would stand in my way. I began to think of all the hurdles I would have to jump. I began to think of all the time I would have to spend, and the big job of writing, and the problem of earning my living all that while—and so forth.

I spent twenty-nine seconds struggling with a negative mental attitude which, had it overcome me, would have affected me negatively ever after.

How do I know I took just twenty-nine seconds? Because, when I found the positive mental attitude which I had lost temporarily, and said "Yes!"—Mr. Carnegie showed me the stopwatch he had been holding beneath his desk. He had given me just one minute in which to show my positive state of mind—otherwise, he felt, he would not have been able to depend on it. I had beaten the deadline by just thirty-one seconds, and thereby embraced an opportunity that was destined to change and improve the lives of millions of people, including my own.

A positive mind tunes in on other positive minds. Once I had accepted that great task and had set my mind confidently toward it, I found that my imagined obstacles simply melted away. Of course my positive mental attitude helped me not only in finding out the success secrets of some five hundred of America's wealthiest men, but also in making considerably more than a mere living. Am *I* a genius? I must say I have positive evidence I am not!

In meeting many men I discovered a very valuable fact: a positive mind automatically obtains benefit from other positive minds.

Are you aware of the general principle of radio broadcasting? It is this: when electrical vibrations of rapid frequency are impressed upon a wire, those vibrations leap into space. Another wire far away—the receiving antenna—can pick them up, and thus a message or a picture is transmitted over thousands of miles, or millions of miles in space-age communication.

There are electrical currents in the brain. They give you a private broadcasting station through which you may send out any kind of thought vibrations you desire. Keep that station busy sending out thoughts of a positive nature, thoughts which will benefit others, and you will find you can receive kindred thought vibrations from other minds whose attitude is tuned to yours.

When I visited such successful men as those I have mentioned, and many others such as John Wanamaker, Frank A. Vanderlip, Edward Bok and Woodrow Wilson, both they and I felt the attunement of mind to mind. Otherwise I surely would have met with opposition when I asked those top-ranking men to give me of their time and experience. Not only did such men spend hours talking to me, but also they served as my teachers and guides for year after year, and charged me nothing.

Believe in what you are doing, and you too will see the great effect of your belief upon those whom you may request to help you. Doubt yourself and the *No* part of your mind takes over and draws defeat instead of victory.

This barely sketches in the all-pervasive power of a positive mental attitude. Let us look at some of the other "control levers" which combine with a positive mental attitude to give you wealth and peace of mind for an entire, victorious lifetime.

The nine major motives. It is not for nothing that court trials often concern themselves with questions of *motive*. Everything you do is the result of one or more motives. In various combinations we use nine basic motives. The seven positive motives are:

1. The emotion of LOVE
2. The emotion of SEX
3. The desire for MATERIAL GAIN
4. The desire for SELF-PRESERVATION
5. The desire for FREEDOM OF BODY AND MIND
6. The desire for SELF-EXPRESSION
7. The desire for PERPETUATION OF LIFE AFTER DEATH

The two negative emotions are:

1. The emotion of ANGER AND REVENGE
2. The emotion of FEAR

In those nine motives you can find the roots of everything you do or refrain from doing. *Peace of mind is attained only by the exercise of the seven positive motives as a general pattern of life.* Rarely if ever does a person who has peace of mind exercise the two negative motives or emotions. You cannot have peace of mind while you fear anything or anyone. You cannot have peace of mind while you entertain the kind of anger which brings you to a desire for revenge or a desire to injure another, no matter what the justification may seem to be.

Great men have no time to waste with a desire to injure others. If they did, they would not be great men. Great men are not immune to fear, but theirs is not the kind of fear that hangs on constantly and takes over all of life. Look to small, mean men to see lifelong patterns of fear and anger. Their minds are so filled with these negative influences that they cannot find the power to shape the circumstances they desire.

Recently I heard about a man, now seventy, who fifteen years ago lost all his money in a real estate venture. Taking the advice of a friend, he had borrowed heavily in order to invest in vacant swampland on the assumption that in a couple of years the land would be in great demand for building lots. This did not transpire, the man's notes became due, and he had to see his retail shoe business sold out from under him.

The friend who had badly advised him also had lost money. Nevertheless this man became filled with hatred toward his friend and said he would get even "if it's the last thing I do." It nearly was. Five years of hatred left him incapable even of doing business. Meanwhile the friend prospered and seemed far out of reach of any puny revenge. The man who had lost his money at length lost the balance wheel of his mind and had to spend six months in a quiet place in the country surrounded by a high wall.

In his last month of confinement, however, he was sufficiently recovered to listen to an adviser who pointed out to him that hatred and the desire for revenge had done him far more harm than had been done by his losing his money. He was persuaded to forgive the friend who had led him into the real estate deal. He even wrote to this man, telling of his change of heart.

When he went back into business it was with love of his fellow men and the determination to keep his mind filled with positive, constructive motives. Beginning at the age of sixty, he built a new career. Now, at seventy, he is fairly well off, and most of all he has peace of mind, the one form of wealth which is indispensable.

I myself have suffered from the effects of negative motives from time to time. When I went into hiding, as discussed in the last chapter, I acted at first upon a very wise motive of self-preservation. Soon, however, this turned into fear and with the fear came misery. Fortunately I saw in time what was happening to me. It cannot happen again.

You can call upon Ten Princes of Guidance to stand at the doors of your mind.   You can make yourself aware of certain principles of personal guidance and guardianship; and to make these principles real and memorable, you can personalize them—see them as so many Princes in armor who stand at the doors of your mind. These Princes challenge every thought-vibration which seeks to enter. They keep your mind positive, effective and free of discord. I shall name my own

Princes, a list which you may wish to modify to suit your own life-requirements.

The Prince of Peace of Mind. He stands at the very outer door and asks all callers if they come in peace to share my peace. If not, they are turned away.

The Prince of Hope and Faith. He admits only those influences which keep my mind alerted with belief in my mission in life.

The Prince of Love and Romance. He brings into my mind only those influences which keep love eternally fresh in my heart.

The Prince of Sound Physical Health. He knows the kind of mental influences which can destroy health, and admits only those states of mind which help the body maintain its vigor.

The Prince of Financial Security. When I desire him to stand on guard, he admits no thoughts save those which bring me worthy financial benefit.

The Prince of Overall Wisdom. He is charged with passing certain thoughts into my store of knowledge when he sees they will benefit me or help me benefit others.

The Prince of Patience. He keeps away all impulses to rush, to tackle jobs half-prepared, to be in any way impatient with the power of time.

The Prince of Normhill. "Normhill" is a very personal word I have created for my own use. Combining certain names, it means to me what it cannot mean to any other. Just so, create your own name for your own very personal Prince. This Prince stands guard along with all the others. The others from time to time may be relieved of duty; for instance, one hardly may wish continually to keep out all thoughts except those which have to do with financial security. Your special personal Prince is *always* there, representing all the special personal influences in your life. Normhill is my ambassador-at-large who performs services not assigned to the other members of my invisible family of guides.

When you have made yourself well aware of your corps of spiritual Princes, they serve to rally all your forces to solve any problem or to set up special lines of defense.

Sometimes I find myself talking to someone whose antagonistic attitude begins to invade my peace of mind. Very well—I send a special alert to the Prince of Peace of Mind. Immediately he takes charge of the ramparts with doubled strength, and I am calm and in control of my own mind once more.

Or, let us say, I feel some physical ache or pain. I call upon the Prince of Sound Physical Health to look into the cause, and I get good results. I believe I have received benefits of healing which are beyond the power of ordinary medical science to explain.

My Princes of Guidance receive a certain compensation for their services. Their "pay" is my eternal gratitude. Daily I express this gratitude, first to each of the Princes individually, then to all of them in their mighty group. You will find this expression of gratitude of great help in keeping your mind alerted to its own powers. I know that if I ever neglect it, I feel a neglect on the part of my Princes. When, once again, I make myself aware every day that I have great spiritual forces at my command—there they are once more, as strong as ever.

Don't let the motive of material gain conflict with the motive of freedom. Freedom of body is easy to see and understand; but freedom of mind is a subtle matter. Fear and anger put the mind behind bars. Guilt wraps the mind in chains. To add a bit of levity to a serious matter: Once there was a man who was encouraged to *know himself*. Immediately he handcuffed himself to his bed, so he would not get up and rifle his own pockets during the night.

All too often the motive of *material gain*—excellent in itself—conflicts with the excellent motive of *freedom of body and mind* because in gaining what is material we give up freedom of mind; we load the mind with guilt and fear because we do not act honestly.

In addition, one who makes his money through taking dishonest advantage of his fellow men has cheated himself of the genuine joy which comes with honest success. When you obey the rules of a game, and win, you have done something for your soul. When you cheat and win, you only *call* it winning, but you have really lost instead.

I believe I was fortunate in starting my career very early in life, so that I learned life's lessons quite early. Let me tell you of an experience I had while I was holding my first job. I was just out of business college and I was inexperienced in the ways of life and the character of men.

My employer owned a number of banks. He had placed his son as a cashier of one of his banks, in a distant town.

One night a hotel manager in that town telephoned me, saying my employer's son was in serious difficulty. He had not been able to reach my employer. Immediately, I boarded the train and arrived in the town early the next morning.

When I went to the bank I found the door closed but unlocked. Inside, I discovered that the vault had been left open and beautiful green currency was scattered all over the teller's counter.

I closed the door and picked up the telephone. I managed to get my employer on the phone and told him why I had gone to that town and what I had found on my arrival. In great distress, he said: "Go ahead and count the money. Balance the books. Draw a draft on me for whatever shortage there may be."

I settled down to counting the money. To my great surprise, not a cent was missing.

I sat there looking at those piles of greenbacks. My youth had been tragic, turbulent and poor. My present state was one of bare solvency. I sat there looking at nearly $50,000 in cash, knowing that I could put at least half of it into my pocket and nobody would be the wiser. My employer's son showed obvious signs of mental instability. Everyone would assume he had taken the money. He even had acted as though he had filled his own pockets—and I was the only one who knew he had not.

The motive of material gain nudged heavily at me. But the motive of freedom said: *Don't do it.* Or rather, it was "something" that kept me honest, for at that time I could not have named the major motives. Perhaps that "something" was the result of certain sessions I had had with my stepmother before I had left home, in which she had instilled into me the fact that I was in control of my own mind and that always I must live with myself.

I locked the money into the vault forthwith, then phoned my employer and told him there was no deficiency to make up; not a cent had been stolen. I walked out of that bank with a mind at peace, a mind that was free and joyously positive.

Forever after I have placed the motive of *freedom* ahead of the motive of *material gain*. I have succeeded in having all the money I need without ever hampering either my inward or outward freedom.

This episode was one of several which led me straight to Andrew Carnegie and my realization of my goal in life. My employer was grateful for the way in which I had protected his son's reputation as best I could. He was responsible later for my entering Georgetown University Law School. This led through a chain of circumstances to my assignment to interview Mr. Carnegie. If I had yielded to the *material gain* motive that day in the bank, the Science of Personal Achievement might never have come into being.

Yes, as Emerson suggested, there is a silent partner in all our transactions, and woe is the lot of the man who tries to drive a sharp bargain with Life.

Life reflects your own thoughts back to you. Thoughts are things, a poet said, and truly they have an existence of their own, so that a curse comes back to curse you and a blessing comes back to bless you, reflected by the mighty mirror of life. Another poet said: "I am the master of my fate, I am the captain of my soul." This too is true, and the two truths harmonize. Send out positive thoughts from a positively oriented soul and the world will reflect back greater and greater positive influences to help you.

Turn back and read the list of nine basic motives. Concentrate on the seven positive motives. Remember it is possible for these motives to come into conflict, as we have seen; but by and large they drive one way, and with a positive mental attitude they take you the way you want to go. We shall not say farewell to the motives till we are finished with this book; but let us now pay our respects briefly.

Love has limitless scope. Handle it in a spirit of reverence, for it is tuned to the Eternal. Give freely of it and you will attract as much as or more than you give; stop giving love and you stop receiving. With no other emotion or motive or desire is the mirror of life so very evident.

Sex is the great creative force of the universe. On its highest plane it merges with love; but love can exist without being sexual. The mighty power of sex can be transmuted into action for the achievement of profound purpose, and so important is this matter that later on we shall devote an entire chapter to it. On the other hand, sex may be debauched and misused, and it is in this guise that it brings grief and trouble to mankind and gives itself an undeserved bad reputation.

Self-preservation can become a negative force when one seeks it without regard to the rights of other people. It is instilled by Nature to help us stay alive. Even so, the human being assumes the prerogative of rising above it. When a ship is sinking it is *women and children first,* and there are many parallel instances which call forth a nobility in human nature.

Self-expression is part of finding one's self. It is part of one's freedom to be one's self. Thus it is positive, constructive and infinitely valuable. Only make sure that your own means of self-expression do not demean or damage others.

Perpetuation of life after death belongs among the earliest beliefs and motives of mankind. It should be bounded by common sense and a true understanding of one's relationship to that change known as death. When wrapped in superstition and fear, this motive leads only to wretchedness. It can turn life into a preparation for death and hamper an entire civilization.

The surest way of finding peace of mind. The surest way of finding peace of mind is that which helps the greatest number of others to find it.

Let this be your guide to your use of the great motivating forces; then you will know you are using them correctly, not corrupting them.

Is there peace of mind in prayer? There can be. There *should* be. But note how many people go to prayer only in the hour of a misfortune, when the motive of *fear* dominates their minds. The approach must be negative in that case, and so, in terms of peace of mind, the results must be negative as well.

Prayers which bring peace of mind proceed from a mind which gives forth a confident message even though that mind may be afflicted with problems and sorrow. Prayers which free great forces to solve problems are born in minds which know that the problems can be solved once the forces are found—and have perfect confidence in the existence of those forces.

Along with many others I see evidence of an Intelligence beyond man's. I believe that the positively conditioned mind may at times tune in on that Intelligence. Yet mind-conditioning through prayer or resolution is something an individual must accomplish for himself. When the Creator made man free to seek his own destiny, and choose between good and evil, he gave man this prerogative as well. Every great accomplishment of any man at any time first had to exist as a thought before it could exist as reality.

Have you recognized the Supreme Secret?

CHECKING ON CHAPTER 3:

Life says Yes when you maintain a positive mental attitude
The mind of man is more wonderful than any computer. Like a computer, however, it seems to process much thinking at a Yes or No gate. A positive mental attitude helps you find every possible Yes in every life-circumstance. Even if your attitude presently is negative, you can change it to positive and open your life to all that is rich and rewarding.

Control your mental attitude with definiteness of purpose
Famous and successful men never show any doubt as to their ability to do what they wish to do. Anyone at any stage of his life can win the benefits of this mind-transforming method. Focus your mind upon a single purpose and you seem to achieve "genius" powers because your mind works far more efficiently. Now you find ways to handle problems that used to stump you, and to set obstacles aside. A positive mind tunes in on other positive minds. Through this mental broadcasting you exchange priceless information and guidance.

Control the major motives that control your life
Seven positive motives and two negative motives stand behind everything you do. Small men allow the two negative emotions, anger and fear, to rob them of peace of mind and prevent their minds from conceiving and achieving greatly. Big men use the seven positive motives to build the kind of lives they want. You can form Princes of Guidance to stand at the doors of your mind and prevent negative influences from entering. When you make use of such spiritual Princes they are always ready to take care of any emergency situation, such as a threat to health, as well as your day-to-day needs.

You can prevent your motives from conflicting with each other
The desire for material gain may conflict with the desire for freedom——but freedom of mind and body is the more important. The emotion of love is yours as long as you give love to others. Sex is a creative force which should not be debauched or mis-used. The belief in a life after death must be freed from superstition and fear. Self-expression and self-preservation are great human rights which benefit you when they do not harm others. All the positive motives will guide

you, and the negative motives, if they touch you, will not harm you if you remember: The surest way of finding peace of mind is the way which helps the greatest number of others to find it.

4

When You Are
Free of Fear, You Are Free to Live

Free yourself of fear, and you free yourself of a man-made devil. Seven major fears reinforce each other: the fear of poverty, the fear of criticism, the fear of ill health, the fear of loss of love, the fear of loss of liberty, the fear of old age, the fear of death. Separate your self-made fears from the fears which are necessary for self-preservation. Make way for self-confident faith in yourself, the indispensable ingredient of a life worth living.

WHEN you fear something, that thing is more likely to find you and harm you.

When you look a threat in the eye and *know* you are going to overcome it—that is when great powers come to your aid.

Fear, the most powerful of negative motives, is like prayer in reverse. Instead of appealing to the constructive forces which surround us, it appeals to the forces of destruction. It becomes a god in itself, demanding endless painful sacrifices. People rarely will admit that lives of bitter privation may be founded on nothing more than constant fear—and yet you can see it happen all around you.

The first fear I shall mention is a terribly "magnetic" fear. The more of it you have, the more you are likely to attract.

1. The fear of poverty. Now and again I have had occasion to meet people I knew in my own poverty-stricken youth. Of late I have been meeting their now-grown children. When I have known both parent and child I often can trace the persistence of a kind of family fondness for poverty. Fearing poverty with good reason as it ground them down—hating it and protesting it—such families have nevertheless allowed their negative emotions to dull their wits and cancel their courage.

In the greatest nation in the world, a nation that fairly throbs with opportunity, they settle down to live in want. Some member of the family may make some gesture toward lifting himself out of his rut, but it always turns out to be a feeble gesture that lacks follow through. Perhaps it salves his conscience to have this gesture to point to for the rest of his life. Worse yet, whole families are brought up in the belief that God intended them to be poor! Surely it must be the final twist of fear which equates the idea of God with the idea of persecution.

To be poor and not to like being poor is a good step toward becoming rich. But put aside your *fear* of poverty. See it rather as merely that point from which you take off. Let your intimate knowledge of the unwanted condition become a sustaining force as you drive toward the condition you do want —prosperity, even opulence.

Let your present necessity for pinching pennies make you aware of the power of money. Let your lack of capital make you aware of the many ways you can make use of other people's money merely by paying them a fair fee for their money's hire.

Know that much education is free, that self-education in some fields can be better than school education, that vast stores of information may be used free, that industry and trade stand with open arms to receive the willing worker. Know that our economy is so vast and various that any special talent can find the place where it is needed; and our economy is filled with unmet needs which *you* can meet.

I forbear from giving you a list of the many well-known men who began their lives in poverty. We have met many of them and shall meet others. *Cast out fear of poverty and drive ahead.*

2. The fear of criticism. Your mind has limitless power to make a dream come true—provided you allow your mind to work unhampered. Few fears hamper a mind so quickly as the fear of criticism. It can stop you before you get started. And yet it is nothing but the influence of another mind or other minds—a negative influence which often is only imagined. A person who is filled with fear of criticism often will not put forth his ideas lest he be rebuffed, and so he loses his great gifts of imagination and self-reliance.

We may examine the careers of men who achieved mighty breakthroughs in their fields and we may marvel at the way in which they found their abilities and put them to effective use. At the same time we may see many of the obstacles they had to overcome. Rarely, however, do we know of the *adverse criticism* many such men faced. Had they feared this criticism and let it take root in their minds, all their ability to conceive and achieve might have been crippled. Indeed, they never might have felt it, for their minds would not have been free minds that drive ahead.

The automobile, of course, "would not work." Nor would the airplane. Nor would space travel. By the time Henry Ford was ready to manufacture automobiles on a mass production basis the automobile obviously worked, but mass production of such tricky devices was sneered at. They were a laboratory curiosity. Nobody could supply the gasoline necessary, nor the rubber, nor insure that such necessities would be available to a motorist wherever he might travel. Furthermore, said the bankers with whom Henry Ford preferred not to do business, people simply would not buy such a high-priced gadget in sufficient quantities. Almost everyone who knew of Ford's plans condemned them on one ground or another. Surely the sustaining power of love helped Ford to know his own mind, for Mrs. Ford said simply: "Go ahead no matter who criticizes."

More recently, a man named Henry Land took a photograph of his young daughter. She wanted to see the picture right away. He explained that first the roll of photographic paper must be taken out of the camera and developed in a darkroom by means of certain chemicals. Once the negatives were obtained, they had to be printed by intense light upon another kind of paper which in its turn needed chemical treatment; and so, at length, pictures would appear.

At this point his unhampered mind took hold. Why not build a camera which produced finished pictures? Anyone who knew anything about photography could have given him a dozen reasons why not—but criticism did not stay the development of the Land-Polaroid camera which does exactly what young Miss Land requested.

Criticism cripples as well in the realm of pure ideas. When I set out to organize the Science of Personal Achievement, I was almost snowed under by the criticism heaped upon my head. Most of the criticism came from my nearest relatives, and this is hard to take. I could not then have put in words the power that kept me going—but I had my mind upon my goal, not upon obstacles, and I kept going. This first practical Science of Personal Achievement has earned more money for its users than was contained in Andrew Carnegie's entire fortune—and he was very likely the world's richest man.

It is one thing to listen to advice from a person qualified to give advice. It is quite another to allow adverse criticism to blunt the fine edge of your own conquering mind. Notice how much of such criticism comes from people who criticize everything—in particular, from people who criticize everybody who tries to succeed. Failure, like other forms of misery, loves company. *Cast out fear of criticism and drive ahead.*

3. The fear of ill health. Probably you know more than one person whose main topic of conversation is health—or rather, ill health.

Such people would rather describe their operations than talk of the benefit they derived—if indeed they needed the operations in the first place. They start each day by searching for symptoms, first from the hair down and then from the toes up, and will find many a "sure sign" of illness with which to bore their friends. They buy every quack remedy that comes along, follow every health fad one year which turns out to be an anti-health fad the next year. They are hypochondriacs; they imagine illness, fear illness, and literally bring illness upon themselves—for such is the *negative power* of the mind.

In my sixty-odd years of adulthood I have been gratified to see that physicians give increasing attention to psychosomatic illness, or bodily illness which originates in the mind. Since man's earliest history, however, it has been obvious that almost all of our illness is caused by *un*-peace of mind. Here is a very partial list of symptoms which can arise from mental conflicts, fears, and tensions:

Headache	Circulatory trouble
Indigestion	Frigidity
Ulcers	Impotence
Arthritic pains	Rashes, other skin afflictions
Constant fatigue	Mouth infection
Sleeplessness	Rectal disorders
Slow healing of wounds	Muscular cramps
Kidney trouble	... and more ... and more ...

Then there are the many mental disorders, ranging from extreme nervous tension to outright insanity, which often are caused or aggravated by a mind which fights itself. The list of ills to which body and mind may yield is almost endless, so let your first step toward good health be this: do not dwell upon the image of illness. The mind tends to transmute *all* beliefs into their physical equivalent. Why, then, see yourself as anything but a person who enjoys good sound health from top to toe and back again?

Even if you do contract some illness or injury, hold to the peaceful knowledge that it is merely an adverse incident of life which of course you will overcome. Moreover, a mind filled with faith and confidence can better see beyond a disability to the healed condition, the *Yes* condition—and this above all is a healing aid which cannot be supplied by medicine. It is *conceived,* and therefore it is boundlessly powerful.

FAITH is the greatest of all healers. FAITH is the great universal medicine which prevents illness, cures illness, builds a resistance to further illness, heals and sustains. Have FAITH in your health, and it is as though ill health starves to death for lack of food. Keep ill health out of your conversation. Keep ill health out of your mind. Reflect your faith in the image of a Prince of Sound Physical Health and that Prince stands by, almost invincible.

Then, to prove conclusively that you have stopped believing in ill health, empty your medicine chest down the drain. *Cast out fear of ill health and drive ahead.*

4. Fear of the loss of love.   Love walks hand in hand with peace of mind. A couple who truly love one another often reflect that love upon the world like a beacon of happiness. They "belong to each other," we say, and in many ways they do. Yet look beyond the trite statement and you will see that *belonging* is not the same as selfishly *possessing.* One who really loves another does not hold his mate in chains of jealousy, for this is fear, fear of the loss of love. True love knows no fear. Moreover, love cannot be *demanded;* it must be *given.* Should it cease to be given it no longer exists.

The end of love is not pleasant. No adverse circumstance is pleasant when it occurs. Yet to fear it in advance, as so many do, is as damaging as to imagine one's self dead in advance of dying.

A particular person's love may be lost, but love itself never is lost. The capacity for love beats with the heart. It seeks another, and love for one person always can be transmuted into love for another.

Know that there *is* another. Know too that love also transmutes itself into great achievement and great Service. Charles Dickens' first love almost ended in tragedy when he found it was not reciprocated. He transmuted his love into his writing, and his most popular book, *David Copperfield,* arose from a heart which *seemed* to be broken.

Love generously. Love fully. Love faithfully. Love is a great power for good when you get it, but love can destroy you when it gets you. Do you think I am cynical in talking thus of the most sublime of all emotions? No, I am following the purpose of this book and showing you the lessons of life itself. Any fear holds you back and hurts you. *Cast out fear of loss of love and drive ahead.*

5. Fear of the loss of liberty.   I read recently about a man who had served a term in prison and had been released. He had difficulty in finding a job, for he was honest enough to say he was an ex-convict. He was for a time unable to come home to his family, for they mistrusted him. Within himself, however, he knew he was a changed man, and with quiet persistence he has won back a place in the world of honest people.

He expressed his thankfulness at having regained the privileges of working for a living, of planning a career, of having a family and a home. "But all these blessings have their foundation in a greater blessing," he said. "I have my liberty."

Millions have learned what happens when an entire nation loses its liberty. The necessities of life may all be present, and many of the luxuries, but without the liberty to speak one's mind and live one's own life, all the rest seems a mockery. I recall a group of men and women who crossed the ocean in a tiny, unseaworthy boat and nearly drowned several times in order to win their way to our land of liberty. This sailing craft began its voyage with two masts, and at one port of call they sold one mast in order to buy provisions—yet still they struggled onward to find liberty.

And I know of many who have given up so much liberty of body and mind that they might as well be in prison or living under a dictator. Also I know many others who so constantly fear the loss of liberty that the fear itself becomes a fetter on their souls—as is the case with fear of any kind.

When I speak of freedom of mind and body I speak of a

basic, personal freedom. It is not a physically absolute freedom. If each of us were absolutely free to do whatever he wanted to do, we would have chaos instead of civilization. Peace of mind includes going along with the laws and customs of our times and our society. It also includes a balanced view toward any temporary loss of freedom.

A little while ago I suffered a temporary loss of liberty to get about as I wish. A light case of influenza sneaked past my Prince of Sound Physical Health and sent me to bed for three days. I could have fretted about the appointments I had to cancel; but if I had, my mind would have lost its liberty. Instead, I devoted the time to peacefully and restfully outlining this book. It had been a task which I had been "getting around to" for a long time. Once again I proved the soundness of the principle that *every adversity carries within it the seed of an equivalent or greater benefit.*

The concept of *time* is closely allied to the concept of *freedom.* Time is wealth, and unlike money when it is gone you cannot replace it. Many a man who arrives promptly for an appointment only to be kept waiting—or who is stuck in a traffic jam—gets into a stew over this infringement of his right to spend his time as he wishes to spend it. I have pointed out to salesmen that time spent in an anteroom can be time spent in reviewing one's sales pointers and thus be the better prepared for selling—or, in many cases, the time may be spent in observing and listening so that one gathers useful information about the customer's needs. For a salesman or anyone else, enforced waiting time can be transmuted into a time of quiet relaxation which restores the strength of mind and body. Even a driver in a traffic jam can keep his mind peaceful and thoughtful, and it is often on such occasions, while one is alert but not heavily concentrating, that the subconscious mind feeds back the answers to questions and problems which may have lain within it a long time.

Peace of mind is a many-splendored thing. Now connect it with the statement you read a moment ago: *Time is wealth, and unlike money when it is gone you cannot replace it.* Peace of mind is so beneficial to your entire well-being, however, that it is almost certain to extend your life and to help you keep active and productive far into your later years—so that "lost" time *can* in a sense be replaced, and at a most valuable period.

Liberty includes peace of mind; peace of mind is a basic liberty. We have too many slaves to the clock, too many slaves to the bankbook, too many slaves to convention and to self-consciousness. Before you say *I am free*, see if you answer *yes* to these questions:

When circumstances require me to use my time in a way I did not plan to use it, do I, in that time, know my own mind and use it beneficially?

Have I set up my work schedule so that I need not live in fear of work overwhelming me and stealing my hours of rest?

When I find a way to express myself, and know it is socially acceptable, do I continue to express myself in that manner even though others may think it strange?

Have I freed myself of any family or regional or cultural custom which has hampered my career or my personal life?

Am I willing to question the ways in which other people do things, and never make an absolute guide out of "That's the way it is done"?

Do I realize I am not working for money, but for that which money can buy?

If you honestly answer *Yes* to all these questions, you are essentially a free person and you do not fear the loss of freedom; you know that freedom cannot be taken away from the soul.

Notice the last question especially. When I became aware of the drives which enable men to make great fortunes, I also became aware that some rich men do not have peace of mind. An appreciation of money is a far cry from the worship of money, which in the end destroys happiness. Remember, this book shows you how to grow rich *and* have peace of mind.

Liberty extends in many directions. Those who fear slavery are the ones who have made themselves slaves, for they have conditioned themselves to it and they know how defenseless they have become. *Cast out fear of loss of liberty and drive ahead.*

6. Fear of old age. "I used to be a good amateur shortstop," mourns a man of seventy-five, "and now I couldn't stop a grounder that was rolling more than one mile an hour."

Such remarks are typical of those who fear old age and so cannot know peace of mind in the years which should be most rewarding. Old age is a handicap, yes, but only in connection with certain types of physical motion. Nature never takes away anything without replacing it with something of equal potential value. When Nature takes away youth, she replaces it with wisdom. It is impossible for a young person to possess the accumulated wisdom and experience of a person of ripe age. Think that over before you say old age is a drawback!

It is pathetic to see people assume extra handicaps because they are past forty or past fifty or even past seventy, when these handicaps exist only in their own minds. They show an inferiority complex, allow younger people's thinking to overwhelm their own mature and experience-backed thinking.

They apologize for being old, as though living past youth were a disgrace. They do not *expect* to feel the impulses of initiative, imagination and self-reliance—and so, of course, they don't feel these so-called "youthful" qualities. They act as though losing youth's springy muscles must mean you lose the power inside your head. This is so only if you wish it—only if you *fear* old age.

Recently I set up an entirely new series of schools in several cities, where men of all ages can learn the art of positive thinking and how to use it to achieve success. Is it "odd" that a man of my age should embark upon such an enterprise? Only to a fearful, hampered mind is it odd. While I remain in direction, I can hire younger, more active men to do the "leg work." In fact, I can do a better job of such direction than I could have done forty years ago. I have that much more experience. Also I have peace of mind *in depth*, as I did not have it forty years ago, when I did not yet completely see the forces which make men what they are.

Part of the fear of old age, with many people, stems from the feeling that an old person inevitably must miss a great deal. You cannot partake in so much that is going on. Because of this, some people of ripe years attempt to masquerade as youths and only succeed in being ridiculous.

It is not necessary to partake physically of the entire world around you so long as you keep in touch with that world. Every few years we see an advance in the means of communication, so that the affairs of all the world can be brought into the living room. Surely the neighbors of my youth would have been less ignorant and superstitious if they had had today's opportunities to know what is going on.

To keep yourself in tune with youthful states of mind, however, I invite you to make use of a procedure I have found very useful. Every year I *subtract* one year at the time of my birthday. Then I pay particular attention to the aspects of the world which appeal to a person of that age. I am now back in my late twenties, renewing my acquaintance with my state of mind in that era, and also with much that is unique with the present late-twenties generation. Viewing as I do from the vantage point of experience, I have doubled fun; and at the same time I gain a perspective on myself as a younger person might see me. The experience is both valuable and delightful.

Look deeply into your own vast experience—refresh your deep knowledge of human nature—find and feel the positive forces which *never* are out of reach. Old age can be the greatest time of your life. *Cast out fear of old age and drive ahead.*

7. Fear of death. My father tried to fill me with the fear of fire and brimstone which would be my lot after death. In fact, he tried to beat the fear into me. Fortunately it never took hold, even though such a dismal belief was fostered by our local church.

If you have to rise above your religion in order to rid yourself of the fear of death, then rise above. Nobody has the right to tell you that *his* way is the way to enjoy yourself after you die. You need only to look down the street where another group of people is being assured that another way is the only way. Again, you may believe, as I do, that nothing you do in your lifetime has any effect upon what the life-spirit may experience or where it may go after death—and it is still a belief, no more.

It is, however, a belief which helps you considerably in living a good, useful, hearty, happy life *right now,* and enjoying every bit of it. As for your being honest and helpful with your fellow men, so that they too may enjoy living—this is part of your peace of mind, part of your success in living.

During my entire life I never have sought anyone's opinion about anything, unless I had reason to believe that another person knew more about a subject than I did. I have found many *opinions* about what happens after death, but I never have found anyone who *knew* anything about the subject. Shall I fear death, then, merely because it is unknown?

No, I shall remind myself that there are two types of circumstances. Type One is the kind of circumstance which one may control, modify or avoid; this type is worthy of one's attention. Type Two consists of circumstances which one cannot control, of which death is the prime example. I shall therefore do what I can to remain in good health and good spirits, avoid obvious threats to life and in other ways make logical use of the motive of self-preservation. But as for giving a second thought to death itself—why worry about the uncontrollable?

You wish to provide that your money or property goes to your loved ones after you die? Very well, this is controllable. We do not delude ourselves into thinking we will *not* die. Yet having mastered the philosophy which accepts death as inevitable and which makes no false attempt to see what lies beyond the veil we cannot penetrate, you will fear nothing. Your mind will turn from death to life—from *No* to *Yes*—from guesses to realities. *Cast out the fear of death and drive ahead.*

Man was made to live in full possession of himself. Whoever created man gave this wonderful new creature a possession not shared by any other creature—the possession of his own mind. Along with this, the unknown Creator provided that man be capable of fear because justified fear is a part of self-preservation. One who meets a tiger on a jungle trail, and has no weapon in his hand, is well advised to be fearful and to take immediate measures toward his self-preservation.

Likewise do we exercise caution in any circumstance of inherent danger. The motorist, one hopes, drives with attention to the rules of safety. The child is taught to look both ways before he crosses the street. Self-made fears, however, are another story. Apparently man's mind must also be capable of entertaining self-made fear, or else it could not have its great breadth of creativeness. Yet both through the study of psychology and through common-sense observation we see that self-made fears are unhealthful and damaging.

Being in full possession of your own mind, you *can* free yourself of this kind of fear. When you relate yourself properly to life you have no need for such fears and no occasion in which to suffer them. I repeat: If you have to rise above your religion in order to rid yourself of fear, go ahead and rise above it. Along with this . . . if you have to become bigger than your local folkways to rid yourself of fear, go ahead and rise above them. If you have to rid yourself of certain people's company in order to rise above your fears, go ahead and rid yourself of such company, knowing the world is full of people who are better employers or better customers or better friends for you. You would take drastic steps to get rid of any poison that found its way into your food. So let it be with fear, the mind poison.

Fear is the tool of a man-made devil.

Self-confident faith in one's self is both the man-made weapon which defeats this devil and the man-made tool which builds a triumphant life. And it is more than that. It is a link to the irresistible forces of the universe which stand behind a man who does not believe in failure and defeat as being anything but temporary experiences.

Again the Supreme Secret has beckoned to you. When at last I give it to you beyond question, you will not be surprised.

CHECKING ON CHAPTER 4:

Fear is like prayer in reverse
With positive prayer we appeal to positive and helpful forces beyond ourselves; with fear we appeal to negative, destructive forces. Anything you fear is much more likely to harm you than it would be if you did not fear it. This is notably true of the fear of poverty, which cancels the courage necessary to leave poverty behind you no matter how many generations of your family may have been poor.

Your mind has limitless power to make a desire come true
To make a beneficial desire come true, your mind must work unhampered. Fear of criticism can cripple even a highly intelligent mind. Many successful men had to overcome obstacles of which we know, but also had to overcome criticism. Of the damaging wishes which, alas, come true, the most prevalent is a wish we generally would deny having— the wish for ill health which is founded on the fear of ill health. A long list of ailments arise from a fearful mind which fights itself. Faith is the greatest health-sustainer and the greatest healer.

Only fear can rob you of love and liberty
True love is not possessive love. The capacity for love remains even when love is denied, and fear should not hamper the expression of your love as transferred to another person —for love cannot be demanded, it must be given. Liberty,

too, lives within the heart despite outward circumstances. Loss of liberty as well may be incurred within the heart even when outward circumstances indicate one is "free." Freedom is a many-splendored thing, and you should search your life to find where you may have lost it and substituted the slavery of fear instead.

The years past youth can be the best years of your life
Nature always provides a compensation for anything she takes away. Giving up the intense physical drive of youth, we acquire wisdom and experience which only age can bring. Modern devices help us keep in touch with the world. Reducing one year from your age on each birthday gives you perspective both on youth and age. The fact of death need not be denied, but nobody knows what lies beyond death's impenetrable curtain so there is nothing to fear from a circumstance we cannot control. No matter how old you are, you can keep yourself so busy living that the fear of death finds no place in your mind.

5

Will You Master Money— Or Will It Master You?

Anything that robs you of peace of mind robs you of life's greatest wealth. You may lose peace of mind by pursuing money too anxiously, or by trying to acquire more money than you can spend wisely. Money you earn through constructive work is the money most likely to benefit you. It is a mistake to deprive young people of the need to know life through work. Anyone can save, and the effort you make toward saving a percentage of your income gives you a true knowledge of the value of money. Saving also prepares you to handle many opportunities which otherwise might slip by.

IN my explorations of the points of view of young people I rarely find a great appreciation of money, most especially when a good sum of money is yet to be earned. This is proper enough. A lack of money makes the business of living so difficult it is very likely to destroy peace of mind.

So the young man pursues money. For a good part of his life he is likely to have no difficulty whatsoever in spending as much as he makes. If he has a family, they help him spend it. A successful man, however, is not very old before he begins to accumulate some money beyond his immediate needs and his household bank account. This money is likely to go into investments, real estate and the like.

Be he a truly positive-minded man, he will soon own considerable amounts of both property and money. And somewhere along the line he will have passed an invisible border. He is now *rich* in the sense that he has a considerable surplus above his needs. Undoubtedly he can fulfill any reasonable want. And so, while his financial records show he is rich, his inward and very private record should show he has peace of mind.

He will have peace of mind—if he has mastered money. He will not—if money has mastered him.

A man who makes a big splash may be a man who has gone overboard. The "big splash" is the big show of one's material wealth. I have freely admitted my own weakness for making a big splash in the days of my Catskill estate—which I was fortunate enough to lose before it permanently harmed me. Not every man is endangered by making a vast show of his wealth, and some seem to thrive on it. Others enter upon such conspicuous display that obviously they have gone overboard—their souls are drowning in their sea of dollars.

Some years ago a man who had earned several million dollars suddenly went bankrupt. When the lawyers searched his assets, they found a large warehouse filled with valuable antique furniture, magnificent paintings and the like. They all belonged to the man who was bankrupt and he had paid for them in cash. But had he ever enjoyed them? Most of those precious items never had been unpacked! He liked to talk about his treasures, however, and make himself sound like a veritable Croesus. Such an accumulation mania is at the opposite pole from a mind that knows peace.

"They are going to take it away from me!" The fear of poverty has a strange and ugly first cousin. It is the rich man's fear that his money will be taken away from him; or that he will not be allowed to pile up his money into ten times the sum he possibly could use—twenty times—thirty times!

I once knew a majority stockholder of the fabulous Coca-

Cola Company. He had gathered money in many ways, and was worth about twenty-five million dollars. Did he have peace of mind? He had a mind filled with hatred and mistrust. His worst hatred was directed toward the government. Although he was then well in his eighties, he always prophesied that the government would cause him to die a pauper.

The last time I ever saw him, he asked me a most significant question: "If you were in my place, what would you do to protect your peace of mind and save your money?"

I had determined that for the sake of my own peace of mind I never would start a quarrel with this man; but, if he ever asked me a direct question, he would receive a direct answer. Even so, I asked him now if he wanted my honest opinion. "Yes!" he said. "Naturally!"

"Well," said I, "if I were in your place and wanted peace of mind I would not save my money. Your peace of mind and your money have become enemies who cannot live side by side. If I were you, I would first convert all my money into United States Savings Bonds so that it would go to work for the benefit of all the people. Then I would pile all those bonds into my fireplace and set fire to them. And as I watched my money go up the chimney, I would watch a great deal of my unhappiness burn away."

My friend snapped, "Don't be facetious!"

"I was never more serious in my life," I replied. "If *I* had *your* fortune and it deprived me of *my* peace of mind, I would first put my money where it would be well distributed and then I would burn every symbol of my government's debt to me. Then I would go to bed and sleep like a child and wake up feeling peaceful and free."

I did not expect this man to follow my advice. To the day he died he lived in fear and bitterness, and I believe that the illness and debility which dogged him long before he died was rooted in his love—not of mankind, but of money.

There are very few people for whom advice to burn their money would be good advice. The *principle* is what holds for every one of us. Nothing, absolutely nothing is as precious as your peace of mind. Few young people see this. Some people see it as they gain more experience. Many never see it. Remember, you can be rich with peace of mind, but if money or anything else gets in the way of your peace of mind, choose peace of mind and let the other go.

Notice I made no attempt to evaluate my friend's complaint against the government. His complaint may in some ways have been justified. It was his attitude I drove at—an attitude of fear and distrust while he was at least twenty-five times a millionaire and could have done so much toward making himself and others happy.

How much money does a man need? Andrew Carnegie certainly had a firm hold on methods for making money. In his later years, his earnest wish was to give this "know-how" to the average man. Mr. Carnegie was one of the first of the enlightened industrialists who saw how important it is for a nation to spread its wealth.

He saw that millions can be rich in the sense of having plenty. He also saw that, in the nature of things, the man who has millions always will be an exception. He saw that a goal of "millions" or even "a million" is not the right goal for the majority of men. For many, such a goal sets up strains which deny peace of mind. They may give up too much that is necessary for men of their personality, and so end with nothing. He admonished me again and again to make this clear, and I have done my best to do so.

How much money, then, does a man need?

As much as will keep him and his loved ones in what he considers solid comfort, along with enough luxury so that he may feel he has tasted the treats of life.

Aiming for this, and always maintaining his peace of mind, he conditions himself to a full use of his self-confident faith. And lo! out of this conditioning he often finds a money-making power beyond his dreams. For such a man, excess money never will be a curse. He knows how to live, so he knows how to broaden his life. He has never tried to cheat others, so he knows how to help others.

The man who wanted a hundred billion dollars. A student of mine once flew all the way from India to have an interview with me. First he sent me a letter in which he stated that his major purpose in life was to accumulate one hundred times as much wealth as Henry Ford had accumulated, or about one hundred billion dollars. He wished to be one hundred thousand times a millionaire.

When at length we sat in my study, I asked him what he would do with that modest little sum of money.

After some hesitation, he admitted: "Honestly, I don't know."

"Well," I said, "the possession of one hundred billion dollars by one individual poses a threat to the world. But let us put that aside. If you desired to spend the sum in helping the people of India overcome the superstitions and outmoded customs which have held them in bondage for centuries, I'd have some sympathy with you. It seems to me that you just want the money for the sake of outdoing Henry Ford."

He thought awhile and admitted this was so. I helped him search himself, and he saw that in using the Science of Personal Achievement he had "taken the bit in his teeth" and was galloping beyond control. What the mind builds in imagination, the mind can indeed build in reality; but we speak of a mind in good balance. Discussing his affairs, he came to see that a quarter of a million dollars would buy him what he really wanted. With that realization, the tense businessman— he was an importer—relaxed and said he felt much better.

This story's sequel involves another of those "coincidences" I do not believe are really coincidences. Before this man returned to India I helped him secure several contracts for the sale of American-made products in his homeland. His profit eventually amounted to just a little over a quarter of a million dollars.

Money that benefits you most often comes from work that benefits you. In the last chapter I planted the idea that one can insure that his money and property go to persons of his choice when he dies. Unlike death itself, the bequeathing of assets is a controllable circumstance.

You are going to make money; and when you do, please be careful that such a bequest does not rob an inheritor of his peace of mind.

It has been said, and with reason, that a rich man's son often does not display the ability his father had. I believe that many rich men's sons are robbed of this ability because they inherit their fathers' money. By and large, the "old man" worked for his money. His money came to him side by side with the development of his insight, his ability, his knowledge of people and his knowledge of the world. He was not given riches by his father; he was given riches by his work.

Now let us look at the son. All his life he has lived in the midst of money and the many comforts which money buys. He knows he is going to inherit great amounts of money. Assuming that he does have the inherent willingness to work hard—what happens to that willingness? In many cases it is replaced by a willingness to get something for nothing, and thus he never learns one of the basic lessons of life.

Great fortunes or modest fortunes are a blessing only when they are used in good part to benefit others. No father benefits his son when he robs him of initiative. No testator favors a beneficiary by making it unnecessary for him to work. You may wish to shield your inheritors from the meanness of poverty. Well and good! Beyond that, do not shield them from life with a wall of money. Let them have the priceless opportunity of building better lives with their own life-taught wisdom and their own constructive work.

In my youth I worked as a secretary to a wealthy lawyer who had two sons somewhat older than myself. These youths attended the University of Virginia. It became my duty to make up for each of them a monthly check for one hundred dollars as spending money. In those days a hundred dollars would buy three or four times what it will today. How I envied those boys!

When I had been in business college, learning how to earn my own living, I had often gone hungry because I literally did not have a cent in my pocket. I vividly recall standing in front of a store and longing for some apples which were priced six for a dime. At length I went in and sold the storekeeper on the idea of trusting me for the dime until I got through school and began to earn money. Such were my memories as I made out those magnificent monthly checks.

By and by my employer's sons came home with their diplomas. They also came home conditioned to easy living and with little idea of what work is all about. Were they inherently as capable as their father? We shall never know. One of them was put into a good job in a bank his father owned, and another was made manager of one of his father's coal mines.

Ten years later they had completely wrecked their father's fortune and his health as well.

I no longer envy anyone, for envy is no part of peace of mind. As I look back, I am grateful that I had to undergo such experiences as negotiating a ten-cent long-term credit. And I am grateful that, when I began to earn money, my earning power became part of my self-fulfillment. I am even glad that when I made mistakes and lost money, I had no rich father to see me through, for I found a mighty teacher in adversity.

My book *Think and Grow Rich* has been read by perhaps seven million men and women. In the twenty years since it was published I have been able to talk to some of these people, and I see that some have used the book to help them become truly rich. But some have used it to help them become rich in money only. It is time to set down once more the twelve great riches of life:

1. A positive mental attitude
2. Sound physical health
3. Harmony in human relationships
4. Freedom from all forms of fear
5. The hope of future achievement
6. The capacity for faith
7. A willingness to share one's blessings
8. A labor of love as an occupation
9. An open mind on all subjects
10. Self-discipline in all circumstances
11. The capacity to understand others
12. Sufficient money

These are the riches which can and should go along with peace of mind. Notice I have set money in the last place, and this despite my insisting that it is very difficult to have peace of mind without sufficient money. I set it there because you yourself will automatically give emphasis to money. Now and then, therefore, I must remind you to de-emphasize it and remember this: Money will buy a great deal but it will not buy peace of mind—it only will help you find peace of mind. But neither money nor anything else can help you find peace of mind unless you begin the journey from within yourself.

Basic steps in building your income. I have been told that it is not good logic to warn people of the dangers of misusing money, when probably they do not have enough money to make them worry about misusing it. I would follow this advice if I were writing a book merely about how to earn money. This book also is concerned with showing you where you are going and how the world looks when you get there. It helps you build correct attitudes right at the start.

As long as we have pointed firmly at those attitudes, however—as we shall point again—I shall set down some practical ways in which a person who has little or no capital can begin to build his wealth. Each of these ways is specific unto itself, so to speak, but is capable of almost infinite modification. It is up to you to pause as you read and apply these procedures to yourself, your talents, your surroundings and, above all, your goals.

1. Get other people to help their own businesses by helping yours. A young life insurance salesman was having trouble in placing policies with heads of families. Using this adversity as a springboard, he wondered why he could not sell insurance to the very same men, not in their role as heads of families but in their role as businessmen. After all, money taken out of the family budget is money gone; but a business expense offers an opportunity of bringing back the expended sum many times over.

He began with a leading restaurant owner in his town. He pointed out to this man that he might very well advertise that the food he served was so wholesome and sustaining that people who ate in his restaurant were likely to live longer. The restaurateur said this was indeed so and he intended to make sure it always was so. Good, said the insurance man, and explained the rest of the plan. The restaurateur was to offer to insure the life of each regular customer for one thousand dollars. Details were worked out and the offer made the restaurant's business boom. Needless to say, it helped the young insurance man.

He extended the idea to a group of filling stations, to a large grocery and to others. I am not positive it was this man who originated the idea of adding life insurance to mortgages so that the mortgage would be paid off if the purchaser died —but he certainly made good use of this angle as well.

Now stop and think: How can you get other people to help their own businesses by helping yours?

2. Show someone how he can get more for his money. Here we are not talking about setting yourself up as a business adviser, so that people seek you out to learn how they can get more for their money. We assume that the initiative must be yours.

Here is how one man did it:

Working at a low salary for a distributor of magazines, he took notice of many different kinds of printing. As with another man I have mentioned in this book, he noticed that many of the printing jobs could have been done with more taste and style.

Now, this young chap was discovering that most jobs of any kind are not done as well as they could be. Take note of this, for a fortune can be made on the idea.

The young man found out more about printing, then went to a large printing firm. He arranged to bring in printing jobs at a 10 per cent commission. He then went to large users of printed matter and collected a great many samples, which he took home and studied.

Selecting two or three brochures which obviously needed improvement, he arranged with a free-lance commercial artist to prepare a sample layout for each, on the promise of a fair fee if the job went through. An advertising copywriter who had spare time contributed his own talents on the same basis. Armed now with a good "rough" of an improved job, the young man took the brochures to the firms which had issued them and simply showed how much better they could be.

Now, let us look into some of the practical psychology at work here.

To begin with, a person or a company may go on almost forever with some condition or process or product that "gets by." He may not realize he is merely getting by; or if he does, he is too busy or too lazy to do anything about it.

Along comes someone who makes him dissatisfied with what he has and in the same moment shows him how to do better. Moreover, the work is all done for him. Why not take advantage of it?

Now stop and think: How can you show someone how he can get more for his money? Extend that: How can you help someone get more for his money in such a way that he will thereafter depend on you to show him again and again?

3. Bring producer and consumer together.   The farmer used to have a tough time bringing his goods to market. Imagine an isolated farm in hilly country, on a road that was mostly mud, and with horse and wagon the only means of transportation. Still, the farmer had to bring his produce to town and so he did by hook or by crook.

Everything in our economy intermeshes with everything else. As the automobile came in, roads had to be improved and they were. Now the farmer could carry his goods five to ten times the distance he used to and still get home the same night. Soon someone found he could set up marketing centers between towns, and draw on the increasing car traffic for customers while the farmers were very glad to be a continued source of supply.

Farmers used to depend on peddlers who came by perhaps twice a year, sometimes on foot with huge packs on their backs. Unrolling his pack on the kitchen table, the peddler would provide the farmer's wife with needles and the like, the farmer with tobacco and fish hooks—and above all, with news. How hungry people used to be for news! The peddlers invariably had more money than the farmers, for they performed the valuable function of bringing producer and consumer together.

When the farmer wanted to sell or buy a horse, he often was assisted by a broker who helped both parties reach an agreement on price, then sealed the bargain by making them shake hands. The broker, too, generally made more money than the farmers because he brought producer and consumer together.

Recently I read of complaints by shoppers in the Soviet Union. It seems they spend endless hours standing on line in front of separate, specialized food stores. Eventually they may adopt the American idea of bringing many producers and many consumers together in convenient supermarkets.

Fortunes have been made in this revolution in merchandising, especially as supermarkets—and their sprawling parking lots—have moved into the suburbs and even far out into the country. Fringe benefits have come to many property owners who saw how to ride along with the trend.

A woman lived alone on twenty poor acres which had mostly been taken over by scrub pine. At last she decided to sell the old homestead. Neighbors told her, sighing, that she would never get much for it. A local real estate man made her a pitiable offer.

This woman, however, was one of those elderly (in years) people who never had seen any reason why her mind should not remain alert. She told herself that her farm must be good for *something*. She decided to spend thirty days in an intensive investigation of what run-down farms are good for. Before the end of that thirty days she had found she could sell it as a base for a riding stable, complete with pasture and pleasant riding trails, for twice what the real estate man had offered.

But also she had studied several supermarkets in the area and had concluded that her farm would make a good supermarket site. She sold out finally to a supermarket for five times what the real estate man had offered.

When roads were paved and transportation by automobile became so easy, it was predicted that the mail-order house would disappear. After all, why should a person buy from a catalog when he can buy from the store itself? Such firms as

Sears, Roebuck and Montgomery Ward nevertheless continue to flourish.

Despite constant rises in postage rates, thousands of mail-order businesses thrive on selling everything from postage scales with the new rates printed on them, to books, household furnishings, preserved and fresh food, vitamins, equipment for hobbies, boat supplies . . . the list is almost endless.

Why is this so? Because times may change but universal needs always continue. Showing a person that he can write his name and address on an order form and drop it into the mail, and be assured of prompt delivery of something he wants, continues to be a good way to bring producer and consumer together.

Sometimes the producer sells directly to the consumer. Far more often the consumer buys from a middle man who assumes retail selling as his special function or from a manufacturer's representative.

Now stop and think: How can you bring producer and consumer together?

Some of the money you earn should stay with you. Certainly we have not exhausted the subject of making money! You may even feel that in giving the subject a once-over-lightly treatment, I have not done justice to it. I suggest, however, that you reread the foregoing three items and see in how many ways you can relate yourself to them. They have a great universality. Stretch them—you need not be too literal —and you will find they cover a vast variety of business situations, a broad horizon of opportunities. Note that they have not been tied to any particular craft or skill, since the fields mentioned are illustrative of many others.

You will find it an interesting exercise to see how many incidents of your own affairs can be fitted into one or more of those three categories. If you will put aside your own work and see yourself as a consumer, you certainly will "fit"! We shall touch upon many other principles which help hardworking men make money.

We still are talking about money and peace of mind.

Nobody who goes too deeply into debt can count on having peace of mind. You may have it for a time, but now and again the debt comes into your consciousness and you feel you are not quite your own master; somebody else owns a piece of you. I am not talking here of ordinary business credit without which business hardly could exist, but more of personal debts.

Having some money laid away is a means of avoiding the uncertainty and often the embarrassment that goes with incurring a personal debt. But saving does more for you than merely make it possible to spend the money you save. Saving gives you the habit of gauging your money against your needs. It helps to remind you that money is good only because of what it can buy in goods and services, and again it helps you gauge what you need in the way of goods and services.

The habit of saving does away with the habit of waste. As saving becomes a need, through habit, many a man finds he can live just as well as he did before, on the same salary, and this even if some prices have gone up. Why is this? Because he stops throwing away portions of his money on needless or frivolous items; he buys more carefully; he conserves his clothing and other possessions. He finds out how to make his money do its absolute most for him. And he does not do this by forcing himself into poverty for the sake of building his bank account. He continues to live at his general level and finds he can save as well.

What should you do with the money you save? There is no single answer that fits everyone.

I have seen and heard of a good many instances in which small saved sums—in one case as little as two hundred dollars—were used as investments in small businesses of good promise. Some of these investments paid back many thousand per cent. Of course you cannot count on this, but bear in mind that an opportunity arose and a person who had saved was able to take advantage of that opportunity without borrowing, without obligating himself.

A young couple had formed the habit of buying "on time." They were always in debt. One day the wife calculated the amount they had paid out in interest and said, *Never again!* The couple was about to give a party and needed a new bridge table with four matching chairs. But the wife said they would play bridge sitting on the rug—and incur no more debts. They called it Turkish Bridge and had a hilarious good time.

This experience caused them to put aside some friends who seemed unable to entertain without making a show, and cultivate friends who valued friendship more than display— friends who turned out to be far more worth knowing. Also they began to save one-tenth of their income every week. One day they went shopping with money in their pockets and found out this great truth of merchandising: merchants sell for less when they sell for cash.

In addition, the husband felt more relaxed and confident now that he was out of debt and also had a backlog of money. This helped him in his job. He was called in for an interview, during which his employer asked him casually if he saved money in any of the local banks (just another way of asking "Do you save money?") The young husband's confident and affirmative answer was the right answer, and he got a promotion which led to greater things. Saving *is* an index of character for it has much to do with a man's sense of purpose and his ability to manage his affairs.

I once helped a man start saving even though he said it was absolutely impossible for him to do. First we set up a goal. It was the purchase of a handsome sport jacket, a sensible purchase in that he could wear it in his business as well as during leisure hours. The price, which would not buy an equivalent jacket these days, was $24.95.

Then I made this fellow set down every cent he spent for two weeks. We went over the list together. The conversation went something like this:

"Can you give up two packs of cigarettes a week?"

"Yes."

"Instead of spending fifteen cents a day on a shoeshine, will you spend a dollar on shoe-shining equipment and shine your own shoes? And get a better shine for perhaps two cents?"

"Yes."

"Will you spend no more than one dollar on your lunch?"

"No, I eat with people who like to eat heartily and . . ."

I told him about a lunch I had had with Henry Ford. I ordered a lobster salad for three dollars. The billionaire ordered a sandwich and his total bill was eighty-five cents. Mr. Ford was not an eccentric about economizing. He was just a big enough and peaceful enough man to feel he could eat what he wished.

The man who could not save now said with determination: "I'll keep my lunch check down to one dollar. Yes!"

"Well, by saying *Yes* three times you've saved yourself at least ten dollars a week."

"Ten dollars a week!" He was astonished, then thoughtful. Without my having to oversee the process, he got himself out from under a great many other small, money-eating expenses. He found he now lived better in ways that counted, and he saved as well.

Whether or not you are short of money, I suggest you fill in a list of your own. Think about expenses you can reduce or eliminate if you really want to. Set down the amounts per week, total them, think about that total, ask yourself what that sum could buy for you in one week, in two weeks, in a month, in a year.

This experience is important. Here is a list to point the way:

Shoe shines	$	Items of which only	
Smokes	$	you know	
Alcoholic drinks	$	————	$
Entertainment of a		————	$
casual nature	$	————	$
Gambling	$		
Bad debts	$	Total	$
(Are you a sucker?)		Grand Total	$
Extra adornment	$		
Fancy food	$		
Total	$		

Chapter by chapter you are growing more and more familiar with the Supreme Secret.

CHECKING ON CHAPTER 5:

Will you master money—or will it master you?
Once you earn a considerable surplus above your needs, you should enjoy both riches and peace of mind. You will have peace of mind if you have mastered money, but not if it has mastered you. Too many men use money merely for conspicuous consumption. Too many, having millions, live in fear of losing them. If money or anything else gets in the way of your peace of mind, take peace of mind and let the other go.

Money that benefits you comes most often from work that benefits you
A man needs enough for comfort and for a good share of the world's luxuries. Aiming at these and retaining his self-

confident faith in himself, instead of straining for many times more than he can spend, he often earns much more than he expected. No father benefits his son when he surrounds him with money and prevents him from learning life's great lessons through honest work. Keep your mind on all twelve of the great riches of life, and know that your journey toward riches must begin within yourself.

Basic steps in building your income
One way to build income is to show others how they can help you succeed by advancing their own success. Another way is to show someone how he can get more for his money. Another is to bring producer and consumer together, which can be done in many ways. Always, some of the money you earn should stay with you. Debts can rob you of peace of mind. Saving is a habit which gives you many benefits besides money in the bank.

How to start yourself in the saving habit
Almost anyone who is short of money can stop the drain of small, unnecessary spending. Doing this, you often find better and more interesting ways to enjoy life. You can live as well as before because you augment your ability to handle money. The ability to save is a good index of character, and employers know it. Make a list of every cent you spend on certain items, and you will open your eyes to the total you spend—a total which can be saved toward purchases which hitherto have seemed beyond your means, or kept as a means of taking advantage of low prices or investment opportunities.

6

The Blessed Art
of Sharing Your Riches

Wealth that is shared creates more wealth, and you can share many forms of wealth besides money. Today's millionaires themselves point out that anyone can become a millionaire because today's wealth is so wide-spread and gives rise to so many opportunities. When you share in your own home you create a basic harmony which adds to your success and peace of mind in everything you do. Start now to share what you have, and when you have plenty of money you will share your money the more wisely and with greater benefit.

YOU are going to make money. If you do not allow negative points of view to trip you up, you will march straight forward on the road to riches. Yes, you are going to make money in solid sums—money that comes to you through your own worthy efforts—money you spend for your own worthy desires—money you spend in helping others.

Will you build your character while you build your fortune? This, as by now you know, is not exactly "another matter." There is a strong connection between the power to make money and the power to know your own mind and fulfill your own self as a fully realized person.

Again we shall examine a technique that goes with being rich and having invincible peace of mind. So far as sharing *money* is concerned, you may see this technique as belonging to your future. So far as sharing other forms of wealth is concerned, this technique is yours right now. Use it and make it part of you. Life proceeds according to a great Law of Compensation. The more you give of what you have, the more comes back to you—and it comes back greatly multiplied.

He gave away 90 per cent of his working hours. One of my distinguished students, Edward Choate of the New England Life Insurance Company of Los Angeles, decided to help his government sell War Bonds during World War II. He devoted 80 per cent of his time to this effort for which he received no direct compensation.

In addition, he gave 10 per cent of his time to counseling and training other life insurance men, his direct competitors. For this he neither asked nor received compensation. He used the remaining 10 percent of his time to sell life insurance on his own account.

One might think that a man who gave away 90 per cent of his working hours would ruin his business. Let us see. A life insurance man is considered to do pretty well if he writes $1,000,000 worth of insurance in a year. During the first three months of one war year, Edward Choate wrote more than $1,500,000 worth. Most of this was written in his own office, on the lives of men who sought him out and asked him to accept their applications. *They were men who remembered him in connection with the services he rendered while he was giving away 90% of his time.*

In giving of his time, Mr. Choate never hinted that he wanted anything in return. Yet such is the Law of Compensation that a return is inevitable. You may wish to look at it this way: every time you share your blessings with another, you become his creditor. Eventually, the debt is paid. Somehow, debts have to be paid.

They gave away a philosophy and it returned manyfold. One of the most valuable gifts you can give any man is the gift of *direction.* Show him how to gather his forces and focus them the way he wants to go, and literally you do more for him than if you handed him a million dollars. Andrew Carnegie gave away multiple millions for the purpose of founding free libraries, hoping thus to disseminate knowledge of all kinds and lift the entire knowledge-level of a nation. Above and beyond this he made available the Science of Personal Achievement in which I have played my own part.

One of the greatest rewards of my life has been to see my book *Think and Grow Rich* given away as a means of spreading the philosophy. Mr. Choate is one of those who have given away hundreds of copies. Often he gives the book to men who by no stretch of the imagination ever will become prospects for life insurance. He gives the book to others because it helped him find himself. Undoubtedly it has brought him business. Undoubtedly it has helped many a man to be able to afford the life insurance he needs.

Another student of mine moved to Oakland, California, with a total capital of less than two hundred dollars. He invested half his capital in *Think and Grow Rich.* He made a practice of lending the book to his neighbors, asking only that each person keep the book one week. At the end of that time, he would pick up the book and lend it to some other person. Later he came to tell me what his habit of sharing his own philosophy had done for him.

"When I started to lend those books of yours," he said, "I had no other purpose in mind than to make friends among my neighbors by introducing them to a philosophy which has so much friendship in it.

"Meanwhile I had started my machine shop with one small drill press. Very soon, some of my neighbors who had read

Think and Grow Rich began to spread the news of my shop and my philosophy of giving as much as I can, and business began to pour in. I never spent a cent in advertising. I never solicited a single order from anybody."

At last report this man had $100,000 worth of equipment in his shop and had grossed more than a million dollars. He said: "It beats anything I ever heard of in my whole life!" But you hear of it when your ear becomes attuned to the great art of giving. It is not a new idea. The great philosophers of all times have pointed out the riches we gain when we give away some of our wealth—of money, of time, of service, of unpremeditated moments of kindness, and especially of love.

Giving to those who help themselves. Any man noted for his millions receives endless requests for money. He knows that most of these appeals come from people who will not use the money for necessities, let alone in any manner which helps them in their careers. He cannot hope to screen all such requests. Often it is far simpler for him to give large sums to a charity or to endow a foundation.

Those who have worked for their money know that the virtue of money consists in its use, not in its quantity. This is equally true whether the amount be a dime or a million dollars.

Henry Ford once was approached by Miss Martha Berry of the Martha Berry School in Georgia. Miss Berry asked for an endowment for her school, but Mr. Ford refused the request.

"Well," she countered, "will you give us a sack of peanuts?"

Mr. Ford obliged by buying her a sack of raw peanuts.

With the aid of her students, mountain boys and girls, Miss Berry planted and replanted the peanuts, selling the crop until she had converted the original sack into six hundred dollars in cash. She then returned to Mr. Ford and handed him the six hundred dollars, saying, "You see how practical we are in the use of money." Mr. Ford handed back the six hundred dollars, along with some two million dollars to build the fine stone buildings which now adorn the campus of the Martha Berry School in Mt. Berry, Georgia.

Mr. Ford made very few gifts of this kind. Experience had taught him that all too often gifts to schools are handled by impractical people who know very little about sound business (or farming) methods. As long as Martha Berry lived, the

Ford private car appeared on the railroad siding near her school once a year, while Mr. and Mrs. Ford paid a visit.

A present-day multimillionaire, Henry Crown, who arrived in this country as a poor immigrant from Lithuania, is now a leading figure in the vast General Dynamics Corporation. Mr. Crown has put a great deal of money into a plan which teaches aspiring young people how to handle capital. He has set up a fund of eight thousand dollars at a good many colleges, and this money is invested each year by the senior economics class. When the class makes a profit, its members share the surplus, and the fund is passed on intact to the next class.

Wealth creates wealth. A large sum of money in the hands of one man generally does not create as much wealth as does money which circulates, provided that those who handle its circulation are interested in creating wealth.

A man's happiness and peace of mind depend on his sharing all kinds of wealth. Business relations cannot properly be described as a relationship of *love* between buyer and seller; yet when the idea of *service to one's fellow men* comes into the relationship, much that is profitable to both parties also enters in. "A little bit of myself," said Henry Ford, "goes into every automobile that rolls off our assembly lines, and I think of every automobile we sell, not in terms of the profit it yields us, but in terms of the useful service it may render the purchaser." Thomas A. Edison said: "I never perfected an invention that I did not think about in terms of the service it might give others."

The idea that a business should give its customers more than a product for a price is not new, and history proves it creates both good businesses and good customers. Good relations between an industrial employer and his employees, however, are not very old as history goes. This is natural enough when we consider that enterprises which employ people by the thousand have not been with us more than a few generations. They are a great way for the owner of the business to make money, and unfortunately many a labor force has been badly treated in the process.

In past years we had our own era of those industrial pirates who never thought of sharing with their employees the wealth their employees helped to create. While they made a great show of their money in New York, Newport or Palm Beach those men would have sneered at the idea that a society needs a large number of well-paid people who are able to buy more goods and lead better lives.

Millionaires are far more numerous today. More than five thousand new millionaires have so declared themselves on their tax returns in the last decade. Also, as I have mentioned, today's millionaires do not seem to want the notice that rich men used to require. Most of my readers will not recognize the names of some of the present-day millionaires and multimillionaires I have cited.

Nor do today's moneyed men seem anxious to form a definite class to which the poor may not aspire. I quote Arthur Decio, who made so much money in building and selling mobile homes: "It's easier to get ahead than it was fifteen or forty years ago. Look at the population growth and the tremendous rise in personal income. . . . This country is just loaded with opportunities."

So it is, and many of the opportunities would not exist if wealth were not better distributed than it used to be. Employers have seen the value to themselves, to their people and to society of taking workers into partnership with industry. A capitalist society proves over and over that it is the best way to create maximum, widespread wealth.

A victory for the Science of Personal Achievement. The R. G. LeTourneau Company is a large employer. Some years ago I received a phone call from a former student who had become one of its executives. "Please come to see us immediately," he said. "We have a difficulty which only you can handle."

When I arrived at the LeTourneau plant I learned that communistic influences had entered in the guise of a labor union. The company wanted help in immunizing its employees against this "ism," knowing that if the crisis could be surmounted the men would realize which way of life was best for them.

They asked me my fee. "Perhaps there will be no fee," I replied. "Give me freedom to act, and if I cannot overcome your trouble there will be no charge. If I succeed in eliminating the communistic influences, I will tell you later what my charge will be."

The deal was closed on that basis. I set up a cot in the plant and I stayed on duty day and night.

The basic trouble was twofold: the men did not realize, first, how the company returned to them part of the wealth they created; and also few individuals had any idea of their own power to take their own abilities and multiply them through the exercise of a positive mental attitude. Fear of poverty and other crippling fears ran rampant among them. Belief in wealth and happiness, and in each man's power to win his own wealth and create his own happiness, had been pushed aside by negative thinking.

Given this ground in which to sow their seeds of discord, the communist-minded organizers were able to make those men believe that their future should be in the hands of others —that they should reduce themselves to cogs in a kind of economic machine; that indeed it was *wrong* for a man of faith and ambition to rise where negative-minded men might not follow.

In combatting the Communists I never mentioned them. Rather, I taught the Science of Personal Achievement and that was all I needed to teach. In a short time the Le-Tourneau employees saw how much greatness each man has within his own mind—a greatness nobody else can or should handle for him. They saw what it really means to work and the rewards work brings to a man who has some goal besides three meals a day and really wants to achieve his ambition. They came to see that the rich men of their time owned no natural power which they themselves did not own, and all they had to do was to find their powers for prosperity and use them.

I succeeded. When I named my compensation, I received it immediately. Eight months later the company increased my fee. Thus it goes when men realize that wealth is not something you grab from another; it is something you build for yourself out of service to others, sparked and enhanced by your own positive, joyful inward drive. This is true wealth and part of peace of mind. I do not know how many of those LeTourneau men became rich, but I know they had reason to bear in mind the true picture of wealth and share it with others.

Sharing the wealth in your own home. You can tell a great deal about a man by what goes on in his home. Men who are successful in living—not merely in mastering the mechanics of some trade—generally maintain homes in which no one person has to be "boss" and there is true love and true sharing.

I have been in the homes of rich men whose wives had to

beg them for money enough to buy needed articles of clothing. I have been in the homes of poor men in which every purchase had to be discussed lest it leave no money for food; and the poor home was the happier because of its atmosphere of sharing, even though the lack of money was sadly felt.

I have at times been asked to give marriage counseling, and at times I have recommended that a marriage be broken. There are many reasons for such a recommendation, and I assure you the reasons are not trifling. I have noticed in such cases that lack of the ability to share invariably shows itself. Let non-sharing take hold at any level, in any aspect of married life, and it leads to other troubles.

You are going to make money, and when you do, make sure that your wife has a fund of her own to spend as she wishes. It will not be "her" fund in the sense that it is sacrosanct, for if you meet financial misfortune she will share this as well in a good and loving marriage. It will be "her" money in the sense that it is your recognition of your wife as a person in her own right, your partner, not your servant.

I am informed that much of the chatter that goes on in beauty parlors has to do with the clever ways in which women get money out of their husbands. Not a few must resort to slipping a few dollars out of his pocket while he sleeps. Others invent charities, or dream up "school expenses" for the children. Apparently, many a woman is literally forced into such tactics if she is to maintain a decent home, for her husband shows no willingness to shell out more than enough for a mere subsistence, if that.

On the other hand, many a woman in the sanctity of Hair-drying Row reveals she has lost her grocery allowance in playing Mah-Jongg or in some similar pursuit and she cannot admit this to her husband. The sum lost is rarely large, and Mah-Jongg is not wicked; it is the lack of frankness with her husband that is the truly damaging condition.

"If you knew how angry my husband can get," such a woman often says, "you'd know why I can't tell him." So it takes two to create the bad situation. Add to this the fact that many husbands never tell their wives how much they earn or how much they may spend on drinks or how much they lose at poker.

By and large when a man shows he is willing to share, a woman by her nature is eager to share lovingly with him. High on the list of information a man should share with his wife is the knowledge of how much money he makes and how he acquires his money.

Women generally stay at home or close to home while a man is out somewhere earning money. When a man comes home from his job, a woman likes him to bring with him some of the outside world. It is a smart man who sees to it that his wife gets a blow-by-blow description of all he does, and where he spends his time, without her having to ask for this information. There are sexual overtones in this, for a wife may work up jealousy for no reason, especially if a man has a job which does not keep him constantly at a desk or a bench within sight of others.

Share and you have a marriage; avoid sharing and you might as well be living alone.

Think back upon the nine basic motives we discussed in a previous chapter. To refresh your memory, they are:

Seven positive motives
1. The emotion of LOVE
2. The emotion of SEX
3. The desire for MATERIAL GAIN
4. The desire for SELF-PRESERVATION
5. The desire for FREEDOM OF BODY AND MIND
6. The desire for SELF-EXPRESSION
7. The desire for PERPETUATION OF LIFE AFTER DEATH

Two negative motives
1. The emotion of ANGER AND REVENGE
2. The emotion of FEAR

It has been said that the first three basic motives—love, sex and money—practically rule the world. I would not say this statement is entirely true, but there is a great deal of truth in it. A man who has not truly shared all of his life with the woman of his choice cannot know the magic of sex and love in their most sublime combination. But when a man lives with these motives, he often connects them like a mighty dynamo to the third. He makes more and more money so that he may share more and more of life's abundance with his wife.

No part of your existence can be lived separately from all the other parts. When you are successful in one area, it helps you to be successful in all other areas. Most especially, when you have peace of mind at home you can count on having peace of mind everywhere.

I'll tell a little story about or perhaps *on* myself. There was a time in my life when changing a flat tire upset me completely. Now, if a flat occurs on one of my long drives across the wide-open parts of our country, I change the tire and am not in the least upset. In former years I had more muscle—but in former years, I did not drive with the woman of my choice beside me, as I do today.

Everyone has something to share and gains by sharing it. When a stranger stops you in the street and asks directions, you share your knowledge when you tell him. You do not have to be rich in money in order to do this. If you are really rich in human kindness you will give the stranger a very careful explanation, and perhaps walk to the next corner with him and point out the way.

The poorest of us has much to share. In some ways a poor man has as much to share as does a rich man. Certainly it is so with love and with kindness.

I shall suggest three general ways of sharing which are available to almost anybody. You may not make use of the particular instances used as examples, but the list will serve to open your mind to the many possibilities of sharing more than money.

1. *Share your special skills or knowledge.* Many of us possess some special skill or knowledge which helps us earn money. We are used to selling our skill. Now look for a way to *give* that skill without thought of gain.

A much-needed clubhouse for boys was built in the slum section of a large city. The basic construction costs were provided by a large foundation, but the clubhouse never would have gotten started were it not for those who gave their skills. A lawyer volunteered his services in drawing up the incorporation papers and other necessary documents. A carpenter installed locker room partitions. A painter gave his own services and also supervised a volunteer crew which painted the entire interior in cheerful colors. A mason installed a concrete ramp at one entrance so that physically handicapped boys could make their way in.

2. *Share by filling a gap where you see one.* Mr. A loaned his lawn mower to his new neighbor, Mr. B, who had not had time to equip himself. This was the beginning of excellent good-neighbor relations between the two families—but for a

while it seemed as though matters were going the other way.

After Mr. B had trimmed his lawn, he returned the lawn mower with a big chip in one blade. Noticing this, Mr. A remarked diplomatically that Mr. B must have had some rocks hidden in his grass which chipped the blade. The new neighbor said gruffly that the blade had been chipped when he had been offered the use of the lawn mower, and walked away.

Since the chip was fresh and shiny, this hardly could have been so. Mr. A said nothing more, however. He limited his contacts with his new neighbor to mere nods if he met him in the street.

One day, Mr. B came around with a brand-new lawn mower and handed it to Mr. A. "I want you to have this," Mr. B said. "You see, I knew I'd broken that blade but I couldn't afford to have it fixed right then. I guess I should have said so, but, well, I didn't. Now things have turned out all right and I want to do more than merely have the blade fixed."

Thus is many a non-money debt returned with interest! Far more valuable than the lawn mower itself, however, was the atmosphere of cordiality which the two families found from then on.

3. *Share recognition and appreciation.* Notice how often you are recognized as being in a certain role—for example, the role of a customer—and so you are treated in a certain way. Now turn around the situation and recognize the other person. You will find it is a limitless form of sharing.

For example, you may stop your car at a filling station on a hot day. The attendant rushes up, mopping his brow, anxious to give you prompt service. You recognize him as a person who has his own problems and you say: "Take it easy. It's too hot to hurry." He will remember you the next time you drive in.

Say you are an employer or a foreman. One of your men does exceptionally good work. Many an employer or foreman would observe that the man is paid to do a good job, so what? A wiser supervisor will make a point of telling a worker that his good performance has been noticed. When a person does a good job, he is favorably disposed toward anyone who gives him recognition. Furthermore, he will try thereafter to keep his work up to a high standard.

You will offer many a kindness, you will perform many a free service, and in many cases you will see no return. Bear in mind there is always a return within yourself, for when you give of yourself you make yourself bigger. And remember the Law of Compensation which *always* works in your favor when you arrange it so. We shall look more deeply into the wonders of compensation later on.

Look for ways to share your wealth? Never ask, "What wealth?" In sharing, you will find you are wealthier than you think. Share more than money, and when you have plenty of money you will be more closely attuned to human needs and your money will give added benefit to those who share it.

The Supreme Secret is like a half-hidden treasure you may pass a hundred times a day without noticing; yet you see it from the corner of your eye.

CHECKING ON CHAPTER 6:

The more you give, the more comes back to you
Even a man who gave away 90 per cent of his working time became richer thereby. When you share your blessings with another, you become his creditor and eventually the debt is paid. You also can share *direction* in the form of a philosophy which leads to peace of mind and great wealth. Giving to those who help themselves is a highly constructive kind of giving.

Wealth creates wealth
When a buying and selling relationship contains the idea of service to one's fellow men, both sides benefit. Many early industrial employers took all they could from their employees and returned as little as possible. Today wealth is more widespread and this helps create more opportunities. A millionaire no longer attempts to make a great display of wealth, there are increasing numbers of millionaires, and rich men no longer see themselves as a class apart.

As you create your own wealth you can create your own happiness
Many people who work for others do not realize the extent to which they share the wealth they create, nor how they can create endless wealth in their own lives through the power of a positive mental attitude. Rich men have no natural powers denied to poor men. Every man carries his greatness within his own mind, and it is he himself, and not an outside power, who is the only one who can bring forth his greatness.

Sharing the wealth in your own home

Men who are successful in living generally maintain love and sharing in their own homes. When couples do not share, other troubles arise. When a man shows he is willing to share, a woman is eager to share with him. Three basic motives, love, sex and money, are said practically to rule the world, and this can be seen in many cases. No part of your life can be lived separately from the other parts.

Everyone has something to share

You can share knowledge, you can share love and kindness no matter how poor you may be. Almost anyone can share in three areas which offer themselves over and over; you can share your special skills or knowledge; you can share by filling a gap when you see one; you can share recognition and appreciation of others and the work they do.

7

How to Develop Your Own Healthy Ego

All your ability and personality show themselves in your ego. For many a man the ego works always at full power and for some it needs restraining. For most, it is as well to find and use some ego-boosting device. Your own ego-booster may be connected with the way you dress, the way you express yourself, your surroundings, some object which has symbolic value —or in some other way which has a special, individual meaning. The ego can be attuned to mysterious forces beyond one's self. Through your ego you can be guided toward an expression of yourself which reflects in your increased prosperity.

I HAVE spoken before and shall speak again on the need for knowing your own mind and going in your own direction. Now let us look at the *ego*, that invaluable mind spark-plug which my dictionary defines as "the self-assertive tendency of man."

People who have peace of mind also have healthy egos. Now, to some the term "healthy ego" brings to mind the picture of a loud, back-slapping type of person. This may be so, but it is not necessarily so. *Your* ego as *you* reflect it to the world has been built for many years out of childhood influences, later influences and a great many other factors. Your ego is as individual as your fingerprints, and what is "healthy" to you will not be healthy for another man.

Often ego seems to have a bit of vanity in it; but it is far stronger and far more subtle than ordinary human vanity. Think of your ego as an invisible part of yourself which makes you strong and resourceful, or puts obstacles in your way, *according to the sort of influence you feed it.*

Even the greatest of minds now and then find themselves with a rundown ego. Truly great men feel this, and quickly restore their egos. The purpose of this chapter is to show you some of the surprisingly straightforward ego-boosters which others have used, and to give you an assortment out of which you may choose and perfect a tailor-made ego-booster of your own.

The ego that was stronger than a clean shirt and a shave. It is old advice and good advice to say that being well-dressed and well-groomed gives a boost to your ego.

Now I want you to meet a man who knew that very well —but whose deeply abiding ego was strong enough to rise above a clean shirt and a shave.

The impact of this story will be stronger if I tell it in sequence as it came to me. It begins with my meeting Edwin C. Barnes when he was Thomas Edison's business associate. Mr. Barnes at that time owned thirty-one expensively tailored suits and in the course of a month never wore one suit two days in a row. His shirts were made to order out of the most expensive fabrics available. His ties were made to order in Paris and cost at least twenty-five dollars apiece.

One day I suggested jokingly to Mr. Barnes that he let me know when he was ready to discard some of his suits so that I might wear them.

"I know you are kidding," Barnes said, "but you might like to know that at the time I decided to associate myself with Thomas Edison, I didn't have the railroad fare to take me to East Orange, New Jersey, where I had to go to sell him the idea.

"My desire to get there was greater than my fear of the humiliation I would suffer by riding a freight train. I packed a suitcase—it didn't take long—and I traveled by boxcar.

"When I walked into Mr. Edison's office and said I wanted

to see him, I heard a titter of laughter all over the place. Finally his secretary consented to let me see Mr. Edison. As soon as I faced the great inventor I started telling him how fortunate he was that I was giving him the first chance at my services. After I'd talked a while, he rose, walked all around me, looked me over with penetrating eyes, grinned and asked: 'What did you come to see me about, young man?'

"That's how I discovered he was hard of hearing. Now I had to explain myself all over, loudly. My clothes were wrinkled and dusty, my shoes were scuffed, I had a two days' growth of beard, and I almost lost my courage. It is to Mr. Edison's credit that he did not judge me by my appearance. But I made up my mind, then and there, that never again would I stand before any man without knowing that I was better dressed than he.

"Now you see why I have all these clothes. And as far as my giving you my discards is concerned, I doubt if you would get from them the same ego boost they give me."

He was right. I never have felt the need to bolster my ego by personal adornment, and I too am right, for ego is a strictly personal matter. During the early part of my career I did stimulate my ego with that large estate and those elegant cars. Later, when my work became widely accepted, I became content with a much simpler style of living. Yet I do not neglect my ego, which functions through my Princes of Guidance.

Still, just like Mr. Barnes and so many others, I see myself reflecting long-ago experiences which I no longer wish to suffer. During my childhood I lived amid poverty and illiteracy, surrounded by poverty-stricken neighbors. Now I am very sensitive to the "feel" of any neighborhood in which I live, and it must be just right. I even inspect the approaches to my home to make sure they do not lead through any unpleasant areas.

You may find it instructive to look back at the early influences of your own life and see how much they may have to do with your actions now. Here are some questions to get you started. Think a while after each to make sure you have found the right answer.

As a child . . .

Did you have sufficient food, clothing and shelter?

If the answer is *No;* was it insufficient by any reasonable

standard or insufficient by some neighborhood or other
standard by which you have come to judge?

Did your parents, or someone else who had influence in
your life, tend to belittle you and make you feel that your
brothers and sisters or playmates were better or smarter
than you?

Were you called basically *bad* when you misbehaved—or
were your actions merely labeled as unacceptable?

If you were *bad* by definition, did you decide you were
going to live up to your badness?

Did you have sufficient schooling in the three R's so that
you never had to feel inferior, later, about your Reading,
Writing and 'rithmetic?

Are you too short, too tall or too fat, so that you feel conspicuous?

Are you exceptionally ill-favored as to appearance, or
scarred or crippled?

How would you describe the general atmosphere in your
childhood home? Peaceful? Antagonistic? Clouded by
worry? Cheerful? Carelessly happy-go-lucky?

Did your parents quarrel in your presence?

Were you conscious of people using you as an "easy mark"
or a "push-around"?

Were you fond of being the leader in games and clubs?

Did you set up a symbol of success early in life, such as "a
big house like Mr. Jones's" or "a job traveling to glamor-
ous places like Mr. Brown's"?

Did your parents encourage you to accept responsibility—
or were they overanxious to do everything for you?

Were you forced to be so much on your own that you
never felt you had anyone who really cared what happened
to you?

Thinking about such questions will suggest many facets of
your past which show themselves in your present actions. I do
not suggest you worry about your past; remember, when we
close the door on the past we close out a great deal which
otherwise might hamper us. At times, however, an under-

standing of past influences helps you to appreciate and enjoy your present ways of bucking up your ego.

A salesman sells through his ego. While I was engaged in organizing the Science of Personal Achievement, I made my living by training salesmen. More than 30,000 men and women came under my guidance while they were being trained to sell.

The first thing I taught my students was that before any salesman sells anything to anyone, he first must sell it to himself. That is, he must so condition his own ego that it is in shape to strengthen his statements, and he must believe that both he and his product are *good*.

An executive of the New York Life Insurance Company gave me an interesting case. One man had been with the company more than thirty years, and had maintained a high selling record. Suddenly his production dropped to almost nothing. The salesman could not tell what was wrong and neither could the company executives. They called me in to doctor the "patient."

I went out with this salesman to observe him in action. Soon I noticed that his basic trouble, after thirty years in the field, was the fear that he had grown too old for selling. He talked constantly about his age. His fear had developed into hypochondria and he felt he must use a walking stick to help him get around.

Somehow he had persuaded himself that he "didn't have it" any longer and so he expected to be rebuffed. He had allowed his ego to become so thoroughly subdued that he anticipated a *No* before he ever heard it—and that is the best way to make sure it is said!

Back in the office I said to this man: "I want you to go out and find one of those old-fashioned ear trumpets which once were used by the hard-of-hearing."

He protested, "But I am not hard of hearing."

"That's right," I said. "You hear too well. You hear the *No* before it is said. Now, I want you to simulate deafness. Place the trumpet at your ear when anyone speaks, pretend you didn't hear him and when he says *No* go right ahead with your sales talk."

We agreed that he could not sell life insurance to someone who really did not need it or want it, so nobody would be hurt. He found a monstrous old hearing trumpet and took it with him on his rounds. In his first week as a trumpet-user he procured applications from six out of nine prospective buyers. The next week he came back with eight applications out of twelve interviews—an almost unheard-of record. His ego restored to the *Yes* habit, he put away the trumpet and had no trouble thereafter.

Although my own hearing is fine, I seem often to come into contact with hearing troubles. My son, Blair, was born without ears. How I helped Nature give him sufficient hearing is another story; I am thinking now of the time when we sent him to public school wearing his hair long to hide the absence of ears. The other children made fun of his long hair, which was damaging to his ego. We promptly had his hair cut short; but first I sold Blair the idea that his affliction would be a great benefit to him when people understood about it. And that is exactly what happened, for people now were kind to him. He soon lost all self-consciousness about being different from people who have ears.

Perhaps I was inspired by Thomas A. Edison's determination to make an asset out of his deafness rather than a liability. I never saw him wear an expression of annoyance or disappointment. Rather, his expression clearly said: "My ego is under my control and it does my bidding without fear or limitation."

Your ego and your opulence. As with the ear trumpet, I have on many occasions been able to prescribe exactly the right ego-builder for a particular person. It requires knowing the person, of course; and when you wish to prescribe for yourself, you will see the importance of that ancient, great advice: *Know thyself.*

Now and again a man will stop working before he should, and find himself at loose ends. This was the case with a former student of mine named Ray Cunliffe. He had owned a Cadillac agency in Chicago, which he sold at a handsome profit. Since he now had plenty of liquid assets he decided to take a year and play around and "rest up," as he put it.

Before the year was out he grew restless. He looked around for a good Cadillac franchise, but found none. Another six months passed and he began to eat deeply into his cash reserve for living expenses. About that time he joined a class in the Science of Personal Achievement which I was teaching in Baltimore.

Ray and his wife had been accustomed to having servants in their home. Now they had had to let the servants go and do their own housework. One day while Ray was in the basement doing the family laundry, it occurred to him that he was making the very mistake I had mentioned at a recent lesson. He wasn't nourishing his ego. He was starving it; beating it down.

In his excitement and anxiety he came to me for personal help. He told me his story, then asked, "Where do I go from here?"

He had told me that for several years his wife had wanted a mink coat which would cost some three thousand dollars. Also I could see that although he drove a Cadillac it was beginning to look shabby; and so did the clothes he wore.

So I said: "Ray, get out your notebook and pencil while I give you a prescription for opulence.

"Number One: Go to the nearest Cadillac agency, trade in your present car and buy a new car of the model you like best.

"Number Two: Go to the best fur store in town and buy your wife a fine mink coat, even if it costs more than three thousand dollars.

"Number Three: Go to your tailor and have a complete wardrobe of suits made up. Then buy the ties and shirts and shoes you need to go with your new suits.

"Number Four: Have the mink coat done up in gift wrapping. Place the package in your new Cadillac, hire a liveried chauffeur, and while you are not at home have the chauffeur drive the car to your house and deliver it and the package to your wife.

"Take these four steps immediately. Then come back for the next prescription; that is, if you need another. This one prescription may turn the tide very quickly."

When the new Cadillac and the mink coat arrived at Ray's home, his wife at first refused to accept them. The chauffeur merely handed her the car keys and walked away, leaving the car in the driveway with the coat on its seat.

Ray's wife finally tried on the coat. Sure enough, it was the very coat she had tried on out of curiosity—and longing—a few weeks earlier.

Suddenly she felt a surge of confidence and happiness. The same thing was happening to Ray. Now, what I have to tell you seemed like magic to him and it may seem like magic to you, but it was not magic.

The cook and the housemaid who formerly worked for the Cunliffes showed up and asked if they might return to their old jobs. Without the slightest hesitation, Mrs. Cunliffe told them to come right in.

As for Ray himself: A friend phoned him and said: "I hear that the Baltimore Cadillac Agency can be bought. You might look it over."

Ray looked it over and saw it was good. The deal required $150,000, however, which was quite a sum for him to raise on short notice. His ego had lifted itself out of the doldrums. He said: "I don't know who is going to let me have the money, but I know that I shall get it."

The following day he called on a man he had been avoiding—a wealthy man toward whom he had begun to feel inferior. No inferiority marred his approach now as he explained he needed $150,000 to put himself back into business.

"Fine!" was the answer. "I'm glad to see you getting back into the business where you always made money." He wrote Ray a check for $150,000 and added, "You can pay this back year by year as your profits come in."

So Ray Cunliffe was back in a Cadillac agency of his own and doing a good business almost before he had had time to wear all his new shirts. He had only one disappointment; he was disappointed that I did not show surprise over his sudden turn of fortune.

"Well, Ray," I said, "I can't get excited over something I have seen happen hundreds of times." But I was pleased, of course, to see once more that poverty-consciousness can be replaced by success-consciousness which invariably draws success as though with an all-powerful magnet. Ego is the key to this—an ego filled with self-confident faith, and bolstered by the means that is right for *you*.

You can paint an ego-picture of yourself and use it for first-aid. Sometimes a man faces a single situation on which a great deal depends. Often such a situation involves another person who must in some way be persuaded—for whom some situation must be made attractive. When you know that other person, often you can use the power of your ego to give him the picture he wants to see. Even when you do not know him personally, you often can look closely at the values of the situation and come up with a picture that is attractive to him.

Let us now look at myself at a stage in my career when my ego faltered.

I have told how I was associated with Don Mellett, the

newspaper publisher, and how his murder forced the post-ponement of publication of my first manuscripts; also how it saved me from wearing a Big Business label.

As I related, I had to get out of town to hide from the thugs who believed I had been involved in the attacks upon their illegal rum-running. In the time I spent hiding, my spirits were not good. I came close to losing my faith in my ability to carry out the great task Andrew Carnegie had assigned me some twenty years before.

I took hold of myself and decided to break the bondage of fear. I would find a new publisher. Since Judge Gary had died, I had to start from scratch—not an easy task for the unknown author of a trail-blazing work.

As my ego rebuilt itself and my success-consciousness reasserted itself, an insistent inner voice began to tell me that I would find my publisher in Philadelphia. I knew no publisher in that city, but the inner voice became so strong that on a capital of fifty dollars I got into my car and headed toward the Quaker City, half believing I would find the solution to my problem, half believing I was going mad.

Once in Philadelphia, I began to look through a classified telephone directory. I hoped to find a cheap boardinghouse where I could stay for a couple of dollars a day. Now, follow closely what happened, for this story is one of the most startling you ever may read, and it contains—besides its revelation of the power of ego—a revelation of the Supreme Secret that can transform your life.

As I turned the pages of the directory, that inner voice spoke again. It said: "Never mind looking for a cheap boardinghouse. Go to the best hotel in the city and register for the best suite of rooms in the house."

I closed the book and blinked my eyes. I had less than thirty-five dollars in my pocket! But the command was so irresistible that I picked up my luggage, marched to the best hotel in town and took a suite which cost twenty-five dollars a day.

The moment I signed the register, I knew I had done the right thing. My ego and my faith swelled within me. I could not then have put the Supreme Secret into words, but I know it took hold of me.

A quarter was a good tip for a bellhop in those days, but I tossed the boy a dollar. No sooner had I seated myself in one of the luxurious chairs than the inner voice spoke once more.

"You were restrained from registering in a cheap rooming

house because such an environment would have placed you at a great disadvantage in dealing with a publisher. Right now you need an ego-booster, and you are getting it from this finely appointed suite of rooms. Now your mind can conceive on a positive plane that brings success. Ready? Call into your consciousness the name of every person you know who has the financial means to publish your works. When the right name appears, you will recognize it. Get in touch with that person and tell him what you desire."

Without a shred of doubt, in perfect faith, I began to review the names of men who would be able to finance the world's first practical Science of Personal Achievement. After three hours of this my mind went blank. Then a name popped into my mind with such compelling effect that I knew this was the man I wanted. He was Albert Lewis Pelton of Meriden, Connecticut.

All I knew about Mr. Pelton was that he had published a book called *Power of Will,* and that he had advertised this book in my *Golden Rule* magazine several years previously. Immediately I wrote to Mr. Pelton by Special Delivery. I informed him that I was about to confer upon him the honor of publishing the Science of Personal Achievement.

Two days later I received a telegram saying Mr. Pelton was on his way to Philadelphia to see me. I shall never forget the expression on his face when he was ushered into my suite, nor the words he uttered: "Well, an author who can live in a suite of rooms like this must be the real McCoy!"

The manuscript was about the size of an old-fashioned family Bible. It contained 1800 pages, and weighed about seven pounds. I handed it to Mr. Pelton and he sat down and turned through the pages. After about twenty minutes he closed the book and laid it on the table.

He said: "I will publish this philosophy and pay you the regular author's royalty."

We sent for a typewriter and he typed the contract. At one point he said: "I suppose you'd like an advance on your royalties? I'll make out a check right now." I replied nonchalantly, holding fast to the image my ego had built: "Oh, make it any amount you care to."

"Five hundred dollars?"

"Okay."

Some months later the first published set of my work, *The Law of Success* in eight volumes, was presented to me. Those had been successful months in many ways, for I had regained the power of a positive point of view. I hope sincerely that those who read this story will not have to win their own positive points of view the long way around, as I did.

Had I been guided by some unseen power? I believe some outside force was guiding me. I believe that a mind attuned to currents of faith is attuned beyond its own physical dimension. Later in this book I shall relate another experience of the sort—actually the experience which resulted in my writing this book after nearly seventy years of getting ready.

Since that eventful day in 1928, I have helped tens of thousands of men and women to rehabilitate their egos. Most of them I never have met, for our minds contacted each other through the pages of my books. Through my lectures and personal lessons I also have helped many thousands to find the same key to the conceptual and achieving powers of the mind, and here in many cases I had the gratification of seeing it happen.

I have developed a considerable ability to gauge people's needs in this direction and to "press the right button," so to speak. But what takes place when the button is pressed? Whence comes the power that revitalizes a faltering ego? What is it that turns a mind from *No* to *Yes* and so opens great gates of accomplishment? I still am seeking that answer. Perhaps the knowledge has been reserved for me to uncover as a sort of post-graduate course in my own work, for I never shall be finished with learning.

Look for your own ego-booster and you will find it. There are amazing varieties of ways to boost the ego. Although they may be mysterious in their inmost essence, their outward manifestations are clear to see. Consider the following examples; they are universal in their application and may help you find your own.

Among the successful insurance men I have trained is one among many who drives an expensive car. His ego-booster is more individual. It consists of a handsome golf bag and set of clubs he carries in full view in his car.

He thus carries with him the impression—both for himself and for others—that he spends considerable time playing golf and is always ready to drive to the links. I do not know if he would be as successful as he is if he did not always display this intimation of success, but I do know that he gets exactly what *he* needs as an ego-booster.

Another successful insurance agent I trained wears an

eight-carat diamond ring which seems to serve as his magic wand as he talks to prospects. This man is one of the largest producers for the Massachusetts Mutual Life Insurance Company.

Once he took his diamond ring to a jeweler for a new mounting. The job required a few days. During those days he worked harder than usual, used every persuasive argument he always had used in order to write a policy, and yet failed to make a sale. He said that when he began to talk to a prospect he would look down for his ring; the ring was not there and somehow he could not put himself over.

When the ring was back on his finger this man went to work as usual, and out of his first six interviews he received six applications for insurance—a record he never had made before.

As for myself, if I were caught in public with such a searchlight on my finger, I would feel so self-conscious that I would get in my own way and be unable to command my ego. To each his own, and a mighty power comes to the man who knows himself.

When a man comes to himself, discovers his ego and takes possession of it, the fact is revealed to the whole world. It is reflected in the tone of his voice, in his facial expression, in the lift of his motions, in the clarity of his thought, in the definiteness of his purpose, in a positive mental attitude that brings out in others the desire to believe in and work with this man.

Friend, when you become commander-in-chief of that very core of your mind, your ego, you are master of all you survey. You never will want, because you will unhesitatingly find the way to plenty. You never will fear, because your mind will not contain fear. You will be free, gloriously free, living a life that pays you in your own terms.

Some few there are who need reins upon their egos. They are so rare, however, that we need not write any part of this book for them.

A healthy ego is a means of health and peace of mind beyond comparison. Look, then, for the one right method or object or condition which helps you to fulfill yourself in "the self-assertive tendency of man."

Study the ways of any successful, happy people you know. Chances are that they possess and use the Supreme Secret.

CHECKING ON CHAPTER 7:

What it means to have a healthy ego
Your ego is the mind-power which helps you project your-self and your desires. It can make you strong and resource-ful, or put obstacles in your way, according to the sort of influence you feed it. We are familiar with the ego-boosting power of being well dressed, but a strong ego can rise above any limitation. When a man can afford to assert his ego in the ways he prefers, these ways often reflect long-ago influences.

A salesman sells through his ego
A good salesman knows that he is good and his product is good, and this confidence rarely falters. Sometimes a sales-man's success hinges upon some ego-sustaining factor, or some outside circumstance may so affect his ego that he slides from a *Yes* attitude into a *No* attitude. A salesman may even assume his hearing is poor in order that he may filter the *Nos* out of his dialogue with a prospect. With a salesman or with anyone else, a real physical handicap can be a lifelong drawback or lifelong stimulus—depending upon the power of the ego.

Your ego and your opulence
When the ego is strong it attracts success. When the ego falters, it can be restored by making sure that every ap-pearance and self-image is in its favor. A man who is used to living well, but has lowered his standard of living, can restore his prosperity by first restoring the *feeling* of pros-perity that comes with appropriate possessions and actions. Even when an appearance of prosperity is assumed for a short time, it can prove the turning-point because that is what the ego needed. The ego may thus be guided by mysterious, all-pervasive powers.

Look for your ego-booster and you will find it
Ego is a highly individual matter. Observe the ways in which others boost their egos and you may be helped to find your own ways. Sometimes it is in the means of expressing our-selves that we best sustain our own egos, as in writing in-stead of speaking, or vice versa. When you find your own best way to boost your ego, you have found a great treasure.

8

How to Transmute Sex
Emotion into Achievement Power

It is within every man's ability to transmute some of his sex emotion into a dynamic drive which brings success. This ability grows with your willingness to use it. Young men often make the mistake of seeing only the physical side of sex, so that they are in their forties or beyond before they begin to use transmuted sex energy to add value to everything they do. There is no interference with the physical side of sex, which in itself becomes a life-transforming power.

NOW and then a book "catches fire" and the author of that book has the satisfaction of knowing he has added something permanent to the knowledge of the man. So it has been with my book *Think and Grow Rich*. Although it is only one of several books built around the Science of Personal Achievement, probably more copies have been sold than of all my other books combined.

I have asked a number of people why they think *Think And Grow Rich* has sold so briskly for almost thirty years, and why it seems to be off to a fresh start in a slightly revised edition.* These people tell me the book is somehow more inspirational than the others—and I think I know the reason why.

I wrote it twice. The first time was in 1933, while I was on the staff of President Franklin D. Roosevelt, merely as a means of keeping busy while I waited for the crippling atmosphere of fear to pass. As I recall, I just sat down and wrote while I was serving the President without making any effort to condition my mind so that personal magnetism would be projected into the book.

It was some years later that I decided to publish the book. When I reread the manuscript I saw it lacked something. The answer to what it lacked actually was inherent in one of the chapters, a chapter on sex transmutation of which this pres-

* New York: Hawthorn Books, Inc., 1966 paperbound edition, Fawcett Publications, Inc.

ent chapter is a summing-up and a carrying-forward. I had written a book full of information but lacking in transmuted sex emotion. Now I rewrote it from start to finish and the effect has been electrifying. *Anything you do can be electrifying and positive and profitable when it is infused with sex emotion.*

Lest there be any confusion, let me state emphatically what you may be doing need have no connection whatsoever with the physical manifestations of sex. Nor does language have anything to do with it. The "something" I injected into *Think and Grow Rich* during its rewrite has carried over into all foreign-language editions of the book. It is just as inspirational in Brazil, for instance, where it appears in Portuguese, as it is in English.

What is sex transmutation? Let us first look at sex itself. Nature has provided that the vegetable and animal kingdoms know sex activity only in certain seasons. Man, however, knows sex activity in every season. Perhaps that is why sex makes so much trouble for so many people. They may keep themselves willfully ignorant of sex because they are afraid of it; they may debauch the sex instinct because they want to show they are *not* afraid of it or because they simply let it run away with them.

In either case, sex loses the deep force and meaning it has for man and only for man. Consider a certain class of professional religionists who advertise sex as a cardinal sin, who lump hell and sex together and come out against both as being approximately equal and equally evil. Such men say they are saving souls when in reality they are shriveling them.

On the other hand, we have the prevalent phenomenon of vulgar scribblings and pictures in public toilets. This is a twisted, sad outlet for the sublime sex emotion. Too many people are caught up in one extreme or the other; and as for the actual physical expression of sex, too many never find out how much of the spiritual is tied in with the physical.

When you see sex as the great creative force, creative not merely of children but also of all that is noble and enduring —then you are ready to see what sex transmutation can do for you. It is a focusing of sex energy into other channels where it adds immeasurably to one's power of achievement. It is not in any way a lessening of sex energy but rather a shifting of that energy, as though a central powerhouse had, for the time being, sent its pulsations into a different transmission line.

It is also a focusing of *personal magnetism*, which is really no different from sex energy. If you are more familiar with the term *personal magnetism*, well and good; but remember it is rooted in sex.

Successful people tend to be highly sexed.   Some years ago I operated a school of advertising and selling. One day my secretary announced that I had a caller who looked like a tramp. Perhaps because I remembered the man who became Thomas Edison's associate, I asked her to send the tramp in.

He was shabby, he wore a three days' growth of beard, and the cigarette dangling from his lips as he walked in showed he either did not know or did not care about politeness. He was selling advertising space in the *World Almanac*, a medium I never had used because I did not think it was suitable for my business. Despite the fact that this unkempt man gave me a bad first impression—despite the fact that he scattered cigarette ashes on my carpet—he left my office with an advertising order for more than eight hundred dollars.

This man certainly had psychological troubles but above and beyond them he had a tremendous personal magnetism. I heard it in his voice, so I listened to him. I felt it in the aura of his personality. For the first time I really gave deep consideration to the *World Almanac's* advantages—which proved out fairly well. But if that man who automatically used the principle of sex transmutation had straightened himself out in other ways, he might have owned the *World Almanac* instead of merely being one of its "space men."

I now watch for the phenomenon of sex transmutation in everyone I meet and have thought back upon others I have known. It is obvious that those who win the greatest success in all occupations and in all walks of life have high sex capacities which they transmute at will. They may not know they are doing it, but that is what they do.

There is an obvious connection with ego; and as with ego a person may have to search for the best way in which to express himself through sex transmutation.

When I was a member of the Chicago Rotary Club, one of our guest speakers was the late Dr. Frank Crane. Here was a man who had fine things to say, yet he had no gift of *speaking*. Even his appearance was against him. He bored everybody present, including myself.

After our meeting I walked down the street with Dr. Crane and we spoke frankly about the cold reception his talk had received. I gave him great credit for his message, which was unusually good—but unfortunately it had been spoiled by his delivery, and he knew it.

He told me he was the pastor of a small church and barely made a living. He asked me what advice I might have to give him.

I had been thinking. I told him he had a capacity for profound thought which he could put across in a popular, easily understandable way. Rather than do this by voice, however, he should do it in writing. If he worked up a newspaper column of sermonettes and syndicated it, he would reach thousands of people where now he reached only a small flock, and undoubtedly would increase his income as well.

"That sounds like a splendid idea," he said thoughtfully. We shook hands and parted.

After a time I began to see his daily column of sermonettes. Some years later he learned I was his neighbor at a New York hotel and he invited me to drop in. He had just completed his annual tax report, and with a broad smile he handed it to me. His net taxable income after all deductions amounted to something more than $75,000 for that year.

The late Billy Sunday expressed his undoubted sex magnetism in the way which was natural for him—through the spoken word, to tremendous audiences. He chased the devil up one side of the country and down the other, swaying crowds as few other preachers ever have done. He was so successful that his religious campaigns became big-time business ventures which were managed by Ivy Lee, a well-known public relations man.

Some said that Billy Sunday's success was due to his high spiritual qualities. Those closest to him believed his power came from his highly sexed nature, plus his ability to transmute sex emotion into sermons which were so fiery that even the devil could not withstand them.

Watch for the "something extra" and you will see it. In every generation there are only half a dozen men who are universally recognized as "great" violinists. Some hundreds play the violin very well, but beyond them stand the few who have that *something extra*. It is the more successful transmutation of sex emotion.

Of course the same applies to pianists and to other musicians. As I write, Arthur Rubinstein is in his eightieth year, and commentators say that he is not only perhaps the greatest pianist who ever lived, but that his performances always seem fresh and new. Rubinstein is also a great lover of life, a participator rather than an observer—and all this points to a deeply sexual nature and a transmutation of its wonderful emotion.

It is the same with political leaders, with lawyers, with athletes, with craftsmen. I discovered that a highly sexed bricklayer could lay nearly twice as many bricks in a day as a man who lacked that intensity, and lay each brick with the greatest skill, *provided he had learned the art of keeping his mind on his work.*

Looking back into history, we can see that many outstanding men in many different fields were known to have a considerable sexual drive. (History alone may not tell you this; but a study of biography will.) I shall set down a few names which may start you thinking:

George Washington	Robert Burns
Benjamin Franklin	Thomas Jefferson
William Shakespeare	Andrew Jackson
Abraham Lincoln	Enrico Caruso
Ralph Waldo Emerson	

Note that these men were not the victims of their sexual drive; they were its beneficiaries. They transmuted sexual energy into the energy of their individual accomplishments. You are not likely to find a single man in the history of civilization who achieved outstanding success that did *not* arise from his sexual nature. This applies to soldiers, statesmen, great thinkers, great explorers and other men of action, painters—all kinds of men, and not necessarily men of virtue. The sexual drive does not exist of itself, but as a part of the entire personality. Without it, however, much ability remains undiscovered.

I also have seen many instances in which sexual energy appeared to be the igniting spark, so to speak, of the "sixth sense." This great creative faculty lifts brain action far above its ordinary limitations. It is the psychological receiving antenna of those inspirations we call *hunches*. Surely it accounts for the "still, small voice" which now and then gives priceless guidance to the perceptive mind.

I knew a great orator who planned his speeches well, yet

at one point in every speech he would abandon his plan, pause very briefly and close his eyes. What followed when he opened his eyes would be the climax of his speech, so stirring that he often brought an entire audience to its feet. In that pause of two or three seconds I believe he focused all of his sexual magnetism and his creative imagination into a great receptive force which never failed him. In his own words: "I do it because then I speak through ideas which come to me from within."

The late Dr. Elmer Gates was one of the world's greatest scientists, although he never publicized himself. He patented more than two hundred inventions, many of which were created through a very significant method.

He had what he called his "personal communications room." It was lightproof and soundproof, equipped only with a small table, a chair, a pad of writing paper and some pencils. When Dr. Gates desired to focus his forces, he would shut himself into this room, sit at the table, and concentrate upon the *known* factors of the invention upon which he was working. Soon ideas would begin to flash into his mind concerning the *unknown* factors of the invention.

On one occasion he wrote rapidly for three hours, hardly aware of what he was writing. When at last he examined his notes, he found they contained principles which had been discovered nowhere else in the scientific world. These principles solved the problem—and broke ground for other men to follow.

Dr. Gates earned large fees merely by "sitting for ideas." Imagine a large corporation paying an outsider merely to sit in his room and think!

We cannot tell exactly where experience leaves off and intuition begins. It has been said that genius consists of the ability to see the patterns of things and project those patterns. The quiet focusing of inward forces surely is a great aid in summoning odds and ends of knowledge through the subconscious mind and forming them into patterns never seen before. Yet beyond this lies the Unseen which gives life to it all. And can this somehow be a function of sex? Why not—when all the world is male and female, and even the basic building blocks of the universe are oppositely charged particles which constantly interact.

In essence, sex transmutation is the ability to switch a desire for physical contact to a similar desire for expression—in art, literature, science, selling or anything else. The switch may be done so habitually that it is not a conscious act—but it always is there.

Transmutation of sex emotion in no way interferes with the natural sex act when performed at an appropriate time. While the energy is being transmuted, however, there is no desire for the physical act. *Something else that is very vital and important is being accomplished with the same energy.*

Yes, when you watch for the "something extra" you will see it. And when you watch for what could be the *something extra* but instead has become the *something wasted*, you can see that too. You can see clearly that many a man who could succeed does not succeed because he does not understand that sex is more than physical passion.

A lesson to learn while you are young. Remember, it is never too late to start living a wonderful new life. The potential always is there, and the means are available to any person who will reach out and take them.

Undoubtedly, however, certain lessons are better learned while one is young. Thus it is with the use of sex energy.

A highly successful businessman told me that if he had learned the art of sex transmutation during his high school days he could have become a multimillionaire in his early twenties. He was well along in his forties before he discovered that sex is an energy which can be directed into many channels.

This remark caused me to study the ages at which successful men generally become successful. It was interesting to observe that most of them did not succeed in a big way until they were well past forty, often fifty or sixty or seventy.

Success is good at any age, but the sooner you find it, the longer you will enjoy it. Success does depend somewhat upon life-experience; yet notice that I said *most* of those successful men did not succeed till they were past forty. An appreciable minority did succeed before they were forty, and one could see that they had learned the art of sex transmutation.

What generally happens is this: A man who is bursting with the physical energies of youth gives himself to the physical expression of sex. It does him no harm that he can see, so he never realizes how much of that energy could be doing him good in building his career, building his peace of mind, keeping him more alert and receptive to the ideas of his business. Transmuted sex energy could be adding warmth to his handshake, strength to his voice, attraction to his personality. It could help him be known as "one of those people it's good to know" and to be admired for being "one of those fellows who are on the ball." Since his sex energy is being used in purely physical sex expression, however, he does not know what he is missing . . . until many years later when he realizes why he may have missed success.

A man's love life, shared with the woman of his choice, can be a wonderfully sustaining force behind his career— while all the while it is sweet and good for its own sake. Sometimes a woman must point out tactfully to a man that she depends upon him sexually in ways which go beyond the marriage bed. In his role as provider he is still a sexual being, drawing upon sex energy *if it is there* as a basic energy that builds wealth. He should therefore keep some reserve of this energy so that consciously or unconsciously he can transmute it. Moreover, he will be the better off in that he exerts some self-control and self-mastery—a strictly human power which lifts us far above the animals.

A man past forty is more likely to find this out for himself and, as with the businessman I mentioned, wonder why it didn't happen sooner. Men in their twenties and thirties who read this are urged to pause for an hour of thought.

The power of love's partnership. For some people it seems impossible to understand that sex has three great functions in the life of civilized man besides giving pleasure.

(1) It is necessary for the perpetuation of mankind.

(2) It aids in the maintenance of health, as does the *proper* exercise of any other natural function.

(3) Transmuted into other channels, it works hand in hand with *ego* to bring out everything in a man that wishes to achieve, that wishes to excel, and stimulates him with added energy, strength of personality and resourcefulness.

On the other hand, it can wreck a man's career, health and fortune—but this is a misfunction and not the fault of sex but the fault of the man.

Some people never really make the effort to combine all of the functions of sex in their lives, perhaps because they think they are "overemphasizing sex" in giving it such importance. This is a prudish attitude and like all extreme attitudes must do harm.

Some insist on believing that when a man channels sex energy into his business, he takes the first step in wrecking his home. Of course homes have been wrecked by men so much in love with making money that they forgot they were married; but let us look at a brighter side of the picture.

This particular story came to me not long ago from the man who is living it. It is not, however, the first time I have heard a similar story. I could tell you the same anecdote about a manufacturer of trolly car conductors' uniforms (about 1910); about an operator of an early "flying circus" (about 1923); about a subcontractor of World War II lifeboat equipment. In short, the story is timeless. Right now it happens to concern a man in the rapidly growing field of micro-electronics. He is involved in a technology which has to invent itself as it goes along, and his problems are multiplied beyond ordinary business problems.

When this man faces an important decision, he never makes up his mind until he has had a sex relationship with his wife. Then, in love's partnership, he feels both rested and invigorated. On the following morning he makes his decision and acts upon it. His record of making good decisions is reflected in his success, and I am certain he transmutes a good deal of sex energy into his business. This couple is known for the happiness of their marriage and the harmony of their home.

Another man told me privately that in the very climax of the loving sex act with his wife he receives flashes of inspiration which have guided him correctly in all his affairs. I daresay this is unusual, yet it serves to show that sex does not exist in a separate compartment of our lives, but permeates our entire existence.

The women who make a man's world. It has been said: "Behind every man stands a woman." This statement is not 100 per cent true; but when you find an instance in which it is not true, you are well advised to ask: *Why not?* You will occasionally meet some rip-roaring character who says he is man enough to do without the influence of women, but the chances are he is not able to get along with women or with men either; or he may have such deep inner doubts of his own manhood that he overcompensates for his lack.

Man's greatest drive comes from his desire to please and protect women! The hunter of prehistoric days who brought back two bears to the cave when his neighboring caveman brought only one, surely looked forward, not merely to eating the extra bear, but also to the pride he would take in showing it to his woman. Today's "hunter" brings home the means to buy comforts and luxuries far beyond what is needed merely to maintain life, and if he is honest he will tell you proudly that he does it for his woman.

That strange and great man, Abraham Lincoln, was not happy with his wife. She was not the woman he had intended to marry. That woman, Ann Rutledge, died before she could marry him, and her death was one of the many misfortunes which molded his greatness. The power of the young frontier girl has extended from her grave into all of our subsequent history.

I am pleased when a man who has made a great deal of money, or wields a great deal of power, or both, expresses his homage to his wife. Often she is a quiet little person, yet you know the influence she has had upon that man and you know they always have been and always will be partners. You see success, you see the symbols of sex—a man and a woman— and you know that this life has been lived completely.

Your mind has many powers, and when you find the Supreme Secret you will know you have found the key to every mind-power you possess.

CHECKING ON CHAPTER 8:

Transmuted sex emotion can electrify your life
The same book can be written twice and gain a great force because the second time it was written with transmuted sex energy. Unlike the animals, man knows sex activity in every season, and this may be one reason why sex is so often misunderstood. Sex often is labeled as a cardinal sin to be avoided; often it is debauched; often it is made vulgar. When it is seen and used as the great creative force of life, it can, at the right times, be focused away from the physical act and become a source of lifelong achievement.

Successful people are highly sexed
Even a salesman who looks like a tramp can put over a difficult sale through the power of transmuted sex emotion. Religion often receives its force through sex emotion. Great artists know how to channel their sex energy into their artistry. Expert workmen as well show the good effects of transmuted sex emotion. Looking into history, we can see that many men made their mark upon the world by transmuting

sex energy into the energy of their individual accomplishments.

Sex energy and the "sixth sense"
Because it is strongly allied to the ego, sex energy can lift brain action far above its ordinary limitations. A great orator used his sex energy to give him climactic ideas with which to sway his audiences. A great scientist used the same dynamic force to solve the problems of invention. In essence, sex transmutation is the ability to switch a desire for physical contact to a similar desire for expression in some other field. This transmutation in no way interferes with the natural sex act.

A lesson to learn while you are young
Most men do not become really successful till they are past the age of forty. Their success often is delayed because in their earlier years they placed too much value upon the physical expression of sex and never realized how much it could add to their money-making power. Sometimes a woman must point out to her husband that sex energy has significance beyond the marriage bed. In a well-rounded life that knows the partnership of love, the physical act of sex becomes both a source of happiness and a source of strength that builds a career.

9

To Succeed in Life, Succeed in Being Yourself

Only the man who has found his true self can know himself, find his own best talents and achieve his own high success. We need to live our own lives, and this attitude should be instilled in childhood. With being yourself comes self-control, a mighty source of strength in handling both circumstances and people. Beware lest in trying to pile dollar upon dollar you give up too much of yourself, for that man is truly rich who owns his own mind as well as his own fortune.

"LIVE your own life!" I said in the first chapter. Now, as planned, we return to the same great theme. I hope you are now completely receptive to the idea of being yourself and living your own life. By now you have seen how much this inward quality has to do with setting free your mightiest powers.

Likewise you have seen that in this book I have paid some attention, but not very much, to the "nuts and bolts" of earning a very good living. The reason is not that "nuts and bolts" are not important; they are very important. This book, however, is devoted to helping you find and use *the basic drives that make a man.* When you have read this book— when you have read *and mastered* this book—the "nuts and bolts" come readily to your hand and you possess the skills which transfer those nuts and bolts into a mighty edifice of good fortune. When the basic drives are not under your conscious control, the components of a rich, rewarding life lie scattered and you may spend most of your life searching for some missing part.

We return, now, to the art of living your own life and being your own self, and shall look further into the ways in which this master skill strengthens and sustains you.

One of these days you will be in a clothing store. If some salesman tells you: "This is what everyone is wearing this season," don't be persuaded. Be yourself. Select colors, fabrics and styles which suit *you.* Tell the salesman that you prefer something that everyone is *not* wearing. Either walk out of that store without having made a purchase, or buy with regard to your own tastes only.

One of these days you will be in a restaurant. Waiters often receive word from the proprietor or from the cook to "push" some item, perhaps because it brings a high profit, perhaps because there is too much of it at hand. If your waiter urges some item upon you, smile, shake your head, and order exactly what you would like to have from the menu.

You may greatly admire some person for a particular skill or talent he shows. Wishing to exercise a similar skill, you may decide you are going to "be" that person. You will have wasted a great deal of time and effort before you discover that personality is a very subtle thing and that nobody can "be" anyone else without harming his own personality and crippling the drives that can make him great in his own right.

In my youth I decided to write the way Arthur Brisbane wrote. He was a very versatile and capable writer with a huge following, and I thought I was being smart when I set out to copy his style. A friend brought me up short when he remarked that if I copied Brisbane I would never develop a style of my own. Right then I put Brisbane aside, and the success of my writings has justified my decision not to be Arthur Brisbane but to be Napoleon Hill.

Children try to imitate older people, which is understandable. I see many a grown-up child trying to keep up with the Joneses financially, or trying to keep up the social pace that the Smiths set, with disastrous results. Until you are willing to be your own self, at your own level, you cannot know yourself, nor know what *your* mind can accomplish.

Let nobody bribe you away from being yourself. You are going to make money, and as soon as you do, others are going to see you have what it takes. Fine!—but this is the point at which many a man loses himself. Having built himself from within himself, and having thus attracted attention, he yields to a "big opportunity" to stop building his own wealth and peace of mind, and ties himself to another's business.

I have been told about a man who sits in a plush office in a huge company that supplies essential components in the field of aerospace. He does not work hard, earns a six-figure salary and bonuses besides. He can gratify almost any reasonable desire that can be gratified with money. But he cannot buy back himself; he allowed himself to be bribed away. So he sits gloomily behind his five-hundred-dollar desk and wishes he had not let the big company buy out the small, growing company which once had been his own—and with it buy all the adventure and personal satisfaction he had known.

Back in the days when $25,000 would buy what $75,000 buys today—and I was not earning half of $25,000 a year, but I was absorbed in what I was doing—I worked hard and happily at publishing the *Golden Rule Magazine*. Perhaps because I had been an adviser to Woodrow Wilson I was approached by Ivy Lee, the public relations expert I have mentioned. He wanted me to join his staff and become a ghostwriter for one of his clients—the Rockefeller interests.

For a moment I was tempted. I listened to his terms: $25,000 a year on a five-year contract, and of course I was to knock *Golden Rule Magazine* in the head.

The moment passed and I was myself again. I replied, "Nothing doing, Mr. Lee." If the salary had been a million dollars a year, my answer would have been the same.

Later, of my own free will, I gave up my association with *Golden Rule Magazine.* Did I then wish I had accepted Ivy Lee's offer? Not at all. My name and my career remained my own. I retained and still retain the right to travel under my own name in any direction I wish to go, assuming full responsibility for my mistakes, taking full credit for my successes.

People told me at the time that I had made a great mistake in turning down that handsome offer, and even urged me to get in touch with Mr. Lee and see if the offer still was open. If indeed it had been a mistake, I told myself, I had only to remember that every misfortune carries within it the seed of a greater benefit. And when I look back at what I have accomplished by way of extending the secrets of happiness and life-success over a large portion of the world, I see that only in being myself have I succeeded in being successful.

Today—right now—start doing all you can toward being yourself. As you enter a clothing store, or a restaurant or any other establishment in which you will be served—in exchange for your money—decide firmly and quietly that you are going to be yourself. In your talks with others, in your own personal dealings, in whatever you may do that is shared with others or affects others—be yourself. I mention other people because it is most often in our relations with others that we neglect to be ourselves—and you can be completely yourself, and appreciated for what you are, while you still respect the rights of others.

In the Foreword I listed a number of blessings which are associated with peace of mind. I pointed out that peace of mind is the peaceful base upon which we erect a good deal of life-dynamic. Now, somewhat overlapping the same list and somewhat extending it, I am going to set down forty-three items which pertain to being yourself. Few people will recognize themselves completely in this list, but if you will take a pencil and check each item that you sincerely believe applies to *you,* it will be most revealing.

1. The man who consistently is himself maintains his poise under all circumstances, whether the circumstances are favorable or unfavorable.

2. He has control of his emotions at all times.

3. He has perfect self-reliance and self-confidence in everything he undertakes.

4. He does not allow himself to be hurried into any careless action.

5. Increasingly, as he succeeds, he controls his own working hours and the conditions under which he works.

6. He never gripes or complains about anything or anyone.

7. He never slanders or condemns anyone.

8. He never talks about himself unless it is necessary, and then never in a spirit of boasting.

9. He is open-minded on all subjects, with all people.

10. He does not fear anything or anyone.

11. He moves about his affairs with quiet definiteness of purpose.

12. Before expressing an opinion he makes sure he has the facts, and he is not afraid to say "I do not know."

13. He has no racial or religious prejudices.

14. He eats moderately and avoids every other form of excess.

15. Without pretending to be an expert on all subjects, on all subjects he thinks for himself.

16. He is a dependable citizen who cannot be influenced by any "ism" which may be detrimental to his country or its economy.

17. He gives nobody any reason to be his enemy (but you cannot help it if someone dislikes you because of your success).

18. He is at peace with himself and with all mankind.

19. He cannot ever be poor or miserable, for, come what may, in his heart he remains happy and prosperous.

20. All the members of his family love him and thrill to the sound of his footsteps when he comes home.

21. He expresses his gratitude daily for all of his blessings, and shares his blessings with all who have a right to claim a share.

22. He seeks no revenge for any wrongs or injustices done to him.

23. When he speaks of others he makes every effort to avoid mentioning their faults no matter how much their faults may have affected him.

24. He looks into the future by studying the past, and recognizes that history has a way of repeating itself, that eternal truths do not change with the times.

25. He maintains a positive mental attitude.

26. He is slow to accuse, quick to forgive.

27. When others make honest mistakes, he makes allowances for them.

28. He will not profit in any transaction if it harms anyone else.

28. He keeps himself free from the bondage of debt.

30. Having acquired all the wealth he can use beneficially, he does not strain after more: yet he knows with full assurance he can earn more if it should be advisable.

31. He converts all adversities and defeats into assets.

32. Facing defeat, he knows all defeat is temporary.

33. He has a major objective in life and keeps himself busy attaining it.

34. If he has been turned aside from his objective, he analyzes the experience and profits thereby.

35. His life is what he wishes it to be, and he always expected it to be exactly that.

36. As he successively pictures success within his mind and then attains it, he lets his deeds, not his words, display his success to others.

37. He is well-liked by a great many different kinds of people; people of all races and creeds.

38. He is a living example of what a man may be in the United States of America when he takes possession of his own mind and is willing to live and let live.

39. He is no more disturbed by panics and business depressions than he is by matters which affect only himself.

40. He finds it easy to win the full and hearty co-operation of others.

41. He is fair to his adversaries, but he is practically unbeatable because he possesses a power unknown to most men.

42. He is fortified against disappointment because he

knows that anything may happen with or without an obvious cause.

43. He does his best at all times, and never feels the need to apologize when circumstances turn against him.

How many items did you check? If you have three-quarters of these virtues, you probably are aware that you are "your own person," living your own life, knowing your own mind, being yourself without fear or self-consciousness.

In reading through the list you can see how wide a field it encompasses. Any one of those topics could be expanded into a considerable discourse, and many other constructive points of view are inherent in the ones mentioned. If now you will leaf back through the book, and glance over the Table of Contents, you will see how many other areas of mind-conception and physical realization are related to this list. This is as it should be. We are speaking of a universal way of life.

You can help others without interfering with their own possession of themselves. I have given a number of instances of how I have been aided by and how I have aided others. Please note that really effective aid comes not from "bossing" another person but from helping that person find and use qualities or success which are waiting to be used. One cannot carry others along the highway of success; but one may point the way by *helping others to help themselves.*

A child can be beaten into a course of conduct acceptable to his parents—sometimes—but that child has learned nothing. I well remember the thrashings my father gave me because I resisted sitting in church for endless hours while five or six "hardshell Baptists" did their best to make the congregation partake of the miseries of Hell.

One Sunday morning my father followed me down to the river where I had organized my fishing equipment. He broke it up completely and gave me a whipping that would have brought the Society for the Prevention of Cruelty to Animals down upon him if he had whipped one of his horses that way.

My wonderful stepmother heard my screams and came running to my aid. She pulled my father away from me and said: "If you ever strike this child again, I will leave you forever. *Can't you let him live his own life?*"

Much as I remember the beatings, I better remember the

one sentence which settled into my young mind like a glorious light. My father never whipped me again, and I believe I gave him no reason to whip me. Yet I did live my own life, perhaps compromising here and there as a child must, yet always winning more and more freedom to *be myself* because my mind conceived so firmly that to be myself was what I wanted. Let me add that my stepmother's influence at length made a fine person out of my father. A child also can be so mercilessly preached at, endlessly corrected and admonished "for his own good" that soon no *self* respecting remains. The child becomes an adult who forever will lean upon others.

Never interfere with anyone else's possession of himself. Do not preach unless you are a professional preacher. Do not insistently and remorselessly teach unless you are a professional teacher; and even then, teaching should be limited to the teaching of definite skills and background knowledge.

Do not expect any other person to meet your definition of "perfect." Do not expect anything to appear perfect to you, and bear in mind that imperfections give variety to the world. In saying this I am reminded of a man who said that if there is a Heaven, he did not wish to go to Heaven when he died. Interested, I asked him to explain.

"Well," he said, "I don't see any enjoyment in living where everything is perfect."

I do not think it is an accident that this man is one of the best-known businessmen in America, and that he owns a large measure of peace of mind. Also, I have never heard of his trying to reform anybody. He says, as I too wish to say, that it is perfectly possible to get along with people as they are, with their faults—and with all their virtues.

One good way to maintain possession of your own mind and to allow others to possess their own minds is to keep certain views to yourself. You are not required to go through life explaining yourself, and often it is a mistake to do so. This applies particularly to controversial subjects such as religion and politics. Exposing your views in these matters is almost bound to cause unnecessary conflict.

No one knows how I stand on either religion or politics. No one, therefore, can get me riled or rile themselves in regard to my standpoint.

Many busybodies have tried to pry into my mind to see what they will discover in those areas. Once a woman wrote to me: "How come I see no mention of Jesus in any of your writings?"

To which I replied: "Madam, if you will read any of my books in the spirit in which I wrote them, you will find Jesus on every page—between the lines, however, not in the words that are printed."

Self-control gives you strength. To be yourself, practice self-control. Few people have difficulty in controlling their physical actions, but they may never stop to realize that physical actions begin in the mind. A man whose mind conceives only a small, frightened view of life will *act* just like a man whose mind conceives only a small, frightened view of life.

A person who has self-control has strength—I repeat, *strength*—denied to many another. Above all, he has the strength to see situations clearly, judge them for what they really are, greatly increase the percentage of life-situations he swings toward his own good and the good of others.

Please look back at the list of forty-three items earlier in this chapter. Number 22 says that a person who is his own master never seeks revenge on anyone. Let us take this as a very good example. Revenge can be spuriously sweet, but it is a sweet poison to the personality and no more will merge with peace of mind than oil will merge with water.

Who is in a better positon to revenge himself on a person who has hurt him, but seeks an appointment to public office, than the President of the United States? Very well, let us look at one of our Presidents—first some five years before he attained that high office.

When I mention he was then a lawyer in Springfield, Illinois, you will have no trouble in identifying Abraham Lincoln. One of our earliest big industrial companies was in legal difficulty, and Lincoln was appointed by the court to work with two other lawyers on the case. But these two lawyers were famous big-city men. They snubbed the gawky country lawyer. When he painstakingly prepared papers on the case, they would not even read them.

Worse yet, they would not even sit at the same table with him. This was a public humiliation, and it must have hurt bitterly.

Five years passed. The lean, sad-faced man was elected President. Soon it was time for him to choose his cabinet, including a Secretary of War. One man stood out as the best choice for this ominously important post—Edward M. Stanton. And Lincoln remembered Stanton as one of the lawyers who had treated him so badly in his Springfield days.

Yet he appointed Stanton his Secretary of War. Is there any question that Lincoln was his own master—for his own good, for the good of all?

Many men date their discovery of self-control from some one dramatic experience. I know that is so in my case. I have mentioned that I learned peace of mind the hard way, by trial and error—and this experience is a good example.

I had an office in an old building. One day the janitor and I had a misunderstanding. After that the janitor decided to show his contempt of me. Many times when I stayed late at work, he switched off all the lights in the building and left me in the dark. I was then still capable of boiling with suppressed rage, and this I did increasingly.

One Sunday I entered my office to prepare an address I had to deliver the following evening. No sooner had I seated myself at my desk than the lights went out.

I leaped up and ran recklessly to the basement. There I found the janitor stoking the furnace and whistling merrily. All my pent-up wrath burst loose and I damned him with adjectives that were hotter than the furnace.

When I ran out of words he straightened up, grinned and remarked: "Why, you're a little excited today, ain't you?"

He had maintained his poise. *I*, a student of advanced psychology, an exponent of the philosophy of the Golden Rule, a student of the works of Shakespeare, Emerson, Socrates and the Bible—I stood there before a man who was scarcely literate and knew he was the better man.

I went back slowly to my office. I sat and thought, and after a while I knew I must apologize to that man. No, I said, I could not and I would not. Yet in time I rose, knowing that I must find peace with him and peace in my own heart.

When I got to the basement, the janitor had gone into his little apartment. I tapped gently at his door. He opened it, and in a calm, kindly voice asked me what I wanted.

I said I wished to apologize for the wrong I had done him in cursing him.

His simple smile spread all over his face. "Nobody heard you outside these four wallls," he said. "I ain't goin' to tell about it and I reckon you ain't goin' to tell about it, so let's forget the whole thing."

We shook hands. There was no more friction between us and no more spite work. And something within my mind took hold of itself. I resolved that never again would I lose my self-control, never again would I lose sight of the *self* which existed as a mind-conception and which henceforth never would falter.

Once I had made that resolution, my pen began to take on greater power. My spoken words were received with full attention. I began to make friends with ease, and I was far better able to show others how to find themselves and be themselves, and use self-knowledge to win a fortune.

Did I make a *perfect* change? Not quite. I had been aware for some time of a series of bitter attacks against me which came from a certain journalist. For four or five years I ignored these attacks, but they became so outrageous that I decided to lay aside my policy of peace and hit back. I sat at my typewriter and began to write. I wrote at length, and filled pages with bitter invective. The more I wrote, the more angry I became. At length I wrote my last line—and then a strange feeling came over me. It was not a feeling of rage against the man who had tried to discredit me, but a feeling of sympathy and forgiveness. I never mailed that letter.

What had happened? As I see it, my furiously tapping fingers had transferred my repressed emotions of hatred and resentment onto paper, and I was rid of those emotions. In a way I had psychoanalyzed myself, and had cleaned the dark sub-basement of my sub-conscious mind.

The experience gave me two benefits. The first and greatest was the realization that, any time rage took hold of me, I could "write it out of my system." It is a great method, and you might try it. Some get the same effect with a long, fast walk; others indulge in violent athletic activity and then feel their self-control return. Others take out their bad temper on their wives—but of course this is harmful to both parties.

My second benefit came from filing away some of my writings-in-anger and looking at them years later, when I had gained greater understanding. Try this too, and you will find it a very interesting process, for as you know yourself you will increasingly know a better self. I am glad to say I have not needed any such release of rage for a good many years, for rage no longer can evade my Guardian Princes.

Your mind is your only master. You had nothing to do with your coming into this world. You may have little or nothing to do with your leaving it. But you have almost everything to do with your life while you possess that life. You can be the master of your fate, the captain of your soul by the simple process of taking possession of your own mind and using it to guide your own life *without meddling in the lives of others*.

Notice the connection between mastering yourself and *not* attempting to master others. A major reason for unhappiness is the tendency to meddle with the lives of others while we take too little time in trying to perfect our own.

Nobody else can do the job of taking possession of *your* mind, nor should you permit anyone else to try. *Your* mind is *your* master; yet your mind can be such a kindly master that it responds to your needs and desires and finds ways to make them come true when they are definite. All other creatures on earth are bound throughout their lives by a fixed pattern of instinct from which they cannot escape. YOU are bound only by the pattern you set up in your own mind. YOU are limited by nothing else.

Be patient in your search for peace of mind. If peace of mind were a quality which could be attained in one easy lesson, I would be glad to show the way in a short letter rather than by writing a book. This book, which approaches the subjects of riches and peace of mind from so many angles, is built on a grand plan which may be compared to the farmer's plan in ploughing his fields, sowing his seeds, tending his crop and waiting for his harvest. Remember the farmer and be confident and patient. And, like the farmer, use thought and action in ways which have proved their power to bring a desired result.

If you meet with adversity, see it as a valuable lesson. During the days of my youth I used to flinch from adversity. Now, when I see it coming my way, I say: "Hello, little fellow! I do not know what lesson you have come to teach me, but whatever it is I shall learn it well so you will not have to return a second time."

After I had learned to live my own life, I observed that adversities became fewer and fewer, weaker and weaker, until at long last they ceased to appear.

Living your own life may take some "house cleaning." By the time we reach adulthood, most of us have acquired a good deal of clutter in our lives. As you begin to know yourself and know the image of the life you want to build, you will recognize this clutter. Throw it out!

You might begin by discarding some of those acquaintances who waste your time, interfere with your efforts and try to manage you. Clear them out! You need not turn them into enemies, but when you want to be yourself you will find ways to avoid any person who tries to deny you the inalienable right of being yourself.

There is also the self-made clutter which results from not having a clear idea of how you wish to use each day. Make up a time budget. Allot your time in favor of the "musts" which apply to anyone who wants to live his own life profitably and pleasantly.

Eight hours a day is a good allotment for sleep and for rest.

Eight hours a day is a good allotment for work at your business or profession; but as your pattern of life-success grows stronger, probably your hours of work will grow less.

The remaining eight hours are particularly precious. You should divide them into various periods, each of which will be devoted to something you *wish* to do, not something you *have* to do. What do you *wish* to do? Stop now and think. Make a list, such as:

Play
Social life
Reading
Writing
Playing a musical instrument
Extending your knowledge in some field that has nothing to do with your making a living
Tending your garden
Building gadgets in your home workshop
Hiking
Boating
"Just sitting" and watching the clouds or the stars

I repeat, those remaining eight hours are particularly precious. They are YOUR FREE TIME in which you may live your own life precisely as you wish to live it. You may find this takes some courage. You may have acquired an exaggerated sense of duty toward others (often a pretty description for plain meddling). You may too well remember being told in childhood such nonsense as "the devil finds work for idle hands." But then, it takes courage to be one's self and avoid the pressures to be like other people and let them live your life for you.

In the earlier stages of winning success you may very logically give over some of that time to get a business education, or in other ways to improve your earning status. But do not let a day go by without taking some time for yourself—some time you spend in pure pleasure, as you see it. This is part of being yourself. It helps you always to keep in touch with yourself, so to speak. With increasing success, increase your hours of pure enjoyment; do not allow those hours to be eaten away by business or by anything else.

Some time ago a close friend came to visit me. He found me dressed in my shorts, lying on the grass in the back yard and playing ball with my dogs.

"What a picture," he exclaimed. "I guess you wouldn't want your public to see you as you are now."

"I wouldn't mind it a bit," I replied. "I'd like people to know I practice what I preach. Here I am, doing precisely what I wish to do at this moment. Can anyone be better off than in doing what he wishes to do?"

If any man needed simple freedom, my friend did. He spent a good deal more than eight hours a day as the operating executive of a large financial house, and often worked far into the night. With millions of dollars, he had no peace of mind and his health had begun to suffer.

He telephoned me the next day. "Guess what I've been doing for the past hour!"

"I can't imagine, but I'd certainly like to know."

He laughed gaily. "Playing with my dog, and it's wonderful!" A moment of silence; then he said: "Believe me, I'm going to play and *live* hereafter!"

I set down the key thoughts of this chapter many years ago. Woodrow Wilson read what I had written and said: "It inspired thoughts which were not of this world."

On another occasion I received President Wilson just as I had received my old friend, in my shorts while romping with my dogs. He was grateful. That harassed man shared, if only for a few minutes, the blessedness of having time to be one's relaxed self.

When you see yourself as your own master and carry the vision into action, you use the Supreme Secret.

CHECKING ON CHAPTER 9:

The basic drives that make a man
The "nuts and bolts" of earning money are important, but

your basic drives are what build the nuts and bolts into a mighty edifice of good fortune. In a clothing store, in a restaurant, wherever you may go, exercise the art of being yourself. Beware of imitating anyone at any time in your career, for in doing so you may suppress talents which are uniquely yours and can build your fortune.

Let nobody bribe you away from being yourself
Because you are going to make money, you are likely to receive offers which amount to tying yourself to someone else's affairs instead of your own. This may work out well, but for some it amounts to selling one's peace of mind and sense of individuality. Check the list of forty-three items which help you see yourself as you are and as you can be— a person truly in charge of his own mind and invincible in his self-possession.

Every human being needs to live his own life
You help others not by interfering with them but by helping them find and use their own qualities of success. It is important to give a child as much freedom as possible. Do not preach unless you are a professional preacher, nor teach too heavily. Accept people's faults as well as their virtues, for even their faults make the world more varied and interesting.

Self-control gives you strength
When you keep most of your views to yourself, you strengthen your sense of self-possession and also avoid unnecessary friction with others. Self-control helps you control many life-situations which otherwise might not turn out in your favor. It helps you act for your own good and the good of others despite your anger or other emotions.

Your mind is your only master
Your mind first must conceive anything you accomplish, but your mind is a kindly master and will find ways to win what you sincerely and consistently desire. Other creatures are bound by a fixed pattern of instinct, but you are bound only by the pattern you set up in your own mind. Be patient in your search for peace of mind. Above all, learn the great lesson that every day should contain a good amount of time in which you enjoy your own personal pleasure.

10

The Master Mind Group—
A Power Beyond Science

The great achievements of your life—first built as mind-concepts, then made real—are not limited to the power of your own mind. A myriad of other minds can tune in upon yours and give you their thoughts through ethereal vibration. Forming a Master Mind group is a good way to begin the process of tuning in, and when you form your group you will know you are using a technique which has mightily proved its benefit among many well-known men. All great achievements are the result of a multiplicity of minds working together harmoniously.

WAS Henry Ford ignorant?

Rather than attempt to form your answer, which must come from within yourself, I shall tell you of an experience the founder of Ford Motor Company had in a courtroom. The experience really included everybody in that courtroom and a good many outside the courtroom as well.

As we know, Mr. Ford had little formal schooling. Perhaps because of this fact, the *Chicago Tribune*, which took exception to some of his views on war, called him an ignoramus. Mr. Ford brought suit, charging the newspaper with libel.

When the attorneys for the *Tribune* had Mr. Ford on the witness stand they cross-examined him in an attempt to prove their statement was true.

One question they asked was: "How many soldiers did the British send over to subdue the rebellion in the colonies in 1776?"

With a dry grin, Ford replied: "I don't know just how many, but I have heard it was a lot more than ever went back."

There was laughter from the court, the jury, the spectators, and even from the frustrated lawyer who had asked the question.

Ford kept calm through an hour or more of similar questioning on "schoolbook" topics. At length, in reply to a ques-

126

tion which was particularly obnoxious to him, the industrialist let off some steam. He observed that he had a row of electric push-buttons hanging over his desk, and that when he wanted a question answered, he placed his finger on the right button and called in the right man to answer that question. He wanted to know why he should burden his mind with a lot of useless details when he had able men around him who could supply him with all the information he needed.

This trial occurred many years ago and I dare say that only a minority of my readers recall how it came out. If you do not know, exercise your own power to develop information by going to the library and finding out. I will say, however, that Mr. Ford's remarks resounded through that silenced courtroom, through the nation and around the world. Surely Ford's friend Thomas Edison appreciated them, for he was another who had surrounded himself with able men through whom he vastly extended his own abilities and his own mind-power, school education or no.

Thomas Paine, whose keen mind helped both in drawing up the Declaration of Independence and in persuading its signers to translate their concept into reality, spoke in memorable terms of the great storehouse of knowledge which waits to be transferred to our own storehouse. I quote him in part:

Any person, who has made observations on the . . . human mind, by observing his own, cannot but have observed that there are two classes of what are called Thoughts: those that we produce in ourselves by reflection and the act of thinking, and those that bolt into the mind of their own accord. I have always made it a rule to treat these voluntary visitors with civility . . . and it is from them that I have acquired almost all the knowledge that I have. As to the learning that any person gains from school education, it serves only like a small capital, to put him in the way of beginning learning for himself afterwards. Every person of learning is finally his own teacher. . . .

Whence come the thoughts which do not originate within our own minds, out of our own experience? Often it is apparent that such thoughts are suggested by other persons in words or in writing, and later they "play back" from within our subconscious memories; or they may be a completely conscious process, as when we sit in conference with another.

All of us, however, receive thoughts which are *silently broadcast* by other minds and received by our own. This too is a "planted" idea we touched upon previously and now shall examine in more detail.

What is the Master Mind? I visualize the Master Mind as a formless, boundless reservoir of thought-vibration. Not all of it can be available to any one person at any one time. When you are in harmony with another person or with a number of other people, however, the attunement of mind to mind results in a "tuning in" of incalculable value. A man who has a corps of assistants with whom he maintains amiable relations has at his disposal far more than the knowledge his assistants may give him by obvious means. Their minds constantly feed his through mental broadcast power, and receive information from his mind as well. The same is true when friends or business associates form a Master Mind group at which they discuss various topics or problems. Their several minds focused on the topic obviously add great power to the mind most occupied with it; but also an exchange of broadcast thoughts is effected right then, and also later, when the persons involved may be far apart. This is not obvious as is speech or writing, but its power goes beyond anything science can completely explain.

I have been greatly interested in observing how the science of this atomic age gives "faith and credit" in this direction to the science of fifty years ago. At that time we could list eighty-odd forms of physical matter (we list many more now) and we knew that matter is made of incredibly tiny particles with space between. We had begun to know there is so much space within matter that, in a sense, nothing is "solid." You and I, the desk at which I write, my typewriter, this dot (.) are made of atoms; the atom in turn contains electrons which either revolve in orbits or vibrate rapidly to and fro. Other particles such as neutrons are now postulated, but the principle remains the same. Whether you observe the largest star that glitters in the sky or the smallest grain of sand among billions on a beach, it is a collection of particles, space and electric charges.

Fifty years ago we had begun to have some proof that even the most minute particles are not "things" but bundles of vibrations. We knew, too, that various forms of energy proceed through air and space in their characteristic forms because of their varying frequency of vibration. Thus, vibrations beginning at about 15 per second and going up to about 15,000 per second are perceptible to the human ear as sound. Above that we no longer hear vibrations; but at around 1,500,000 vibrations per second that form of energy called heat begins and we can feel it with another of our senses.

Higher up the scale of vibration comes light, often combined with heat, and our eyes perceive this. The lowest light-vibrations begin with deep red, the highest are violet, with all other colors in between. Above the vibrations of violet—some 3,000,000 per second—lie ultraviolet and other vibrations invisible to the eye but detectable by instruments.

Still higher up the scale—we cannot yet say how high—may lie the vibrations of *thought,* and these are the invisible, inaudible vibrations which flash from mind to mind.

Dr. Alexander Graham Bell, whose name we justly associate with the telephone, was an authority on vibration. He noted that we have no ordinary sense that can appreciate the effect of any vibration between heat and light. He said: ". . . there must be a great deal to be learned about the effect of those vibrations in the great gap where the ordinary human senses are unable to hear, see or feel the movement. The power to send wireless messages by *ether* vibrations lies in that gap, but the gap is so great that it seems there must be much more. . . . It seems to me that in this gap lie the vibrations which we have assumed to be given off by our brains and nerve cells when we think. But then, again, they may be higher up, in the scale beyond the vibrations that produce the ultraviolet rays [my own theory].

"It would be possible to cite many reasons why thought and vital force may be regarded as of the same nature as electricity. . . . We may assume that the brain cells act as a battery and that the current produced flows along the nerves. But does it end there? Does it not pass out of the body in waves which flow around the world unperceived by our senses, just as the wireless waves passed unperceived before Hertz and others discovered their existence?"

Field theory and thought-transference. Einstein showed mathematically that vast fields of force pervade the universe. A field of force comes out of every wire that carries current —or we would have no electric motors, no radio or television and would lack quite a few other conveniences. Why should not a field of force emanate from the electricity which constantly passes to and fro along the conducting nerves and cells of the body? Why should they not go around the world, into space, on forever?

Now our world is both threatened and uplifted by the physical realization of Einstein's great mind-concept of nearly sixty years ago: $E = mc^2$. This formula governs the conversion of mass into energy, and accounts for the enormous energy put to use in atomic power plants and the atomic bomb. In using atomic power we *prove* once and for all, for everyone to see, that mass *is* energy. Since energy is vibration, everything undoubtedly is vibration. You and I now know we are vibration—beyond the shadow of a doubt.

Tune your radio to the known vibration-rate of any radio station as indicated on the tuning dial, and you sensitize your radio to that particular vibration; the radio then changes it into vibrations you can hear. Is there anything strange about a natural "tuning" to the omnipresent thought-vibrations of another mind which already has shown its empathy with your own mind? It is no more strange than radio. Radio's laws at length were discovered. So shall the laws of thought-broadcast and reception some day be discovered, and the natural aparatus we now use but dimly shall be at everyone's command.

How to form and use your own Master Mind group. You understand now that whenever two or more minds are blended in a spirit of perfect harmony, for the pursuit of a definite purpose, there is born of that alliance a power which is greater than that of all the individual minds combined.

This is the Master Mind principle. It does not interfere with your possession of yourself. In fact, one who is himself in all ways is all the more able to accept ideas from the minds of others peacefully and usefully, since he is in no danger of being overwhelmed. The Science of Personal Achievement was born out of a Master Mind alliance, my allies having been those five hundred and more successful men whom I interviewed and worked with in the course of many years.

A person who has peace of mind always gives as well as receives. As you apply the Master Mind principle, you not only share your knowledge with others but also place yourself in a position to receive generously from others—and that which you receive can multiply your power to grow rich far beyond your present conception.

Here, then, are the steps to take in order to avail yourself of the boundless benefits of the Master Mind principle:

1. Your Master Mind round table Begin by inviting two or three people whom you know well to join you in your undertaking. Be sure that these people are in harmony with you and with one another. Explain that the major purpose of the alliance is mutual growth mentally and spiritually, while you certainly will accept the material benefits which naturally attend such development.

2. *You are not a debating society*   Make it clear from the beginning that such controversial matters as politics, religion and similarly touchy topics have no place in your group meetings. Your aim is to aid one another with knowledge based on the experience each member has gained from life.

3. *Your discussion is confidential*   Discussion and co-operation must stay within the group. Knowing this, all will be encouraged to speak freely.

4. *The group will be allowed to grow*   From time to time, the group may be enlarged by additional members. It should not be allowed to grow so large as to become unwieldy. Any new member must be subject to a unanimous vote of acceptance.

5. *Provide for a trial election*   With the exception of the original members of the Master Mind group, members may be elected for one month or for some other convenient period. You should be perfectly frank about the necessity of making sure that any new member is in harmony with the others, and that if you ask him to leave the group it is no reflection upon his personal worth.

6. *Agree on general principles of life-success*   Bear in mind that if any one of your round-table members does not believe, for instance, that he should give completely of his knowledge and experience, he will create disharmony and you may get nowhere. I suggest that you all agree on the principles set forth in this book in the lists covering the qualities of peace of mind (Foreword) and self-possession (Chapter Nine); also sit down together with the summing-up list at the end of the book.

7. *Rotate your chairmen and your "board of directors"*   Each person should serve in turn as the chairman. He should see that all members take part in the discussion; that questions are asked freely and personal experiences freely described. He should ask each speaker to stand as he speaks, to help him develop poise while speaking "on his feet." He should enforce any time limit agreed upon, so as to prevent the more verbose members from consuming more than their share of the time. Rotation of the chairmen will automatically result in the rotation of members of the "board" who listen to the speaker, who thus wins a variety of minds to serve him.

8. When a group consists of fellow-workers   When a Master Mind group consists of the employees of a single business, it should contain members of management as well as members of the rank-and-file. This plan has been followed with a great development of friendly co-operation, benefit to the business as well as benefit to the individuals concerned.

9. Adopt a major purpose   In addition to the individual purposes and problems which will be aired, the group as a whole should adopt some major purpose or project, to be carried on jointly by all its members *for the benefit of people who are not in the group.* One such project was that of conducting a Personal Problem Clinic once a week, at which the public was invited to bring in personal problems for consideration by the group, sitting as a Personal Problem Court. When a project is completed, another should be chosen.

Further instructions on your Master Mind alliance.   Since part of this book's purpose is to spare you from learning by trial and error, I shall set down some lessons already learned that way—by myself and others.

I suggest that you do not reveal the private purposes of your Master Mind alliance to those outside the group. Remember the many who are wedded to failure and who channel their efforts—not toward success—but toward trying to tear down others. Such persons will scoff at the Master Mind principle. Their scoffing need not annoy you, but it may; and at any rate, you need nobody's opinion but your own so far as forming your group is concerned.

When you sit down with your Master Mind group, make sure you leave all negative points of view behind. Your meetings should be your greatest signal to find and hold a positive mental attitude. Moreover, as leader of your Master Mind group it is your duty to show your own enthusiasm and allow others to share this valuable emotion. (Don't worry about the mechanics of sharing your enthusiasm, for there is no other emotion that is so "catching"!)

Take care to see that every member of the group receives something out of every meeting. Enthusiasm and co-operation will grow in proportion to the rewards each man bears away with him.

A Master Mind group is not a place in which to bring competitors together. Nobody in the group should have reason to feel antagonistic toward any other member, nor have any motive for keeping secrets from him. Remember that confidence is the basis of all harmonious relationships. Form your group out of people in whom you have confidence; make sure they have confidence in you.

Millions of people need a Personal Problem Clinic. I purposefully repeat that every Master Mind should have a group purpose which benefits those outside the group. This principle is so important that I shall enlarge upon the idea of the Personal Problem Clinic, surely one of the best public services any group can perform.

Let us look at a number of typical applications.

If I were a life insurance agent, I would conduct such a clinic twice weekly, if possible. The modern life insurance man is looked upon as a counselor in several fields of family concern, budget for example. While giving of your time and telling your own life-experience and that of others, you may well form an indelible impression upon men and women who need life insurance.

If I were a clergyman, I would conduct a Personal Problem Clinic going far beyond the members of my own congregation. I would have sitting with me, as Board of Counselors, the ablest members of my church, representing a wide variety of businesses and professions. I would expect no direct reward, but would be gratified if my services helped to fill the pews of my church every Sunday.

If I were a schoolteacher, I would recognize that parents who are led to a harmonious solution of their problems are better parents, better able to help their children. I would conduct a clinic in the hopes that both generations would benefit and that the benefit would be reflected in the ability of my pupils to retain what I teach and grow into better citizens.

If I were a physician, dentist, osteopath, chiropractor or naturopath, I would conduct a clinic for the benefit of my patients and I would invite them to bring their friends and neighbors with them. Knowing that much illness originates in the mind, I would take this opportunity to heal where I could and in other cases to speed the processes of healing.

If I were the head of a family that included growing children, I would conduct a Personal Problem Clinic for each member of the family. I might very well invite my neighbors to join.

I have pointed out some of the benefits which may accrue to you from running a Personal Problem Clinic. You may see no benefit; but rest assured that any benefit you send out into the world will come back to you in some way, at some time, perhaps a thousand times multiplied.

The late Mahatma Gandhi made himself one of the greatest benefactors of all time by the simple process of serving his countrymen without limit and without thought of financial reward. He was probably in the hearts of more men than any other man who ever lived. He drew several hundred million of his Indian countrymen to him of their own free will, and his reward—the independence of his nation—was a reward greater than most of us ever dream of achieving.

Your Master Mind group of necessity will be a small group. Yet when you extend it out into the world through a Personal Problem Clinic—through adopting the sponsorship of a Boys' Club or some other welfare agency—or whatever other group project you may choose, your mind will automatically feel the effect of many other minds in harmony with your purpose. Here are illimitable riches!

The Master Mind principle in politics. In speaking with some men who hold political office, I have been saddened momentarily by what they call their "hard-headed" attitude. Once they are voted into power they tend to wield that power like a club, arbitrarily swinging their influence with little regard to those who must obey the rules they set. This is not so with the truly great men; but unfortunately, a good many small-minded men achieve public office.

If I were the mayor of a town or city, I would set up a People's Personal Problem Clinic in the City Hall. The counsellors in the Clinic would be the keenest minds in the city—lawyers, doctors, teachers, bankers, builders—a cross-section of such a variety of human talent that any citizen could rely upon finding an understanding ear.

I would hold clinic sessions at some stated hour at least once a week. As the clinic attracted more and more people, I might find it advisable to organize it into subgroups. I certainly would arrange for private counsel to be available in emergencies between meetings, and to follow up on particular cases if need be.

My reward? I believe that any mayor who did this would maintain himself in office for as long as he wished. Yet this is only a secondary reward. The real reward would lie in knowing that I have lifted government to a new, high plane of individuality and humanity.

Your mind is strengthened by peace and harmony. Do you expect your life to bring you only harmony and peace? Life indeed would be dull if it did not have its times of conflict, of problems to be solved. We grow as we overcome difficulties. If the solving of problems were not so important a part of the learning process, we would learn few of the lessons of life.

When peace and harmony remain as the veritable foundation-stones of thought and emotion, however, problems are solved with a strength which truly "passeth understanding."

Even temporary peace is a great sustaining force. Doctors often recommend a change of climate for certain types of patients. The climate itself may or may not have something to do with the healing process; more important is the change of *scene*. New faces, new landscapes bring the mind away from its accustomed squirrel cage of worries. "Miracle" cures have been effected when a patient walked out peacefully among the trees and the hills.

As you become better and better acquainted with your own mind, you will find it possible to hold harmony within your mind no matter what goes on around you. Meanwhile, try consciously at some time of the day to attune your mind to peace, not conflict—rest, not striving.

After a while, as you sit or walk or lie quietly alone, you may feel as though harmony is flowing into your mind from sources outside. Indeed this is true, for it is possible for any harmonious mind to tune in to yours when you have made your mind receptive.

The importance of harmony in your home. Now you can see that when I have spoken of harmony in your home I have spoken of more than a merely pleasant situation. Harmony in the home is a pervasive force which flows continually in and out of the mind-circuits and conditions the mind to keep itself in peace and continued harmony.

We live in a home where harmony and affection are the dominating spirits. Everything we do in our home gives us pleasure, including our work, which is a work of love.

Now and again, my wife and I take a long walk, or perhaps

a drive into the country. We return refreshed with thoughts of new faces, new scenes, perhaps new experiences—and glad to return to a home that is good to come back to.

Find your own way to get rid of worry—but keep it simple. In II Kings, Chapter Five, you may read the story of Naaman, captain of the host of the King of Syria. This rich and powerful man was afflicted with leprosy. He called upon the prophet Elisha to cure him, expecting Elisha to come up with some complicated and mysterious rigmarole. But Elisha merely said: "Go and wash in Jordan seven times and thy flesh shall come again to thee, and thou shalt be clean."

Perhaps this story is a parable, showing us that there generally is a simple way out of our troubles. I do not deny the existence of very serious troubles; but I have noticed that the great majority of troubles are minor annoyances which lead to a *pattern* of annoyance and worry. Feed your mind on little worries and it will develop quite an appetite for big worries.

The greatest buttress of worry is—sitting around and thinking about your worry. This adds strength to the worry, which thereupon sends stronger and stronger roots into the mind which nourishes it.

The greatest destroyer and uprooter of worry is—transmuting the worry-reaction into some sort of constructive activity. By going into action, make your mind focus on that action. By using your muscles, however mildly, you give a rest to your mind.

I have a friend who has a novel way of dealing with worries. He goes out into his garden and hoes vigorously until he has worked up a good perspiration.

Others, perhaps not so vigorous, may cancel worry by attending to some bit of craftsmanship or carpentry. And then, of course, there is the excellent procedure of turning your mind toward helping someone else solve *his* problem, a method available even to the bedridden.

But nothing complicated! In this book we talk of many things, and you would do well to come back to this section now and then to refresh yourself with the idea that peace of mind is essentially a simple state of being. It is often remarked that some successful, highly placed men are really "quite simple fellows" when you get to know them. Indeed they are—no matter of how high an order may be their intelligence. An efficient mind attains a basic simplicity upon which all else is built.

I am reminded of a man who was greatly benefited by participating in a Master Mind alliance. He said that his greatest benefit came from being helped to see his problems through others' eyes and thus to see, at last, how simple his problems were. He said he had been in the habit of multiplying his problems by each other and looking at the sum, which was tremendous. When he took his problems one by one they were quickly solved, and his mind began clicking as it never had before.

The Supreme Secret is as inherent in this chapter as a book is inherent in the mind that conceives its plan.

CHECKING ON CHAPTER 10:

Your mind can reach beyond itself

Men such as Henry Ford and Thomas Edison were expert in using others as sources of information and skills which multiplied their own talents. We also receive ideas from other minds without the mediation of speech. "Every man of learning is his own teacher," and as he learns from life he also learns from thoughts which "come from nowhere," it seems, but really are transmitted from other minds to his own.

The Master Mind: a boundless reservoir

Fifty years ago, scientists postulated the vibration theory of matter which since has been well proved by the discovery of atomic power. All energy proceeds in varying frequencies of vibration. The vibration of thought must lie somewhere in this spectrum of vibration. When you tune in your radio you sensitize it to receive the signals of a particular broadcasting station. Just so does your mind sensitize itself to other minds and receive thoughts from them.

You can form your own Master Mind group

Make your group out of people you know well. Make it clear you are not to discuss controversial topics. Keep the discussion confidential. Require unanimous consent before you admit a new member, and provide for a trial election. Agree on general principles of life-success. Rotate your chairmen and your "board." Let your group contain both management and rank-and-file members. A Personal Problem Clinic has proved to be a favorite purpose. It can be headed by an insurance man, a clergyman, a physician or anyone else. The mayor of a town can do great things for his city if he sets up a Clinic and provides for following through on any problems brought to the attention of the Clinic Staff.

Your mind is strengthened by peace and harmony
Life would be dull without some problems and conflicts, but peace and harmony deep within the mind help many problems to solve themselves. Some change is good for everyone. To avoid worry, take physical action to focus the mind on other things; or help someone else solve his problems. Some of us tend to multiply our problems by each other, but a Master Mind group helps you solve your problems one by one.

11

Win Mighty Aid from the Eternal Law of Compensation

The Law of Compensation can work for you or against you depending upon the way you guide it. It may take many years for punishment to follow transgression or for reward to follow virtue, but the compensation always will find you out. Nature makes sure that any excess is followed by a leveling. Fear gives way to the Law of Compensation, and envy and malice also disappear from life when one understands how the Law of Compensation can lead anyone to great success—because anyone can control the way it works for him.

DROP in at any public library, even a very small one, and ask the librarian for Ralph Waldo Emerson's essay on Compensation.

She will almost certainly be able to direct you to the exact shelf where Emerson's works are lined up—just a sober row of books, but I think of them as buzzing and humming with success-potential.

It will be easy to spot the volume that contains *Compensation.* It will be the volume most thumbed. Yet alas, that volume may be missing. Some over-eager student has borne it off to help him write his term paper, and has kept it, or some man who wonders why he never got ahead has made it his own, to read over and over.

Spare a sigh for those who do not realize the failure-potential that is inherent in stealing—and do your bit for others by buying the library another copy.

Secure a copy for yourself, too. Once you have read *Compensation* three times, you will read it a hundred times. You will want it at your bedside. It is a *must* for people who want to understand themselves, understand the world and find wonderful peace of mind that will stay with them.

The Law of Compensation in action.   Before we finish this chapter, we shall come back to that essay which is perhaps the most important ever written. Now I want to tell you a story in several parts. I know it is a true story. I lived it.

As you know, I have made mistakes and I have yielded at times to the wrong kind of emotions. Had I not learned from my mistakes I would not consider myself worthy of giving advice; but, very definitely, I have learned from them and built success and peace of mind upon my hard-won knowledge.

Well, there was a time, some decades ago, when I had been through a personal crisis and it "got" me. This was connected with an adventure which, while it brought me valuable experience, brought me little else. I found it necessary to make a fresh start financially, mentally and spiritually.

Being in the downtown business district of Atlanta, Georgia, I visited my friend and former business associate Mark Wooding. He recently had opened a large cafeteria right in the heart of the business section.

Mark told me his business was in serious difficulty. He had not taken into account the fact that downtown Atlanta business houses close early each evening—or at least they did in that era. After that early close of business, the district was as quiet as a graveyard.

The result was that he did splendidly at lunchtime, but had very few customers at the dinner hour when he had counted on making a good part of his income. Was there any way of persuading people to have dinner at his cafeteria? He hadn't thought of any.

My mind had been filled with my own problems. But I had learned long before that when one cannot find the solution to his own problems, the best thing he can do is to look for someone with a greater problem and help him find its solution. I switched my thoughts to a consideration of my friend's predicament.

Looking around, I noted he had a beautiful, large dining room which could seat several hundred people. His equipment was superb. The location was good, on a corner near transportation and parking facilities. People could reach the cafeteria easily and they would eat well and pleasantly when they got there. How to bring them in?

I decide to give away information I had been in the habit of selling. The answer flashed into my mind. I suggested to Mark that I give a lecture course on the Science of Personal Achievement. I would lecture each night, right there in the dining room. The lectures would be free to all who came for dinner and remained for the lectures.

We announced this plan through the local newspapers. We sent printed announcements to all the business houses in the district. And—

The first night we turned away more people than we could seat. There was seldom a night thereafter when we did not have to turn away a large number of people from the completely filled dining room. Mark's dinners became the major source of his income in record time.

The cost? Just the cost of the advertising. I had been in the habit of charging for my services as a lecturer, but now I donated my services without charge to a friend who needed a helping hand. That set certain invisible forces going. And that is the first part of the story.

The Law of Compensation begins to work in my behalf. We are not gifted with crystal balls with which to foretell the future. If I had had this power—which an All-Wise mind wisely has withheld from us—I would have seen that my unselfish giving marked the most important turning point of my life. Even now, in considering the compensation I eventually received for my services, I realize I am still being well paid. Before we go any further, remember this: *I cured my own ills by helping a friend cure his.* Pause right now and think how you can apply that mighty principle which *always* pays, and often in far more than money.

My lectures on the success philosophy attracted a wide variety of people to Wooding's cafeteria. Among them were several business executives, including an executive of the Georgia Power Company. This man was so impressed by the lectures that he asked me to be the guest speaker at a private meeting of the leading officers of several southern electric power companies.

The Law of Compensation was humming and buzzing all around me.

In the audience at that private meeting was Homer Pace, an executive of the South Carolina Electric & Gas Company. After I had spoken, he introduced himself. He told me he had been a student of the Science of Personal Achievement for many years.

He said: "I have a friend I'd like you to meet. He is president of a small college and owns a good-sized printing house. He speaks your language so well that I strongly suspect he is another of your long-distance students. You ought to know each other. Will you write to him?"

I wrote promptly. The college president and publisher came immediately to Atlanta to call upon me. Perhaps the shade of the Sage of Concord—as Emerson was called—smiled over my shoulder during the two-hour conversation. The college president and I made a verbal agreement. I would move to his home town and re-write my entire Philosophy and he would publish it.

Patterns appear in many lives. As you see, when I have needed a publisher, merely following my own Philosophy always helped me find one.

On the first of January, 1941, I began work on the Science of Personal Achievement now being taught in schools which I sponsor throughout this and other countries.

I find a very special Compensation. Looking back, I see that the reversals I had suffered just prior to meeting Mark Wooding had left me in something of a state of shock. Now I transmuted that shock into hard work, a labor of love. *Every misfortune always carries the seed of an equivalent or greater benefit.* Soon I found peace of mind such as I never had known.

Before I describe the third episode in this many-sided story of Compensation, let me make clear that *romance* definitely was not on my mind. As for marriage, it did not seem like anything that ever would happen to me. Yet a peaceful and active mind is not afraid of new ideas—or new conditions.

When I had moved to that little South Carolina town I took an apartment that happened to be near the home of the publisher's secretary. For several months after my arrival I saw the secretary only at her desk, in the ordinary course of business.

She had been the support of her family since her father had died while she was quite young. She now had been associated with two generations of the family that owned the business, she had a responsible position, and she was quite happy in her work. Between family responsibilities—she helped to educate her younger sisters—and the demands of holding down an executive job, she was very busy. She had given little thought to marriage; one might say it was the last thing on her mind.

And now perhaps a little pagan cherub with a bow and arrow smiled over my shoulder. Now and then I invited the secretary to join me for dinner. Now and again we went to a show in one of the nearby towns. I found out that the moment she got away from family and office matters, she had quite a different personality. A wonderful personality.

That woman was almost a perfect duplicate of the greatest woman I ever had known—my stepmother. No wonder I admired her! The picture began to develop rapidly. We took motor trips. On Sunday mornings we listened together to the Mormon Tabernacle radio services while we were driving in the country.

The Law of Compensation works in ways that are strange and unpredictable. I parted from this woman who attracted me so deeply.

First of all—the pattern again—I lost my publisher. The attack on Pearl Harbor and the events that followed affected my publisher's affairs so strongly that he brought our arrangement to an abrupt end.

Then I left town. This event arose from the telephone call from the LeTourneau Company which I have related, and I took over that important public relations assignment at their plant in Georgia.

There I was destined to meet the greatest opportunity of my life to demonstrate the soundness of my Philosophy as a builder of harmonious relations between employees and employer. With all modesty I can say that my influence in that plant, with its two thousand employees, changed everyone for the better, including top management. Later I read that the war in the Pacific depended heavily for its success on U.S. ability to move quantities of earth and rock in building airstrips on occupied islands. LeTourneau earth-moving machinery was largely used on those jobs, and perhaps indirectly I made my contribution.

Again one opportunity led to another. I decided on another move to make my Philosophy all the more available to industry. I would prepare a film about it—and this caused a move to Los Angeles, hub of the motion picture industry.

I had not forgotten that wonderful woman in South Carolina. She had not forgotten me. The day before I left for the West Coast, she became my wife. She is also my secretary, my priceless business associate, and the most important member of my Master Mind group. We have now delighted in more than twenty years of this perfect partnership. Talk about compensation!

"Every act rewards itself." That is Emerson speaking. We shall visit with him soon. You realize, I am sure, that the *reward* of any act may not be a "reward" as such, but rather a *penalty* if that is what the act deserves. The act rewards *itself*, not you, in the sense that is meant here, and so the "reward" is fitting.

This, you may say, is nothing but old-fashioned morality. Indeed it is. It is modern morality as well, valid when man invented the wheel, valid when, perhaps, man will invent the means to duplicate himself in a test tube. And it is more than morality. I have shown you the Law of Compensation at work in my life in the hope that you will stop and think of ways it has worked for you. You will see these ways as manifestations of cause and effect. You performed some action and that "got the ball rolling." But can it be an accident that thousands of years of commentary refer to the fact that the act of giving invariably precedes the act of receiving? That when we "cast bread upon the waters" it *does* come back?

We see the Law of Compensation as it brings us a better job, a sum of money, an opportunity to fulfill ourselves, a meeting with someone who turns out to be a lifelong partner in love—and there is much we do not see. Unseen, silent forces influence us constantly. Some are good for us, some are harmful. This volume speaks on many pages of the solid, bread-and-butter aspects of life; but it speaks as well of the unseen and the omnipresent. As I show you how to be rich with peace of mind I also show you how to choose the friendly, invisible forces rather than the unfriendly, and how to make the favorable forces your allies.

Now let us sit down with Mr. Emerson by candlelight in his book-lined study:

Every act rewards itself, or, in other words, integrates itself in a two-fold manner—first, in the thing, or in real nature; and secondly, in the circumstance, or in apparent nature. Men call the circumstance the retribution. The casual retribution is in the thing, and is seen by the soul. The retribution in the circumstance is seen by the understanding; it is inseparable from the thing, but is often spread over a long time, and so does not become distinct until after many years. The specific stripes may follow late after the offense, but they follow because they accompany it. Crime and punishment grow out of one stem. Punishment is a fruit that unsuspected ripens within the flower of the pleasure which concealed it. Cause and effect, means and ends, seed and fruit, cannot be severed; for the effect already blooms in the cause, the end pre-exists in the means, the fruit in the seed.

Think back upon the story I have told you in detail; the four episodes of success in my life which began at Wooding's in Atlanta. The cause behind those episodes was a simple act of service rendered to a friend I was able to help. It brought me blessings which still continue. Had I substituted for my act of service some selfish or unworthy act, I would not now enjoy those blessings but might still suffer under the penalty which the same Law of Compensation surely would have brought my way.

"There is a third silent party to all our bargains." Remember that! The Sage of Concord continues:

Men suffer all their life long, under the foolish superstition that they can be cheated. But it is as impossible for a man to be cheated by anyone but himself, as for a thing to be, and not to be, at the same time. There is a third silent party to all our bargains. The nature and soul of things takes on itself the guaranty of the fulfillment of every contract, so that honest service cannot come to loss. If you serve an ungrateful master, serve him the more. Put God in your debt. Every stroke shall be repaid. The longer the payment is withholden, the better for you; for compound interest on compound interest is the rate and usage of this exchequer.

The third silent party! There is the unseen force which in its timeless way makes sure of "the fulfillment of every contract" we make with the world. And now let us see how Emerson expresses his understanding of the fact that every adversity carries with it the seed of an equivalent or greater benefit:

The changes which break up at short intervals the prosperity of men, are advertisements of a nature whose law is growth. Evermore it is the order of nature to grow, and every soul is by this intrinsic necessity quitting its whole system of things, its friends, and home, and laws, and faith, as the shellfish crawls out of its beautiful but stony case, because it no longer admits of its growth, and slowly forms a new house. . . . And yet the compensations of calamity are made apparent to the understanding also, after long intervals of time. A fever, a mutilation, a cruel disappointment, a loss of wealth, a loss of friends seems at the moment unpaid loss, and unpayable. But the sure years reveal the deep remedial force that underlies all facts.

The death of a dear friend, wife, brother, lover, which seemed nothing but privation, somewhat later assumes the aspect of a guide or genius; for it commonly operates revolutions in our way of life, terminates an epoch of infancy or of youth which was waiting to be closed, breaks up a wonted occupation, or a household, or style of living, and allows the formation of new ones more friendly to the growth of character. It permits or constrains the formation of new acquaintances, and the reception of new influences that prove of the first importance to the next years; and the man or woman who would have remained a sunny garden flower, with no room for its roots and too much sunshine for its head, by the falling of the walls and the neglect of the gardener, is made the banyan of the forest, yielding shade and fruit to wide neighborhoods of men.

If Emerson had not written those lines long before I was born, I might well believe he was writing directly to me. Do you sense, perhaps, that he was writing directly to you? Please, as you read, take my experiences as reminders to consider your own. The lessons I have learned have been learned by millions, and none of us is very different from his brother.

I am particularly indebted to Emerson for his views on the subject of fear. They were responsible for a self-imposed house cleaning which removed from my mind all breeding places of fear, and I hope the following paragraph does the same for you.

Fear is an instructor of great sagacity. . . . One thing he always teaches, that there is rottenness where he appears. He is a carrion crow, and though you see not well what he hovers for, there is death somewhere. Our property is timid, our laws are timid, our cultivated classes are timid. Fear for ages has boded and mowed and gibbered our government and property. That obscene bird is not there for nothing. He indicates great wrongs which must be revised.

And although I once had a tendency to envy seemingly more fortunate persons, that tendency left me after I was influenced by the following excerpt from Emerson's essay on Compensation:

Every excess causes a defeat; every defeat an excess. Every sweet hath its sour; every evil its good. Every faculty which is a receiver of pleasure has an equal penalty put on its abuse. It is to answer for its moderation with its life. For every grain of wit there is a grain of folly. For everything you have missed, you have gained something else; and for everything you gain, you lose something. If riches increase, they are increased that use them. If the gatherer gathers too much, nature takes out of the man what she puts into his chest; swells the estate, but kills the owner. Nature hates monopolies and exceptions. The waves of the sea do not more speedily seek a level from their loftiest tossing than the varieties of condition tend to equalize themselves. There is always some leveling circumstance that puts down the overbearing, the strong, the rich, the fortunate, substantially on the same ground with all others.

Those who have tested Emerson's views find them based on eternal truth. Others who do not really test them may consider them an abstract preachment, or may point to all kinds of "exceptions" which are not exceptions at all, for time is an essential element of compensation, and nobody can tell what time will bring.

Finally, let us join this great mind in thinking about thinking.

Beware when the great God lets loose a thinker on this planet. Then all things are at risk. It is as when a conflagration has broken out in a great city, and no man knows what is safe, or where it will end. There is not a piece of science, but its flank may be turned tomorrow; there is not any literary reputation, not the so-called eternal names of fame, that may not be revised and condemned. The very hope of man, the thoughts of his heart, the religion of nations, the manners and morals of mankind, are all at the mercy of a new generalization.

Thus the power of mind-force to change the world. You may not change the world, but your mind-force is ready, willing and *able* to cause in *your* world the changes you need and want, no matter how mighty they may be. Emerson is not alone in celebrating the power of thought to "move mountains." I do not know of any other great thinker whose works do not show this inherent understanding—that we are thinking beings who act according to our thoughts; so that thought always precedes action, thought always builds before the hands build, thought is mighty beyond measurement— and so is achievement mighty when the thoughts behind it are unfettered and unafraid.

The philosopher as a practical person. We tend to think of philosophers as people who dwell in ivory towers of thought and come up with books that take a lot of learning before you can understand them. There is considerable truth in this picture. Philosophy has come so far since the ancient Greeks first mused upon the world and man that, these days, the philosophers seem to be talking to the philosophers and we ordinary folk are out in the cold.

Consider, however, that the basic purpose of philosophy is to search out the *why* of things. That is why the Science of Personal Achievement is a philosophy rather than a *method* or a *system*. In my previous books, as in this one, I give the truly basic answers to the questions:

> *Why* do some men succeed in life while others fail?
> *Why* do some individuals and couples live in harmony while others live in constant conflict?
> *Why* do some groups get along with other groups in a spirit of mutual help, while others hamper and frustrate each other?

While the *methods* by which you make money, or handle your affairs, or please your wife, or preserve harmony between management and labor are important—and I show you a number of the key methods—it is the *underlying philosophy* which is more important still. When your mind holds firmly to the basic concepts of wealth, peace of mind and life-success, you build on a firm foundation. When you try to apply methods merely in themselves, you may find you are trying to build on sand.

Thus it pays to be a philosopher in a perfectly practical sense. Faced with a problem, or desirous of improving some situation or influencing some other person for your mutual benefit—pause and remember you are a practical philosopher. Thus you focus your mind upon the basic reasons which always have worked and always will, and immediately you are well guided.

The philosopher in action. Does the philosopher meet with some disaster or misfortune? He looks for the cause, he seeks the lesson, he armors himself against the event ever happening again.

Likewise he notices the mistakes other people make. Knowing that human beings are very like one another, he watches for any tendency in himself to make the same mistake and thus almost surely will not make it.

The philosopher can foretell the future no more than can others. He knows, however, that history has a way of repeating itself; he takes inventory of the past and often can evoke a very valid idea of the future.

The philosopher bears firmly in mind that the way to help others is to help them find their best selves. He does not try to become a reformer and let himself in for endless effort which is not likely to do much good.

Being a philosopher, such a man knows that time is the great leveler. He is patient, and the days and years are his allies, never his adversaries.

Knowing that a peaceful mind is likewise an efficient mind, the philosopher allows no heckling from the kind of emotions which upset the mind and make it incapable of conceiving greatly.

Knowing there is no limit to mind-power, the philosopher does not hem in his powers with small, mean thinking, but thinks in those generous and wide-ranging terms upon which achievement is built.

The philosopher-businessman does not confuse today's profit with a lifetime's peace of mind and life-success. He will not, therefore, take unfair advantage of anyone, for "every act rewards itself."

The philosopher knows that thoughts are things; that every thought he sends forth, be it good or bad, comes back in due time, greatly multiplied, to curse him or to bless him according to its nature.

The chains of the past never drag after a philosopher with their mournful clank of looking backward. He knows that success lies ahead, life lies ahead, and only takes from the past whatever may have been a valuable lesson.

The true philosopher never slanders another person, and when he feels he must give way to righteous indignation, he does not do this as though it were his way of life. (It could be, for a philosopher.) He expresses his indignation as though he were writing it on the sand, at the water's edge, and hopes no man passes that way before the tide comes in.

Sharing is part of a true philosophy, so the philosopher shares freely, knowing that as he shares his blessings he prepares for new blessings. He knows that sharing plants opportunity for self-benefit which is well earned and well deserved, and that is the kind of benefit he wants to come to him.

As philosophers, we passed this book in review. Yes, in our role as seekers of the truths behind human nature and human conduct, we have reviewed much of this book to this page. As a philosopher, remind yourself of the usefulness of review, for the human mind learns by repetition and reinforcement until at length the truth is the rule. The very word *philosopher* is made of two Greek words meaning *love* and *truth*. A philosopher is a lover of the truth.

I close this chapter with an anecdote about my grandfather. He believed, as I do, that people learn best from experience. There is a bite in this anecdote, but I believe it helped to teach a bit of philosophy to a certain "city slicker."

The person to whom I refer stood at the side of the country road which I traveled with my grandfather from Powell's River, Virginia, on our way back home with a load of hay. I was very young; young enough to be impressed with the stranger's sharp clothing and superior manner.

He did not ask for a ride, but jumped onto the slow-moving wagon and said: "Give us a ride, hayseed." Grandfather made no reply. The horse ambled on and we left some miles of dusty road behind us.

When we had reached Grandfather's place and turned in toward his barn, the stranger slid off the wagon and said: "Hey, how far is it to Big Stone Gap from here?"

"We-ell," said Grandfather consideringly, "if you start walking back the way we came, it is about twenty miles. If you keep on the way we were going, I'd say it's about twenty-five thousand."

Once more the Supreme Secret has touched your mind, perhaps to stay, perhaps to return later and stay with you always.

CHECKING ON CHAPTER 11:

The Law of Compensation

Emerson's essay on Compensation remains one of the most important essays ever written. It is a *must* for anyone who wants to understand himself and the world in which he lives, and to find peace of mind all his life. Once the author of this book was in serious difficulty, but he still gave his time and services free to a friend; and his compensation from this act has covered many years and still continues. Unseen forces are at work among us, and this book shows you how to choose the friendly forces rather than the unfriendly.

Every act rewards itself

The Law of Compensation in its visible aspects, as for instance when it brings an opportunity following some action, may seem like nothing more than cause and effect. But, as Emerson says, there is a third silent party to all our bargains, and this is the unseen force which balances the books in the end. Men may believe they can be cheated, but it is impossible for a man to be cheated by anyone but himself, and although recompense may seem long in coming, there is a kind of spiritual compound interest which we receive at last.

Strength from adversity

The law of nature is growth, says Emerson. He remarks that this growth often includes adversities of many kinds, yet a deep remedial force operates to turn hardship and sorrows into guides for later life, and these same hardships often serve growth often includes adversities of many kinds, yet a deep remedial force operates to turn hardship and sorrows into guides for later life, and these same hardships often serve to end some period of life which was waiting to be closed. Also, adversity breaks off certain accustomed ways of living and helps us form new ones which may be necessary for growth. The person who is tempered by hardship becomes a stronger person who can do more for himself and more for others.

Mind-force can change your world

Emerson is not the only philosopher who celebrates the power of the mind and points to the changes a great mind makes in the world. Your own mind can change *your* world. Turn yourself into a philosopher and search out the basic reasons for success and happiness; go back to these reasons for guidance before you turn to bread-and-butter methods, and you build on a solid foundation. In considering yourself as a philosopher you can review this book up to this chapter, applying every basic principle you have learned and remembering how each principle is used in action.

1 2

You Are Very Important
—For a Little While

Your success is yours to make or break, but it never can be bigger than mankind. No matter how high you heap your fortune, in the end it counts for nothing. A successful life leaves its own monuments. In the Jungle of Life we walk alone in a way beset with dangers, but within our minds we keep the means to defeat the mind's enemies, build powers of true wealth and abiding happiness. We walk alone yet there is evidence that we are watched from the world beyond our senses. Even this mysterious world is concerned with guiding us to wealth now, *to peace of mind* now.

HE was a youngish man, not yet thirty, and he told me he was "raking it in" on short-term rentals of cars and trucks. He let me know how wise he was to leave the long-term leasing business to others; how wise he was to offer a lot of free mileage and make up the apparent giveaway in other ways; how wise he was in giving people a choice of insurance plans since they invariably chose the broadest protection, which was the most expensive, but did not have to be advertised as part of his daily rental rate; how wise he was in investing his profits in the stock market at the right time . . . in short, how wise he was.

I almost remarked on all the factors which had combined to help him. The development of the modern car, for instance, which costs so much to buy and maintain that it is worth renting by the day; and the development of good highways, and even the development of the credit card system which helped his business thrive. But no, he took no philosophic view of anything—and if the stock market happened to be going up when he happened to invest, chances were he would take credit for that too.

I merely reflected back upon the successful men I have known who made their money in everything from the manufacture of kerosene lamps to the giving of courses in computer programming. Some of them saw where they fitted into the scheme of things, and they were the men I had admired more than the others, who saw only their own ability to ride the crest of the timely wave. The ones who had had perspective upon life also tended to be the ones who had peace of mind. They were very big men, some of them, but they knew the world around them was bigger than they, and considerably more important.

Andrew Carnegie was well aware of this. At one time he believed that I was beginning to assume a feeling of superiority because of my association with him. He had me write out the following motto:

"Don't take yourself too damned seriously, unless you wish to be damned by others."

This motto did me some good at the time, later faded into my submerged memories; perhaps it was at such times as when I could be happy with nothing less than two Rolls-Royces.

Now I see there was nothing wrong with the Rolls-Royces, nor with my Catskill Mountain estate for that matter; it was my attitude that was wrong. I took myself too "damned" seriously. The splash I made in the world mattered more than my respect for the world which had given me my opportunities.

I look back upon that time and upon similar times, and I see I had a peculiarly guilty conscience. I had committed no crimes. In those days, however, if a glance into the rear-view mirror of my Rolls-Royce showed a traffic policeman coming up behind, I grew instantly uneasy even if I was driving several miles an hour under the speed limit. As for a policeman's coming to my door . . . if it ever had happened, I would have quaked in my boots.

Whence came the fear? Surely from the tensions I had worked up. Now those tensions are gone, for I know my place in the world and my mind is at peace. Now, when I see a traffic policeman coming up behind my car, I am glad to see him, for I know that his presence evokes careful driving and fewer hazards on the road.

And finally, a short time ago, a policeman in uniform did ring my doorbell. It was only after he had gone that I realized I *might* have felt some apprehension—but I didn't. I was merely curious to know why he had come to my door. He asked me politely if a certain person lived in my house. No, I informed him, that person once had lived in the house, but had moved away when I had purchased the place. He thanked me and that was that.

Ultimately, nothing matters. I have thought for some time about the best way in which to explain this spirit in which one's affairs are important but not *all*-important; this spirit in which one can find great success and great wealth and yet retain proper perspective upon one's self and one's affairs—a perspective which is so necessary for peace of mind.

Much of what already has been said in this book is connected with this very important matter. Thus, when one continually *gives* to his fellow men he both shows and feels that his personality is not built merely upon his possessions. I know I have given to the world more than I have taken from it, and this is a great source of contentment to me. Again, the ability to relax, play, live some hours of every day exactly according to your own ideas of pleasurable relaxation—this too brings perspective. I hope by now you have found this out for yourself.

After some testing, however, I have decided to emphasize the phrase: *Ultimately, nothing matters.* When you are grimly involved in getting, when the world seems to exist only within your own circle of activities, when something you have built or bought begins to shut out the sight of the sun—remember, ultimately, nothing matters. Say it aloud: "Ultimately, nothing matters!"

A negative counsel? By no means. *Ultimately,* nothing matters. Everything matters in its time and in its place—and give everything its due. Yet reserve a small corner of the consciousness for the ultimate which maintains perspective, which recognizes the ages as well as today. It makes you more peaceful, it makes you more sure of yourself, and it makes you stronger.

How I found out. Beyond that curtain which men can penetrate with the aid of their five senses, I have some friends who now and then communicate with me.

One night during the first world war, as I was about to retire, I felt a strong urge to turn to my typewriter and write *something.* I was then a confidential counselor to Woodrow Wilson and there were matters of urgent national and international importance crowding my mind. Yet when I had inserted a sheet of paper into the machine and placed my fingers upon its keyboard, only three words came into my consciousness. They were so vividly pushed into my mind by un-seen forces that my fingers tapped them out in capitals:

ULTIMATELY, NOTHING MATTERS.

I do not know how to explain what followed, so I shall at-tempt no explanation. Perhaps it was coincidence; perhaps not.

At any rate, on that same typewriter, a short time later, I worked on a message which I helped Woodrow Wilson write. Had the message been made public at the time, it would have changed the entire course of World War I. Certainly it seemed this message *mattered*.

Three days after the Armistice was signed, I saw a newspa-per lying in the gutter. Its front page bore a facsimile of the message. Did it matter? It had become utterly valueless with the lapse of a few days. With a shock of recognition my mind filled with the thought: *Ultimately, nothing matters.*

Some time passed. Woodrow Wilson became the guiding spirit behind the great new League of Nations. He believed that the future of civilization depended on the United States Senate's ratification. The Senate would not ratify. Mr. Wilson took to his bed, and no matter what bulletins the doctors is-sued, we who were close to him knew he was dying of heart-break and despair.

I came to his bedside. He looked at me hopelessly and murmured: "Those men on Capitol Hill have killed me."

Neither he nor I could say at that time that the world was not ready for the League of Nations plan. Yet something prompted me to say what might have been considered unfit-ting—and turned out to be the best words I could have said.

"Mr. President," I said, "ultimately, nothing matters."

He looked at me with a strange, slowly comprehending expression and finally said: "Of course not!"

Perhaps I helped him pass more peacefully into death. I know that the phrase has stayed strongly with me since, and I feel it was not of my own invention—it was placed in my mind by unseen, wiser powers who wished me to have it at that point in my life.

Nothing matters ultimately, so why fill your life with fear?
Often I have noticed men and women who go through life afraid of this and afraid of that—as though they had tuned

in on some cosmic wave-length which made fear an absolute virtue.

They had not tuned in, but rather had tuned out any influences beyond their own tiny affairs, which their own minds expanded to fill their cosmos. Fear is such a *little* thing!

Of course we go through life with "a decent respect for the opinions of mankind," as the Declaration of Independence says, and now and then we defer to others and put their welfare ahead of our own. This is co-operation, not fear. It is civilization rather than anarchy. Yet look around and see how many people stretch their social consciences into consciences full of fear, depression and self-defeat. Why?—when ultimately, nothing matters? Do they think that if they slink through life instead of marching with head up, they will make their lives matter the more after they are dead? Marching through life with confidence and courage is a far more likely way to make yourself remembered; not a sure way, but far, far more likely. Again, if they are not concerned with the size of their tombstones, nor the flowers placed upon their graves, nor the prayers said in their memory—this is all the more reason for living fearlessly.

I once saw a book with the title *I Write As I Please.* I never was able to read the book, but I hope it lived up to its admirable title. Any man who dares to write as he pleases has gone a great distance toward finding peace of mind and holding it firmly.

This too I learned by trial and error. There was a time when an impressive corps of critics went over every line I wrote before my writings got into print. Then I began to see that I was being made to please the reader by pandering to his established prejudices and beliefs. What good would I do in that case?

Now I write as I please and let the chips fall where they may. Perhaps you have noticed this.

Do you remember Elbert Hubbard? Sometimes great men come and go through this world without having their true greatness appreciated. Such a one was Elbert Hubbard. Writing as he pleased in a small town in New York State, he made ripples spread around the world. One of his greatest short pieces was *A Message to Garcia.* One of his books, *Elbert Hubbard's Scrapbook,* used to be found lying open in many a parlor, and you would be well advised to ask a dealer in used books to find a copy for you.

He was a man who had learned how to live his own life and own his own mind despite what others might think about him. He told me that this freedom gave him more satisfaction than all the glory the world might have showered upon him if he had written to please others.

In his earlier years, publishers looked over his writings and pronounced them too advanced for their time. Refused publication, he decided to become his own publisher. He did so well in the publishing business that at one time he employed eight hundred people.

Hubbard was far more than a successful writer and successful publisher. He was one of those rare souls who make life pay off in their own terms; who collect their pay as they go, and never limit it to money; who extract dividends from everything that affects their lives and find a benefit in every experience.

He became rich. He had a good deal more money than he needed. Yet unlike some other rich men, every day that he lived he tarried by the wayside of life. It would be a wonderful world if all men made themselves as free, as useful, as happy and as peaceful as Elbert Hubbard.

Neither Hubbard nor Emerson had to be reminded that *ultimately, nothing matters*. Yet they, and others like them, have left behind them a legacy far greater than legacies left by those who believed that everything they did was the most important event in the world.

Take your cue from nature. What is the only permanent state of affairs throughout the universe? It is *change*—eternal change—as nature forever builds, evolves, tears down, rebuilds in an ever-onward march toward some destiny unknown to man.

The whims of mankind mean nothing to nature. Time means nothing to nature. Of space and of matter she has abundance, and surely it matters not to nature that man now and then finds out a few secrets; there are many more!

Nature balances the births and deaths of men so that we perpetuate ourselves and the race goes on. Forever? That is not nature's concern. If she has set up laws which in time will wipe out man, his earth, perhaps his moon as well, perhaps the entire solar system—then that is nature's law and it is inexorable. If man himself should devastate his planet, nature will handle the charred and lifeless globe with the same forces of gravitation that handled it when it teemed with animals, plants and humanity.

Ultimately, nothing matters in nature.

Ponder this and you will begin to feel the cosmos as it should be felt—neither threatening nor promising. If there is a Heaven somewhere out yonder, I say again that you cannot prove or disprove it; the wisest man alive today cannot prove or disprove it; the wisest man who ever lived could not prove or disprove it. You are far, far better off—and so are your fellow men—if you believe with Emerson that compensation, retribution, punishment, reward, the balancing of accounts and the paying of debts—come in *this* world.

Hubbard and Rockefeller. When I think of Elbert Hubbard, often I think of John D. Rockefeller, Sr. They were so different!

Once Rockefeller asked me if I would like to change places with him. I told him politely that I would not; that I valued my health and my freedom, neither of which he enjoyed. I doubt if my remarks had anything to do with the obvious change which came over him a good many years before he died. But that change did come, and I see it as a new start in his life. Yes, the man who had billions found something lacking and attempted to make a new start in life.

What did he really want? By checking with those who knew him, I firmly believe that he wanted nothing more than what he had missed in his fabulous money-making career—peace of mind. I think that one day he looked at his money and it occurred to him that ULTIMATELY, NOTHING MATTERS. Ivy Lee's association with the Rockefeller interests was part of an effort to present to the world another side of the Rockefeller, Sr. nature. When the Rockefeller money began to flow into scientific, health and cultural projects, it signaled a kind of rebirth.

Elbert Hubbard never needed to change the image he presented to the world and himself. But Rockefeller, Sr. did, and so did Henry Ford, and so did many another man who seemed to be 100 percent successful—until he found that something was definitely lacking, nevertheless.

It is interesting to note that John D.'s descendants seem to have developed many useful social characteristics which simply were not popular among rich men in John D.'s day. Now I see that a great-grandson is occupied with social work—not merely through his money, but right down there where the poor live with their lack. Since John D. did change, I do *not* think he is turning over in his grave.

Through the Jungle of Life with unseen watchers. You know this book has been nearly seventy years in the making. I have intimated, too, that in those decades I did not *know* I would write a book which equates wealth with peace of mind, but somehow felt I would. Obviously I could not write it as a young man nor even as a fifty-year-old man, for I had not gathered the necessary experience. Obviously I could not write it, either, until I had learned well, and tested thoroughly, every bit of advice I give. That advice has been tested in many lives besides my own, and the stories I tell brim with life-lessons you will learn for yourself—which is the best way to learn them.

Now and again I have had evidence that unseen friends hover about me, unknowable to ordinary senses. In my studies I discovered there is a group of strange beings who maintain a school of wisdom which must be ten thousand years old, but I did not connect them with myself. Now I have found there is a connection. I am not one of them!—but I have been watched by them. Here is how I found it out.

I finished this book. And then . . . One day I knew the time had come to write this book. Perhaps the brief illness I had at that time, during which I outlined the book, was planned by those others to draw my mind away from day-to-day affairs. I wrote the book, enjoying it as one always enjoys a labor of love. It took a number of months, during which I felt highly alive and happy.

I completed the last chapter and still sat before my typewriter, musing on what I had written. *Ultimately, nothing matters,* I thought—yet it is good to have achieved that which the mind has conceived for so long a time. I was alone in my study and all was very still.

A voice spoke. I saw nobody. I cannot tell you whence the voice came. First it spoke a password known to few men, that riveted my attention.

"I have come," said the voice, "to give you one more section to include in your book. In writing this section you may cause some readers to disbelieve you, yet you will write honestly and many will believe and be benefited. The world has been given many philosophies by which men are prepared for death, but you have been chosen to give mankind a philosophy by which men are prepared for happy living."

I whispered: "Who are you?"

In a softened voice, which sounded like chimes of great music, the unseen speaker replied: "I come from the Great School of the Masters. I am one of the Council of Thirty-Three who serve the Great School and its initiates on the physical plane."

The Great School of the Masters!

That is the school of wisdom which has persisted secretly in the Himalayas for ten thousand years. Sometimes known as the Venerable Brotherhood of Ancient India, it is the great central reservoir of religious, philosophical, moral, physical, spiritual and psychical knowledge.

Patiently this school strives to lift mankind from spiritual infancy and darkness to maturity of soul and final illumination.

From the remotest days of antiquity, the Masters of the Great School have communicated with each other by telepathy. Eventually they met and organized themselves into the world's oldest association.

"These Masters," says J. E. Richardson in *The Great Message,* "are the Great Teachers who, through all human history, have not only declared their personal knowledge of another life, but have made the personal demonstration of their knowledge in such manner as to leave no possible doubt in the minds of their disciples, or students, as to the fact of that personal knowledge."

The Great School of the Masters always has exercised its powers for the constructive unfolding of individual human intelligence, in harmony with man's unchallengeable control over his individual powers of thought. The Masters believe that this great prerogative, which has been reserved for man alone, provides man with the means by which he may largely control his earthly destiny.

The School has Masters who can disembody themselves and travel instantly to any place they choose in order to acquire essential knowledge, or to give knowledge directly, by voice, to anyone else. Now I knew that one of these Masters had come across thousands of miles, through the night, into my study.

The Master continues to speak. After having paused to allow me time in which to collect my thoughts, the Master

continued in the same great musical voice which surely would
have resounded through the house had it not been audible to
my ears alone.

I shall not set down every word he said, but shall include
the gist of his message. Much of what he said already has
been presented to you in the chapters of this book or will follow in other chapters.

"You have earned the right to reveal a Supreme Secret to
others," said the vibrant voice. "In the journey through life
there is a Jungle of Life, a Black Forest through which every
individual must pass alone. In the Black Forest he overcomes
enemies and his own inner opposition and turmoil. The Black
Forest helps to give refinement to the soul of man through
struggle and resistance, so that the soul may return to the
Great Eternal Reservoir from whence it emerged and become
a part of Infinite Intelligence. You have been under the guidance of the Great School but you have been your own master. You have passed through the Jungle of Life safely. Now
you must give to the world a blueprint with which others
may traverse that same Black Forest.

"And now I shall name the enemies who must be met and
conquered in the journey.

"The foremost is FEAR. The expression of fear denies
man the use of his true power of thought—a power which
can enable each individual to acquire all of his physical needs
and control his earthly destiny.

"The next great enemy," said the Master, "is GREED for
the possession of material things and for power to control
others for selfish ends. No person who is filled with greed and
avarice can pass through the Jungle of Life and successfully
attain and use the Supreme Secret, for he affronts the Creator
when he violates the rights of others.

"INTOLERANCE is third on the list of enemies. Intolerance is the evil partner of selfishness and ignorance. It closes
the mind and shuts out facts. It deprives a person of valuable
friendships he will need in his journey through life and repels
the co-operation of others.

"EGOTISM is the fourth great enemy of man. Self-respect
is a most desirable quality, but self-love is self-deceit and
causes a man to lose his respect for others.

"LUST is the fifth enemy. It prevents sex emotion from
being properly transmuted and properly directed. It leads to
excessive sexual expressions which dissipate the vital creative
forces of mind and body.

"ANGER, the sixth enemy, is a form of temporary insanity. Righteous indignation that is controlled and directed toward the correction of a cause is occasionally necessary, but those who live with rage cannot truly know the Supreme Secret.

"HATRED, the seventh enemy, is anger which has been allowed to dwell in the mind until it has hardened like so much cement. It is a mind-poison which erroneously twists the individual's thinking. One who harbors hate cannot control and direct his power of thought toward constructive ends, and thus he is denied this one and only outright prerogative with which man has been blessed by the Creator."

The Master went on while I listened raptly. He spoke of the enemy of JEALOUSY, that mixture of covetousness and fear; and of IMPATIENCE, which prevents cause from bearing its fruit in effect. He listed DECEIT, which in the end deceives the deceiver; FALSEHOOD, which weaves a noose with which the liar spiritually hangs himself; the related enemy of INSINCERITY; and VANITY, which makes men vulgar and forms a repulsive force.

In the midst of a great silence the representative of the Great School told me I had been chosen to tell others of all the enemies, including the enemies of CRUELTY, which attracts all the other enemies like a pack of wolves, and MERCILESSNESS, which turns its back upon those in need and makes the soul shrivel. He spoke of INJUSTICE, of SLANDER and of GOSSIP. He pointed out that one may know the Supreme Secret in words but cannot use it if he ever attempts to destroy others. He showed me how the Black Forest closes in for a lifetime upon those who do not vanquish the enemies of UNDEPENDABILITY, DISHONESTY, DISLOYALTY and REVENGE.

In concluding with the names of four more enemies against whom I was to warn the world, the Master said they were fully as important in their menace as any of the others. They were: WORRY, which reveals that a man is no bigger than that which he allows to worry him; ENVY, a form of jealousy which most particularly destroys initiative and self-discipline; HYPOCHONDRIA, which prevents the mind from conceiving the continued good health of its bodily temple and so gives ill health its first foothold, which often is in the mind; and INDECISION, which grows stronger the more it is indulged until it rides one's back and one can fall and lie lost in the Black Forest.

"There are other enemies of man," the Master said, "but who conquers these twenty-six will conquer all the others. Know that one who seeks earnestly to conquer these twenty-six lurking enemies becomes an Initiate of the Great School. We know him, and he has access to the mind of a Master. The means of communication is telepathy. The Initiate may at times convey his need for instruction through what is commonly known as prayer."

The principle of prayer. The Master then told me the principles which lie behind prayer that can bring true help and guidance. You who read the mere printed words should read this section several times until its great meaning is clear to you.

"Prayer," the Master said, "is to be based upon a real need for help to accomplish something of constructive value.

"In true prayer one asks for help only after he has proved, by his own effort, that his own powers are not sufficient to enable him to accomplish his purpose.

"The person who prays for help should not assume he gives over his own individual freedom of action, but rather should know he is to co-operate with the helping agencies he cannot see.

"He must know, with confident self-respect, that his first duty is to improve himself and his condition; and that out of this, when it is well done, flows his second duty, which is to help humanity.

"These are the principles we look for in any prayer. However the prayer may be said or thought, under whatever conditions, these principles come through when they are present and bespeak the suppliant's fitness."

The Master now gave a word of caution for the Initiate who is on his way through the Jungle. He told me—as I now tell you—that now and then open spaces appear in that Black Forest, and as one walks clear of clinging underbrush he may think he has conquered all of the twenty-six enemies. This may be a deception on the part of the enemies. A dependable way to keep track of the enemies one has overcome is to list them on a chart, thus:

FEAR	CRUELTY
GREED	MERCILESSNESS
INTOLERANCE	INJUSTICE
EGOTISM	SLANDER

LUST	GOSSIP
ANGER	UNDEPENDABILITY
HATRED	DISHONESTY
JEALOUSY	DISLOYALTY
IMPATIENCE	REVENGE
DECEIT	WORRY
FALSEHOOD	ENVY
INSINCERITY	HYPOCHONDRIA
VANITY	INDECISION

The list should be checked at least once a year. Done honestly, and with the insight and self-knowledge one has gained, such a check enables one to search his record and know the names of the defeated enemies. These are crossed off the list. As long as one enemy remains, the person who made the list still wanders in the Jungle of Life. When every enemy has been accounted for, he has passed through the Jungle.

What happens at the end of the great journey. The Master explained: "When the Initiate has truly conquered all of the twenty-six enemies of success, peace and harmony, he will receive a communication from a Master of the Great School. He will be assured of his success in having passed through the Jungle, and he will receive definite instructions for his future conduct.

"First, he will be shown that a reasonable part of his time is to be devoted to directing others who are struggling to pass through the Jungle, and to helping his fellow men in every other possible way. He will know already that a benefit to others benefits himself, but now he will realize those benefits in their fullest measure.

"Second, he will be given the power to handle all adversities so that their eventual benefit to him always is revealed and he is conscious of his power to turn adversity into benefit.

"Third, the Initiate who masters the twenty-six enemies of man will quickly recognize the nature and purpose of any special mission to which he may be assigned in the future, and he always will have the courage to carry out that mission."

The Master went on quickly: "The Initiate retains the power to neglect or deny any of these requirements, but, should he do so, the penalty may be the complete revocation of the powers he has gained through many years of devoted effort. The powers include great blessings:

"Hope, faith and courage to carry out any desired objective.

"Benevolence toward his fellow men, and compassion for their problems.

"Self-understanding which reveals to him the nature of his own stupendous powers.

"Endurance and persistence enough to enable him to overcome all obstacles in his path.

"Sound health, both physical and mental.

"The wisdom with which to evaluate all things, and the self-discipline to give him complete mastery over himself.

"Patience with which to deal with adversities.

"Tolerance toward all, and a true spirit of brotherly love.

"Freedom from worry.

"Material abundance to meet all his needs and desires.

"A keen evaluation of time.

"Freedom from all vices.

"A magnetic personality and a spirit of generosity which attracts friendly co-operation.

"The ability to profit from his mistakes of the past.

"A listening ear, a silent tongue, a faithful heart, a keen sense of loyalty.

"A profound love of truth.

"The capacity for telepathic communication, including communication with Infinite Intelligence.

"A true understanding of scientific prayer, along with the capacity to get aid from the Masters when it may be needed.

"Immunity against the acts of all evil persons.

"Release from all inherited negative traits.

"Complete mastery of every kind of fear, including the fear of death.

"Understanding of the over-all purpose of life, along with the glorious ability to live according to that purpose."

The Master concludes his message. Another pause in the deep silence, and the Master said: "He will not only understand the true purpose of life, but also he will have at his command the power to fulfill that purpose *without having to experience another incarnation on this earthly plane.*

"And the Masters of the Great School, on this earthly plane and all other planes, will rejoice at his triumph and will bid him godspeed toward his own Mastership. His cycle toward Mastership will not have ended, but he will have spread before him the chart by which to navigate successfully."

The voice ended. I began to hear little sounds of the world around me, and I knew the Master had returned to the Great School of the Masters.

The inherent lesson in a few words. Ultimately, nothing matters. Read once more and see how much of the Master's message is concerned with *here* and *now*, the time in which we insure, by ourselves, whether life will reward us or punish us; whether we will win our dreams or die unfulfilled. Notice the several ways in which we are enjoined not to become too meanly important . . . *meanly* important in a big show of property or power which counts as nothing in the scheme of things and can destroy health and happiness.

As for the Ultimate beyond our earthly ultimates, we see a vision of a great reservoir of life-spirit, but we are not enjoined to walk in awe nor to walk apart from the affairs of life in some kind of self-assumed sainthood. Goodness in life devolves upon *living*, and life was not planned as a bed of roses, but as a wholehearted adventure in training one's self to know and win and enjoy the good.

Already you are qualified to use the Supreme Secret in many ways. As soon as you know it—if you do not already know it—you will see why this is so.

CHECKING ON CHAPTER 12:

You are very important—for a little while
When you take your affairs too seriously you steal from your peace of mind. A really big man knows the world around him is bigger than he is. The tensions incurred in trying to "live big" when it is not in your nature may bring you a guilty conscience and other troubles. Many really big men stop by the wayside of life and enjoy themselves, but small men are afraid to do this. Andrew Carnegie had a memorable motto which teaches us not to attempt to borrow the bigness of others.

Ultimately, nothing matters
When you are grimly involved in getting, it is time to remind yourself that, ultimately, nothing matters. Everything matters in its time and place, but maintaining perspective gives you

a recognition of the ages as well as of today. An experience in "automatic writing" at my typewriter seems to have been a communication from the world beyond the five senses to tell me that nothing matters, ultimately, and to enable me to pass on the word.

Why fear anything?

Too many people stretch their social consciences into consciences full of fear, depression and self-defeat. Marching through life with courage and confidence does away with fear, and there is no need to be concerned with the size of your tombstone. A fearless, peaceful man named Elbert Hubbard wrote as he pleased, published his own works and made a fortune. Neither Hubbard nor Emerson had to be reminded that, ultimately, nothing matters.

In the Jungle of Life there is unseen guidance

The author based much of this book upon a revelation from the Great School of the Masters. Twenty-six enemies lie in wait in the Jungle of Life. Defeat them and you acquire new ability to live a life of peace, abundance, success and enjoyment.

13

Not Too Much, Not Too Little

When your mind truly perceives your potential for wealth, you take advantage of the wealth-building opportunities all around you. Peace of mind is an essential ingredient of wealth. Giving in the spirit of the Golden Rule is closely allied to the enjoyment of wealth and all else of life's goodness. When you give service, as in a job, in the end you will be paid what you are worth, for you cannot fake the Golden Rule—it is eternal and immutable, and goes hand in hand with the immutable Law of Compensation.

THE abundance of the earth waits for *you* to gather it in. We have been told this by the Masters of every school of every century, and thus we learn from life itself.

What constitutes abundance? You know by now it is a relative term. Surely one who does not have enough to eat can not be said to enjoy abundance; but there are those who do not believe they are wealthy until they can eat their meals from golden plates. Be wealthy in your own way and you will know that you are wealthy . . . and bear in mind that even a beggar enjoys the beauty of the earth, the drift of white clouds and the sight of a rainbow or a twinkling star.

This is a practical book nevertheless, and I am sure you have noticed that I do not suggest any outright substitute for sufficient money. Let us look again at the question of sufficiency; let us look at its very beginnings.

Wealth comes to the man who can see a potential for wealth. I was brought up on something we called a farm. Well, it was land, all right, and one could observe certain crops growing in the fields and certain animals grazing. A good, efficient farmer would have noticed, however, that a good deal of our "farm" wasn't a farm at all. It included too much untilled land which produced the need to pay taxes, but no food to be eaten or produce to sell.

We lacked training, we lacked capital and we lacked quite a few other things—but still I do not quite know why we let a potential for (relative) wealth lie there without being used. It wasn't till years later that I heard about scientific farming which can produce more income from ten acres than my father could have produced from a hundred acres of equivalent land. Recently I met a truck farmer who makes a splendid living from only five acres by scientific rotation of his crops— and I knew I had met a man who could see and use his wealth-potential.

Notice, however, that the farmer's *basic* wealth-potential is not in his land. It is in his mind—in his willingness to learn good farming methods and use them, or, going even farther back, in his willingness to learn what constitutes good farm-land and make sure he gets it.

A recent newspaper item mentioned that in some parts of Africa, today, it takes eight people to grow enough food crops to feed nine people. Fortunately, good farming methods are spreading across the world along with good farming machinery, and modern fertilizers can do wonders with poor land. Yet when the same eight dirt-scratchers are turned into eight tractor drivers planting pedigreed seed, and their labor feeds eight hundred or eight thousand—still, first, their minds will have to accept the idea that this has been done by others and that they can do it. Wealth ALWAYS begins in the mind.

Wealth always begins with a mind-concept of wealth-potential. Putting farms aside, you can trace any fortune back to this one principle.

When you seek *enough,* therefore, look first into the mind that interprets the world around it. It is in your mind that you not only conceive the kind and amount of wealth you want; it is also in your mind that you take the raw stuff of circumstance and make it into *opportunity.*

Peace of mind is wealth.   I have not made the above statement before in exactly those words, but I am sure they do not surprise you.

The principle is so important that I shall give you yet another story about a man who was wealthy in money but did not know how poor he was because he did not have peace of mind. Also, he did not know what he was missing until he found it. And in order to find peace of mind, he had to abandon a business principle and substitute a human-kindness principle which he always had sneered at—so you can see, this shapes up into a pretty important true story.

The hero is . . . but who *is* the hero of this story? You have to decide for yourself. At any rate, a major character is a man who had made a fortune in real estate, largely through the rental of cheap property he owned. He found one aging couple to be long in arrears in their rent, and so, following his invariable principle of "good business," he decided to evict them.

He told his lawyer to follow through on the procedure. The lawyer, however, did not present him with an accomplished eviction, so the property owner and the lawyer had a talk.

The lawyer said: "I shan't press your claim. You can get someone else to take the case, unless you'd rather withdraw it."

The property owner decided he knew what was on the lawyer's mind. "So you think there isn't any money in it?"

"Oh, there'd be some little money in it, since I understand you want to sell the house once it's empty. But I don't want the case anyway."

The property owner wondered what was going on. "Did you get frightened out of it?"

"No, not at all."

"Ah-ha! Then the old coot who doesn't pay his rent begged to be let off."

"Well, yes."

"And you softened? He begged you and you went mushy? That's a terrible way to do business. Why, if he'd tried that on me, I'd have—"

"He didn't beg *me* to let him off. He didn't say a word to me."

"Well, he certainly didn't beg *me*, so may I respectfully inquire to whom he did address himself?"

The lawyer said quietly: "He addressed himself to God Almighty."

"So he fell on his knees when you asked for the rent and he—"

"No. He didn't know I was there. It wasn't for *my* benefit. You see, I knocked on the door and nobody answered. The door was ajar. I thought the old couple might have left already, so I walked in. The place is pretty bare, and I found myself looking through a half-open door into a bedroom where a white-haired old woman was propped up in bed, on pillows. I was just about to clear my throat—let her know I'd come in—when she said to someone else in the room: 'I'm ready now. You go ahead, Pa.'

"A man who was very old came from the other end of the room and knelt beside the bed. I couldn't move or say a word then, for the life of me. And that old man prayed, with his hand in the old woman's hand. First, he reminded God that they still were His submissive children, Ma and he, and no matter what He saw fit to bring upon them, they wouldn't rebel at His will. But it was going to be hard for them to be homeless in their old age, with Ma so sick and helpless, and, oh! how different it might have been if He had spared only one of their three sons, but the boys were no longer on this earth . . ."

The lawyer wiped at his eyes. "I cried then," he said, "but I still kept very quiet. And I listened to him remind the Lord about the safety of those who put their trust in the Lord, and how it wasn't going to be pleasant to go to the almshouse after a life of living together in a home of their own. And yet, he told the Lord, he knew there is such a thing as a just bargain with one's neighbor, and he ended by asking the Lord's blessing on . . ." The lawyer choked up.

"Not on *me!*" the property owner said hoarsely.

"Well, he mentioned no name. But he prayed for the Lord's blessing on those who are about to demand their just due. Well . . . I tiptoed out. And that is the end of that case so far as I am concerned. I'd rather go to the poorhouse myself than evict that old couple." He seized the other man's arm. "Look! I'll pay their back rent myself, right now if you'll let them stay in that house."

"No," the property owner said. He rose and walked to a window. After a moment he too dabbed at his eyes. "I'll let them stay there as long as they wish." He turned and said ruefully, "I wish you hadn't listened to that petition not intended for your ears or mine."

The lawyer shook his head. "No, it was intended that I hear it and tell it to you. My old mother used to sing about God's moving in a mysterious way. . . ."

"I've heard that too," the property owner said. He twisted the claim papers in his hands, then tore them up. "Well, why don't you go over there in the morning and—uh—take this ten-dollar bill and bring them a basket of groceries."

"I'll match that ten and bring them a bigger basket."

"And—uh—just tell them the rent has been paid, will you?"

"Yes. Paid in a mysterious way." The two men smiled at each other.

This real estate owner dates his wealth from the day he broke the pattern of his life—the day he stopped grasping and started giving—the day when he felt the first stirrings of what came to be wonderful peace of mind.

Do not limit what you give, limit what you take. Of course, practically speaking, there is a limit to what one can give of his time and his resources. I have mentioned that your first duty is to help yourself, then help other people, and when this rule is applied correctly it still works wonders.

So when I say: *Do not limit what you give,* I mean there should be no limit on the *spirit* of your giving. The property owner, for example, had given charity before. But it was charity given as charity, to local causes which gratefully acknowledged his name—so it was good publicity for him and for his business.

One day he gave when the last thing he had counted on was giving—and that made the difference. One day he felt that something bigger than himself was working through his wallet—and that made all the difference in the world. It changed the entire spirit of his life from that day on.

I make a speech. The above subhead is about as much news as "Dog Bites Man," for I have made a great many speeches. Its significance is this: I made the speech at a small college, and while I was at the college I made a good many notes on some of their activities in the work-and-study area.

When the chairman of the meeting handed me my fee, I handed it back. I thanked him, but said I had gathered enough material for two or more articles in my *Golden Rule* magazine, so I felt more than amply paid.

Later, subscriptions to *Golden Rule* poured in from the neighborhood of that college. The students had decided that since I had done something for them, they would do something for me, so they had gathered those subscriptions. I was paid many times over. And so it goes!

What is the Golden Rule—really? Do you know that the Golden Rule in one form or another was old already at the time of Jesus? He gave it to us in the form most of us know, but here are a few versions which go further back in history:

He sought for others the good he desired for himself. [Inscription on an Egyptian tomb, about 1600 B.C.]

What you would not want done to yourself, do not do unto others. [Confucius]

We should behave to the world as we wish the world to behave to us. [Aristotle]

You can see that the Golden Rule has been set up for quite a few thousand years as a major rule of conduct among men. Unfortunately the world remembers the letter of the rule while too often missing the spirit of this Universal Injunction.

Say it this way and you are more likely to associate it with the kind of conduct that helps both you and others:

The Golden Rule means we should do unto others as we would wish them to do unto us if our positions were reversed.

Think about that. It is not quite the Golden Rule you will find in the Bible. It goes another long step, for it implies your judging the other fellow's needs in *his* terms, seeing the world through *his* eyes.

Forgive a bit of levity in the middle of a serious subject,

but it can help you remember. There is an old story about a missionary who spread the Word among the primitive inhabitants of a South Sea island. Among other things he taught them his version of the Golden Rule, which is the general version: *Do unto others as you would have them do unto you.* The chief of the tribe was greatly impressed. One day he knocked at the missionary's door and announced he had brought the missionary a present . . . six extra wives!

Apply the lesson seriously and you will see that the real goodness of giving lies in giving the other fellow what *he* needs.

It is this kind of giving which so fully accords with the Law of Compensation, and which accords with so much plain human experience that shows giving comes before receiving —when the giving really fills a need.

There is no point in repeating the many examples of such giving I have shown you in this book. If you will check back on a few such examples you will see the Golden Rule in action. Also you will see its connection with another famous saying from the Bible: *Whatsoever a man soweth that shall he also reap.*

We should not content ourselves with the merest crumbs from life's table, and we should not attempt to grab too much. The Golden Rule often seems to act as a great leveler in assuring that this shall be so. It creates an ever-present spirit of kindly consideration for the needs and rights of others, so that without thought of gain (which so often is twisted by small minds into *grabbing*) the mind infused with the Golden Rule acquires a sense of what constitutes its own true ability to give. Giving begets receiving; there is a to-and-fro passage of wealth which may not reflect itself in a swollen bank account, but does reflect itself in a mind which has known such wealth. In this lies happiness, peace and health which a man merely rich in money may never know.

A suggestion: Look around in your community and find some man who you know lives for the purpose of accumulating money. Find some man—and alas, you can find such men —for whom any amount of money is too little and no amount is too much. He will almost certainly be a man who has little conscience about how he acquires his money, for conscience can be a hindrance when your horizon is nothing but a line of empty money bags to be filled.

Observe this man. Look for warmth in his soul; you will not find it, unless the subject of discussion is money. Watch

for a warm, human welcome in his smile; you will not see it
—he smiles like a shark. Notice how little he displays an enjoyment of life. Oh, he may go through various expensive
motions of enjoyment, but that is something else again.

In the humane sense of the word, such a man is not really
human. He is an automaton—a money-making machine. Yet
many will envy that mechanical man. They will point to what
they call his *success.*

Can there be success without happiness? Any really human
person knows the two must go together as partners in a worthwhile life. No man who thinks that happiness lies in having
too much ever will be happy. No man can be truly happy
until he translates the words of the Golden Rule into deeds,
and shares happiness with others. Moreover, the Golden Rule
was not meant to be *enforced* like taxes. The sharing of happiness brings happiness when the sharing is voluntary, with no
other object than to *give.*

How much is too little pay? How much is too much? One
of the reasons I have been glad that my name is not associated with Big Business—as it almost was—is this, which I
say again: I have always felt free to point out that Big Business should share more generously with its employees, both
in opportunities and in profits.

Galley slaves of times past were chained to their oars.
They were fed just enough to keep them going. As you may
read in that stirring tale *Ben Hur,* when a galley was on the
point of sinking, nobody unchained the men at the oars. They
went down with the ship as though they were so much machinery. In spirit, that is all they were.

Labor conditions in the first century or more of the Industrial Revolution were reminiscent of that philosophy. The
owner of an enterprise took from his workers all he could
squeeze out of them, and gave them as little as he could. A
good deal of this approach still persisted in my younger days.
I count it a blessing that I have lived to see some spirit of
sharing enter the world of the factory and the office. Now we
look back in horror at the twelve- or fourteen-hour day
worked at starvation wages, and wonder how we could have
been so stupid as not to see how this hurt both man and his
society; but that is the way it was.

Today, reward for work often comes in "fringe benefits" as
well as in direct payment. The question of—How much is too
little pay? How much is too much?—still remains, and I dare

say always will be with us. It is not to be treated as an absolute, for the value of money keeps changing.

By and large, however, one great absolute remains: Within the context of his times, a man's services are worth as much as he gives. Most men of fifty or more years of age can look back upon their pattern of income from jobs and see that this is so.

Moreover, we instinctively know this and we show we know it. I cherish a story told me by Henry Ford which illustrates the point beautifully.

During the early days of the business which is now so big, Mr. Ford advertised for a general sales manager. He weeded out the applications and interviewed some of the more promising prospects. In talking to one man, he finally got down to discussing salary. They did not seem able to fix a sum, so Mr. Ford said: "Suppose you come in and show us what you can do for a month, then we'll pay you all you are worth."

"No," said the applicant, "I'm getting more than that where I work now."

"And," Mr. Ford chuckled, "subsequent events proved that with his slip of the tongue he spoke the truth. At the end of the first month, we had to fire him."

I do not know why Mr. Ford hired the man, but presumably he appeared to have the experience and other qualities needed for the job. Then it turned out that the appearance of giving was all he had to give—and the reward was commensurate.

You cannot fake the Golden Rule. Does the Golden Rule, then, apply even in cases of hiring and firing? I shall not say this is invariably the case, but on the long average—yes, it does apply. The Law of Compensation, with which the Golden Rule works hand in hand, applies to every form of compensation. The advisability of not settling for too little and not grabbing for too much also applies. There is no valid rule of life which stands alone.

Do not think you ever can fake the Golden Rule. It will avail you nothing to *appear* to give what someone else wants, while at heart you are covering up a dishonest and selfish nature. Emerson said:

Human character does evermore publish itself. It will not be concealed . . . it rushes into light . . . I heard an experienced counselor say that he never feared the effect upon a jury of a lawyer who does not believe in his heart that his client ought to have a verdict. If he does not believe it, his unbelief will appear to the jury . . . and will become their disbelief. . . . That which we do not believe we cannot adequately say, though we may repeat the words ever so often. . . .

A man passes for what he is worth. What he is engraves itself on his face, on his form, on his fortunes, in letters of light which all men may read but himself. . . . Every violation of truth is not only a sort of suicide in the liar, but is a stab at the health of human society. . . . Trust men and they will make it their business to trust you; treat them greatly and they will show themselves great.

You now have read the Supreme Secret in many different ways. You will have no difficulty in accepting it as a proved and valued guide to peace of mind and wealth in great measure.

CHECKING ON CHAPTER 13:

What constitutes abundance?
Many a farmer's land gives him the potential for abundance, but he remains poor because he does not realize that potential. Every man has the potential for abundance within himself, but he may remain poor. Wealth comes when you see your potential for wealth—when you first conceive in your mind how you can turn the raw stuff of circumstance into wealth-building opportunity.

Peace of mind is wealth
Peace of mind evades many a man who thinks he is wealthy but is not. When he finds peace of mind, he knows what he has missed and his life is changed from that day on. Peace of mind often comes at last when a man discovers how to give without planning to give; how to give when the need is evident and without thought of gain. There has to be a limit on physical giving, but the spirit of giving knows no limit.

What is the Golden Rule?
See the Golden Rule as a way of helping others as you would wish them to help you if your positions were reversed. This focuses your attention on what the other fellow needs and results in true human consideration. The Golden Rule acts as a great leveler in assuring that you will have not too

little and not too much, but that great wealth will nevertheless pass through your hands. Nobody who lives only to accumulate money can know happiness, and there is no real success unless one is successful in being happy.

14

The Magic Power of Belief

In the power of belief lies the Supreme Secret. Belief is the key to basic mind-power which turns concepts into realities. Goals can be attained in ways which seem miraculous, yet we use only natural forces available to everyone. Even physical changes in the body can be caused by deeply implanted belief. The key to having quantities of money often lies in a simple process of auto-suggestion. Concentrate on precisely what you want, and you will see signposts that point the way. The forces of human evolution now have been brought under human control, and you can control your own evolution as a better, more successful person.

ANYTHING the human mind can believe, the human mind can achieve.

Please read that again, slowly: Anything the human mind can believe, the human mind can achieve.

If you had been presented with that statement at the beginning of this book, you might have found it a bit too much to digest all at once.

By now, however, you have seen many of the patterns of success and failure, of happiness and unhappiness, of mind-turmoil and peace of mind which man gives to himself.

Now, when you read: *Anything the human mind can believe, the human mind can achieve,* you know that the conception of achievement, which turns into the achievement itself, is our great human prerogative.

Anything the human mind can believe, the human mind can achieve. That is the Supreme Secret.

Truly, deeply believe you will have great wealth, and you will have it.

Truly, deeply believe you will have sound physical health, and you will have it.

Truly, deeply believe you will have a mind at peace, and you will have it—and all the wonders that go with it.

Anything the human mind can believe, the human mind can achieve. This is the secret known in bygone times; this is the secret which governs present-day accomplishment; this is the secret which will follow man to the stars. This is the secret of the ages.

What do we mean by BELIEVE?   "Wishing won't make it so," runs an old saying. This is true, and helps you remember a *wish* is not a *belief*.

A wish takes place, as it were, upon the surface of the mind. *I wish* . . . you may say, and follow with any wish that tickles your fancy . . . to have a million dollars drop into your lap . . . to be able to flap your arms and fly. A wish is not limited by natural forces. That very apparent fact, however, is not the main difference between a wish and a belief.

A *belief* is created, as it were, in the depths of the mind. A belief becomes part of you. That is why a true, deep belief can change your glandular secretions and the content of your bloodstream, and work other physical changes beyond the power of medical science to explain. Again, a belief, radiating its unknown wave length from the depths of your mind to the depths of another mind, accounts for a good deal of "personality power" and much else on which we can put only the clumsiest of labels. It is *belief* in a cause—much stronger than a *wish* to stay alive—which causes people to transcend even the instinct of self-preservation. It is belief that founds religion, sustains nations, stands behind anything great that ever is achieved. A belief, I repeat, is part of you; that is why you can achieve what you believe. Moreover, when you hold a great belief you believe all the time, just as, all the time, you go on living.

Conscious and subconscious.   As someone expressed it, the conscious mind gives us "thoughts we know." You want to put on your shoes, for example, or listen to your radio, and knowing the conscious thought, you take the appropriate action.

Now, there is hardly any physical reason why one should not put on his shoes or turn on his radio if he wishes to do so and has the use of his hands. But let us now suppose that there may be some reason not to turn on that radio. Suppose it is the moment at which a certain foreign broadcast may be heard, and your government, an oppressive one, has set up punishments for people who listen to that broadcast. Morever, you know you cannot listen to that broadcast in complete safety, for you suspect there are spies in your house.

Do you or do you not reach out and turn the switch that will bring in the forbidden broadcast? That will depend a great deal upon your subconscious mind. It is not in the conscious mind that we are basically fearful or brave, but down deeper. And so the subconscious will instruct the conscious, unknown to you, and in the conscious will appear the thought known to you:

Don't do it, you'll end in prison! or

I'm going to assert my freedom to listen to what I want to hear, under any circumstances, or even a compromise such as *I'm going to see if that nosy fellow in the furnished room upstairs is at home, and if he isn't, I'll turn on the radio.*

Take this a step farther. Suppose you say in your conscious mind—*I am going to turn on that radio at 9 PM no matter what!* But you wish it, rather than believe it, while all the time, in your subconscious, dwells a fear which amounts to a direction that you will *not* turn on the radio. Now the subconscious mind will feed all kinds of evasions and excuses to the conscious. You will somehow manage to come home late, or you will rush into the house just in time and "accidentally" bang into the radio, knock it off the table and smash it. (An honest enough accident, since you will consciously believe it was accidental.) Or you may make an appointment to do something else at the time of the broadcast, and then suddenly remember—when your subconscious allows you to remember consciously—that this is the broadcast time, and how *silly* of you to have committed yourself to another obligation.

Do not read any implication of dishonesty into all this, nor any implication that no consideration should be stronger than one's right to turn on one's radio. Look at it broadly. See that your subconscious mind is your hidden boss.

You probably have recognized this many a time when you have said there is something you simply will not do; it is against your principles. A true principle is a firm belief that is part of you, and can of course be a very useful and necessary thing.

Your subconscious mind is your hidden boss, then, and gives orders to your conscious. But your subconscious, as you surely know by reading this book, is a very special kind of boss. It will go into conference with you, so to speak, and consider changing any of its standing orders, canceling them, substituting others if need be.

Decide upon the belief you want, set it firmly into your subconscious mind, and your subconscious will thereafter instruct your conscious mind to "live up to" that belief.

Let your belief include the concept of achievement and your subconscious mind will discover ways and means toward that achievement which, on the strength of a mere wish, would completely escape you. You may talk of "good fortune" and "lucky breaks," but what you mean is a sharpening of all your senses toward the achievement you want—a focusing of all your forces away from other matters and toward that achievement—a mighty access of strength and resourcefulness—a tuning in upon other minds whose aid otherwise would have escaped you—and more! The best of words limp when they talk of the power of belief. Only feel your belief propelling you toward the goal of your achievement and you will know at last that an irresistible force is at your command.

Is there a limit to what belief can achieve? If there is a limit, nobody has seen that limit yet. I have mentioned often that we may at times avail ourselves of powers beyond our ordinary senses. (Not *super*natural, but natural powers we are only beginning to understand.) Deep subconscious belief aids mightily in winning the aid of these unseen powers.

Once, when I was a child, I had typhoid fever—the only serious illness I ever have had. I was ill for weeks without showing any sign of improvement. At length, as my father informed me years later, I lapsed into a coma. The two doctors who had come out to our farm told my father there was nothing else they could do; my end was only a few hours away.

My father walked into the forest. There he knelt down and prayed to another Doctor beyond earthly doctors. With his prayer he generated a mighty, all-embracing belief that I *would* recover. He remained on his knees for an hour or more, and at length a great peace came over him . . . that peace of mind which is the condition in which the mind works at its mighty best. And suddenly, from nowhere, and yet beyond the slightest shadow of doubt, he knew peacefully that I was going to recover.

I do not know where my father's prayer might have been heard, nor if it was heard, nor if the mere fact of the prayer gave him the focusing and intensifying agent which is part of deep subconscious belief. But I know that when he returned to the house he found me sitting up, which had been impossible for me to do a couple of hours before. Sitting up, crying for water, and with my fever "broken" as we used to say.

Another generation, another goal. I have been privileged to see in my own generation, and with my own son, how deep belief can bring "impossible" achievement.

When my son Blair was born without ears, and without many vital parts of the usual hearing equipment, I conceived the idea that he *would* hear. Let me make short shrift of the obstacles that were put in Blair's way and mine—the denunciations I received for not allowing him to learn finger-talk, the attempts to wreck his life by making him self-conscious about being "different," and so forth. At any rate, I knew that the subconscious mind can work wonders toward establishing health and proper function in the body—when it is so conditioned.

The conscious mind often serves as a sort of sentinel which guards the entrance to the subconscious. Thus, as we say, "A man convinced against his will is of the same opinion still," because his agreement was merely conscious, perhaps a peace-maker rather than a subconscious "change of orders." Or in extraordinary circumstances we are "carried away" and do not act in our accustomed manner, but later return to our ordinary ways of conducting ourselves because no deep-down impression was made.

Hypnotism appears to bypass the conscious mind at some times, and with some people. There is a better and less risky way, however, to reach past the barrier of the conscious and implant instructions in the subconscious, where they will be absorbed and fed back. That way is to give instructions to a sleeping person. The conscious mind sleeps, but the subconscious does not sleep. Recent studies suggest that there are certain stages of sleep in which the mind is more receptive than when it is in other stages, and I am glad to see this modern investigation of the technique. I may have wasted some of my efforts, but my efforts were so long-continued and backed by such belief that they achieved what many others said I never would be able to do.

I spoke to Blair while he slept. I spoke directly to his subconscious mind and told it what I expected of it. He received added stimulation of his nervous system through chiropractic adjustment.

With this method I induced nature to build an extra set of auditory nerves from Blair's brain to the inner walls of his skull. Now, he did not grow ears, but he achieved ability to hear equivalent to about 65 per cent of the normal level, and with that he got along quite well. Some may call this a miracle of healing, but I would rather call it a demonstration of the power of natural forces.

Just how does Blair hear? Through bone conduction to those new nerves inside his skull. Now we know that some of the marvelous new transistorized hearing aids depend on bone conduction.

Can the method be extended? My method worked, but it required that some devoted person remain on duty many hours a night. Later I experimented with a phonograph which repeated a recorded message every fifteen minutes, piping it to a hearing device beneath the sleeping person's pillow. I myself have received great benefit from this device.

We know, too, that corresponding devices are sometimes offered for sale. These devices have been benefited by modern developments in sound recording and transmission, but their principle is the same. Concurrently I have become aware of other recent research into the techniques of sleep-learning which suggests some of the difficulties people may encounter:

First of all, the machine alone is not enough. First there must be *belief* that the subconscious mind can and will receive messages while the conscious is asleep. A skeptical mind may make nothing of the messages. A mind filled with fear and inferiority, or both, will soon decide the "gadget" is too much trouble to use.

Then too, some people have their sleep so disturbed by the mere existence of a machine at their bedside that their conscious minds never really go out of action. Probably they could condition themselves to sleeping, machine or no machine, but I suspect that most such people are more anxious to return the machine within the time limit of its guarantee!

Many people also seem to go to lengths to negate any benefit they may obtain through sleep-learning. The subconsciously recorded message needs time in which to take root, so to speak, in the myriad cells of the mind. It will not do this if the conscious mind is allowed, even encouraged, to use its waking hours to throw in negative thoughts—the memory of a past failure, for instance, or overconcern with what other people will think of some course of action, or whatever.

And finally, I discovered this: The recorded messages must be reinforced when the individual is in a conscious, wide-awake state. He should memorize the recorded messages—which, of course, have no concern with anything but what is to be achieved, and carry no clutter of imagined handicaps. He should repeat these completely positive, focused messages to himself many times a day so that his conscious mind becomes accustomed to them, and through repetitive conditioning can talk to his subconscious.

Eventually, sleep-learning may be so perfected as to open great new worlds of achievement. It may help you greatly right now, but I wish rather to mention it as an illustration of the way in which the subconscious can and will accept orders which forever after guide you, and may, as I have shown, even cause marvelous changes in the body.

This book emphasizes the fact that each of us carries *within himself* the means of finding his own greatness. Knowing the Supreme Secret—what the human mind can believe, the human mind can achieve—you see that you have what it takes—your mind—and you have available the only other ingredient you need . . . a world that is bursting with riches and throbbing with opportunity.

Put the two together.

The art of auto-suggestion. There is a man in Cleveland today who is worth about ten million dollars. He made his money first by putting TV sets into super-markets, thus reaching shoppers with special programs he broadcast to them at the point of purchase. This did not require any new inventions nor the instilling of a new way of life into millions of people. It did not even require a head start by way of great capital or special position, for this man—his name is Art Modell—began as a shipyard worker. He conceived an idea and brought it upward and onward into achievement.

A man named McVicker, from Cincinnati, is quoted as saying: "You have got to believe so strongly . . . that you overcome the doubts of others." He believed that a doughy material used to clean wallpaper would appeal to children—and their parents—as a non-sticky modeling material. Others told him he was wrong. He achieved a business worth about four million dollars a year.

Like Henry Ford or Thomas Edison, these successful men of today *believed* and *achieved*. Their belief showed them the way to their achievement. So it was with Columbus. So it was with Paul of Tarsus. So it can be with you.

The art of auto-suggestion is completely self-contained. We shall see it clearly, in plain print, in a moment. First ask yourself: *What do I want?* This is not a question to be answered lightly. What *do* you want? Once more I give you a list to aid your thinking:

Improvement of your general health
Improvement of some specific health or functional factor
Cure of any bad habit
Abolishment of fear
The ability to transmute sex energy
The ability to find the right mate in marriage
Weight reduction or gain
The ability to break away from outworn customs or outmoded ways of life
The ability to get along better with other people
The ability to sway others to your way of thinking
Inner guidance in the selection of a business or profession
Money

When you know what you want, you are ready to go after it. You need a Definite Chief Aim. Vague mind-conceptions are little better than mere wishes. Decide *where you are going*—then, and only then do you begin to see the signposts that point the way.

You are going to make money, and I trust you to see it as only one form of wealth—but, as I have pointed out, a form of wealth which helps us attain many others. The chances are that you automatically accept *money* as a goal, so let us take this goal as a prototype in illustrating auto-suggestion.

How much money do you want to make? You will recall the stories of W. Clement Stone and other men who set up specific sums of money as their goal and attained the ownership of those sums. They did not fill their minds with thoughts of the difficulties in their way, nor the menace of competition. They believed they would make money . . . they achieved what they went after.

Now, this is the way to use auto-suggestion to help you

achieve the sum of money you want. It is done in six steps which stimulate your subconscious mind:

One: Find a quiet spot where you can be alone and undisturbed. Many find that as they lie in bed, just before going to sleep, the mind becomes receptive. Close your eyes and repeat aloud, listening to your own words, the sum of money you intend to make—the time limit you have set for its accumulation—and a description of the service or merchandise you intend to give or to sell in return for that money.

Two: Put the same words in writing. (You may do this first if you wish.) Write it out carefully and in detail. Memorize it. When you go into your quiet place to repeat your goal to yourself, say it word for word as you have written it. You may change it here and there until it is absolutely specific. Add a statement of this nature, in your own words:

I believe that I will have this money in my possession. My belief is so strong that I now can see the money before my eyes. I am holding it in my hands. I know it exists, and it is awaiting transfer to me in return for my services rendered with full honesty and all possible skill and diligence. A plan exists which will transfer this sum [state the sum] to me by [state the deadline date] and my receptive mind will see that plan and cause me to follow it.

See yourself rendering the service or delivering the merchandise. See yourself receiving your payment. This is important!

Three: Place a written copy of your statement where you will see it night and morning. Read it upon rising. Read it again just before retiring. You may also carry it with you and read it several times a day, but to read it first thing in the morning and last thing at night is particularly important.

Again, as you read, see yourself going through the actions which will bring you the money. Feel the money in your hands. Feel with *feeling.* Merely reading the words (or saying them to yourself) will mean nothing unless they carry the emotional charge of desire. It is well known that the subconscious has less regard for *reason* than it does for *emotion.*

Four: Put the Master Mind Principle to work. It is not always possible to form a Master Mind group according to the directions you have read in a previous chapter—and you are better off without one than doing it the wrong way. You can, however, make good use of the principle by conferring with the right people. These are people who can help you and, if possible, people you can help. Don't forget, if you want to see a banker about financing your business, *you* are helping *him* run his business. (And don't forget, many a "cold-blooded" banker has been swayed by the confidence and belief and enthusiasm he sees in a would-be borrower—with good reason.)

The more people you talk to, the more information you will receive. The more they know—the more you know. Choose the right people, however. Now and again you will meet, among them, one whose mind tunes in to yours. Speaking with such a person is a mighty tonic for the subconscious drives you have at your direction.

Five: When your plan appears, act upon it. You will know it. The subconscious is like a fertile garden spot in which any seed will grow, be it the seed of a weed or the seed of your fortune. Through auto-suggestion you work wonders in keeping out the weed seeds. When a seed of your fortune falls in the garden of your subconscious, however, it grows in relation to the attention you give it.

Do not sit idly waiting for your plan to appear. You may not precisely know, for example, where you are going to set up your business—but until the right place draws your attuned attention, you can be contacting sources of supply, learning more about the business and filling your mind with the process of your achievement in a hundred other ways. Remember how publishers came to me when I needed them.

Six: Once you have a matured plan which covers every detail, put that plan in writing. Read it over night and morning. Stick to it, but be ready to change it if circumstances point out the advisability of a change. Your mind will not constantly flutter from one alternative to another. Your subconscious will sift the alternatives with a great power to show you *what you must do to attain your goal.* . . .

I could set down *Faith* as a seventh factor of auto-suggestion; but faith is all-pervasive. Faith is called, in another of my books, the head chemist of the mind. As faith blends with thought, it becomes the perfect ingredient for true subconscious belief. As faith becomes part of you, it rides along with every message you repeat to yourself. It becomes part of your character, part of your personality. Faith helps you emotionalize your thoughts, bring them beyond the power of reason into another realm of mental being where thoughts become their physical equivalent.

Now, with a sense of *faith,* read the six steps of auto-suggestion over again.

A new look at your mind and your body. The Supreme Secret is: *Anything the human mind can believe, the human mind can achieve.* It would be as valid to say: *Anything the mind can believe, the mind can achieve,* but I wish to emphasize the power of the *human* mind. No other living creature can take hold of its mind as we do, sense and explore its powers, find ways to increase those powers to an extent almost beyond imagination.

You are used to being human. Take time now and then to realize the uniqueness of your human state.

One of the great modern commentators on man and his mind is Dr. Pierre Lecomte du Noüy. I have a favorite passage from his great book, *Human Destiny,* which I am fond of showing to people who cannot see how it is possible for the mind to heal the body. I quote this passage now:

The human body is constituted of distinct beings, the cells, each endowed with totally different properties. There are the common and prolific plebeians, the fibroblasts; there are the independent chemists of the liver and the marrow; there are the chemists who obey the orders transmitted by the brain and the nervous system, and who know how to manufacture instantaneously, at the tip of the nerves, acetylcholine which contracts the muscles and adrenalin which decontracts them. There are the noble cells, the pyramidal cells of the brain, living in proud sterility and never reproducing themselves; there are the nervous cells which transmit orders and reactions; there are those which defend, those that protect, those which heal. From the co-ordination of the whole emerges the autonomous personality of man.

And this brief description barely touches upon the stupendous group of factors available to man in his body and brain, for the organization, projection and use of the power of thought.

It is a major indictment against the world's educational systems that most people come into this world, live their span of years and pass on without being made aware of their thought-power and the fact that their lives are made or unmade by this thought-power. Worse yet, we are taught all kinds of things and yet rarely taught to use our minds for the attainment of the one indispensable form of wealth—peace of mind.

It is a major indictment against the religionists that they seem to have learned so much about how to prepare to live in Heaven—but have done so little about preparing us to live prosperously, peaceably and happily here, now.

It is a major indictment against our civilization that the

vast majority of people keep most of their thought power centered on their fears, rather than on conceptions and deep beliefs which can bring them what they want—not that of which they are afraid.

Every man can surpass himself. Dr. du Noüy points out dramatically the power of the human being to reach beyond his limitations and thus forever to extend his powers:

We all have our role to play individually. But we only play it well on condition of always trying to do better, of overreaching ourselves. It is this effort which constitutes our personal participation in evolution, our duty. . . . If we have children, we will have collaborated in a measure modestly, statistically, *but unless we develop our personality* we will have left no trace in the true, human evolution. [The italics are mine.]

Obviously Dr. du Noüy recognized the importance of each individual's exercising his privilege of choice in thinking as a means of mental and spiritual growth, for he continues:

"An intelligent being," said Bergson, "carries within him the wherewithal to surpass himself." It is needful for him to know it, and it is essential for him to attempt to realize it. The incomparable gift of brain, with its truly amazing powers of abstraction, has rendered obsolete the slow and sometimes clumsy mechanisms utilized by evolution so far. Thanks to the brain alone, man, in the course of three generations only, has conquered the realm of air, while it took hundreds of thousands of years for animals to achieve the same result through the process of evolution.

Thanks to the brain alone, the range of our sensory organs has been increased a millionfold, far beyond the fondest dreams; we have brought the moon within thirty miles of us [du Noüy is a modern writer, but see how he already needs to be updated!], we see the infinitely small and we see the infinitely remote; we hear the inaudible; we have dwarfed distance and killed physical time.

We have enslaved the forces of the universe, even before we have succeeded in understanding them thoroughly. We have put to shame the tedious and time-consuming methods of trial and error used by nature, because nature has finally succeeded in producing its masterpiece in the shape of the human brain. But the great laws of evolution are still active, even though adaptation has lost its importance as far as we are concerned. We are now responsible for the progress of evolution.

We are free to destroy ourselves if we misunderstand the meaning and the purpose of our victories; and we are free to forge ahead, to prolong evolution, to cooperate with God if we perceive the meaning of it all, if we realize that it can only be achieved through a wholehearted effort toward moral and spiritual development.

Peace of mind and power of mind. Since what you achieve in life depends on what you first conceive, and this depends first of all upon your deep, inner, subconsciously founded *belief*—you see that your life depends upon your power to believe.

No, your mere life-processes do not depend upon this power. The Eternal has made it possible for the supreme achievement of evolution, man, to stay alive even without knowing he is alive. The beating of the heart, the pumping of the lungs, the processes of digestion and other vital functions are taken care of by a part of the brain which takes care of itself.

Beyond this, man creates an ever better species. He aspires —and climbs to the heights of his aspiration. Seeing heights yet beyond, again he aspires—and achieves that peak, beyond which lies another and another.

Significantly, philosophers always have recognized the power of the quiet mind, the peaceful mind. This is far from being a mind empty of aspiration. It is, rather, a mind which can hold, judge and evaluate the highest forms of aspiration. Nor is a peaceful mind the exclusive property of a person who does not move about in the world and busy himself with the world's manifold affairs, for some of the most peaceful minds are the busiest. Remember, we speak of inner peace, like a quiet center about which all else revolves, like a great rotating dynamo doing useful work and filled with energy, yet referring its rotation always to the unmoved pivot at its middle.

A mind at peace is a mind that is free to conceive greatly. It bears no great conflicts within its subconscious which may hamper the conscious mind and therefore conscious action. A mind at peace is a *free* mind. Its power is limitless.

Form your great beliefs on the basis of inward peace and they will be truly great—and they will be possible of achievement. Not possible to everyone, perhaps, but possible to the man who knows that peace of mind and power of mind are the same.

Who told you it couldn't be done? What great achievement has he to his credit that entitles him to use the word *impossible?*

CHECKING ON CHAPTER 14:

Anything the human mind can believe,
the human mind can achieve

This is the Supreme Secret, forever the foundation-secret of man's efforts to control his destiny. Conceive a great step forward in your life, form a deep subconscious belief, and the belief becomes the very foundation of reality. "Wishing won't make it so," for a mere wish does not penetrate the depths of the mind; but a true belief becomes part of your complete being.

Conscious and subconscious

Your subconscious mind is your hidden boss. Although your conscious mind controls your conscious actions, the subconscious dictates the pattern of those actions. If, subconsciously, you are afraid to do something, you may fill in with excuses and evasions which prevent you from taking that action. But your subconscious can be persuaded to change any of its standing orders and thus completely change your life. Your subconscious mind is the seat of deep belief which becomes your constant guide.

The subconscious knows no limit to its power

The proper use of the subconscious mind puts us in touch with forces beyond the ordinary senses. Thoughts can be transmitted to the subconscious mind of a sleeping person, by-passing the guard of the conscious mind. This is the secret of seeming miracles of healing. Methods of sleep-learning may eventually be so perfected as to open great new horizons of mental power.

Auto-suggestion and your success

Knowing that what the human mind can believe, the human mind can achieve, you can see that deep belief opens great vistas of opportunity. In order to get what you want, you must focus your belief on a Definite Chief Aim. Money is a goal to be handled with judgment, but it is an acceptable goal and a definite one. Techniques of auto-suggestion should be focused on the precise amount of money you want and the means by which you are going to attain that sum. Peace of mind and power of mind go hand in hand, and the mind at peace is the mind most capable of great conceptions, great beliefs and the enjoyment of those beliefs as solid realities.

15

Enthusiasm—
And Something More

Enthusiasm is the great tool of persuasion. Ask for a favor with enthusiasm, add certain psychological factors shown here, and your request becomes irresistible. Behind enthusiasm must stand the honest desire to serve, and a favor done for you should also benefit the person who does the favor. When you look for a job, follow key rules to make sure you get the right job, with every prospect of rapid advancement. Make sure you do the kind of work in which you can express yourself—for it is a long step toward wealth and peace of mind.

I HAVE been looking at a couple of old letters. I reproduced them in a book some time ago, and the comments I have received make me sure they should be reproduced again.

The letters were part of a discourse on Enthusiasm—a discourse I have changed and improved with the years. I never have seen reason to change the principle, however:

Enthusiasm is a state of mind that inspires and arouses one to put ACTION into the task at hand. It is the most contagious of all emotions and transmits the impetus toward agreement and action to all within reach of your words.

Now I give you the letters exactly as I wrote them. You may read them and say: "Letters are not written that way any more." True; styles change. I hope always to be aware of that fact. But remember the principle enunciated above and see which is more important, the style or the principle. Read the letters first; then I shall tell you their history.

My dear Mr.——
I am just completing a manuscript for a new book entitled *How to Sell Your Services*. I anticipate the sale of several hundred thousand of these books and I believe those who purchase the book would welcome the opportunity of receiving a message from you as to the best method of marketing personal services.
Would you, therefore, be good enough to give me a few minutes of your time by writing a brief message to be published in my

book? This will be a big favor to me personally and I know it would be appreciated by the readers of the book.

Thanking you in advance for any consideration you may care to show me, I am,

Yours very truly,

My dear Mr.——

Would you care to have the opportunity to send a message of encouragement, and possibly a word of advice, to a few hundred thousand of your fellow men who have failed to make their mark in the world as successfully as you have done?

I have about completed a manuscript for a book to be entitled *How to Sell Your Services.* The main point made in the book is that service rendered is *cause* and the pay envelope is *effect;* and that the latter varies in proportion to the efficiency of the former. The book would be incomplete without a few words of advice from a few men who, like yourself, have come up from the bottom to enviable positions in the world. Therefore, if you will write me your views as to the most essential points to be borne in mind by those who are offering personal services for sale, I will pass your message on through my book. This will insure its getting into hands where it will do a world of good for a class of earnest people who are struggling to find their places in the world's work.

I know you are a busy man, Mr. ——, but please bear in mind that by simply calling in your secretary and dictating a brief letter you will be sending forth an important message to possibly half a million people. In money this will not be worth to you the two-cent stamp that you will place on the letter, but, if estimated from the viewpoint of the good it may do others who are less fortunate than yourself, it may be worth the difference between success and failure to many a worthy person who will read your message, believe in it and be guided by it.

Very cordially yours,

The letters say the same thing . . . BUT. The second letter bears a quiet but definite enthusiasm, and other factors of mind-to-mind suggestion which I shall explain. The second letter did the trick. Both letters went to eight or ten men who indeed had made their mark in the world and indeed were busy; men such as Henry Ford and Thomas R. Marshall, at that time Vice-President of the United States. The first letter brought no replies. The second letter, written after I had realized my mistake in writing the first one, brought back replies *from all to whom it was sent.* Some of those replies were masterpieces and served beyond my fondest hopes as valuable supplements to my book.

Now, the first letter is not entirely unenthusiastic. But about what? About my own self-interest. It is true that people often will respond to a request for a favor—but it is truer that they will respond when that favor will in some way benefit themselves or, in any event, benefit some third party or parties who seem worthy of such benefit.

Thus, if I were selling scuff-proof shoes (if there is such a shoe) by mail, I might send you a letter asking you to do me a favor by wearing a pair of my shoes for ten days and seeing if you could scuff them. You would do this at my risk —but you would see that if you wore them for ten days and could not scuff them, you would have done *yourself* a favor in discovering such wonderful shoes. Or, writing to a parent, I might ask him to do me a favor by taking the X Encyclopedia into his home for thirty days and seeing the wonderful effect on his children's marks in school . . . wherein the favor actually is done for a third party.

Now look at the closing paragraph of the first letter. What implication lies in: "Thanking you in advance for any consideration you may care to show me"? There is a strong undertone to the effect that the writer anticipates refusal! Well, why not refuse? This writer has advanced little reason for a busy man to take the trouble to write a letter. The recipient did read that those who purchased the book would welcome an opportunity, and so forth, but that hardly hits home, and it is buried in the body of the letter.

The entire letter reminds me of a salesman who once wanted me to subscribe to the *Saturday Evening Post*. He held up a copy of the magazine and said: "You wouldn't subscribe to the *Post* to help me out, would you?"

Well, I am the one who wrote the first letter. At least give me credit for having later improved it!

Now look at the second letter. Notice that the first paragraph asks a question—and the question can be answered in only one way. The question, moreover, is asked in such a way as to set up an entire viewpoint toward the matter at hand.

The reader is now conditioned. The second paragraph carries him along. It mentions me and my affairs briefly, but it is mostly taken up with a statement of fact that will make him nod his head and know I am talking his language. Even if he never has thought in terms of cause and effect, as regards pay envelopes, he will see the point as being clear and helpful.

The next paragraph might be said to contain flattery—or it might be said to contain nothing but the truth. The men to whom I wrote had truthfully come up from the bottom to enviable positions in the world. Having acknowledged this, I have taken the reader another step on the psychological journey which leads straight toward compliance with my request. Then comes the request itself—but couched in terms of service which the reader can render, because of his qualifications, to a third party who is worthy of his help.

The closing paragraph tactfully conceals the suggestion that the reader cannot refuse a request which costs him (in those days) a two-cent stamp, especially when he compares himself with those less fortunate. The letter hardly could be laid aside without a feeling of guilt in not replying. After all, the recipient has been appealed to in the name of those who *will read your message, believe in it and be guided by it.*

Not only did the letter bring me valuable answers, but also, with one exception, the men I addressed replied in person. The exception was Theodore Roosevelt, who replied over his secretary's signature. John Wanamaker and Frank A. Vanderlip wrote magnificent replies. William Jennings Bryan and Lord Northcliffe wrote fine letters, and so did others. Moreover, only four of the entire group knew me, so surely the majority of the group did not write to please *me;* they wrote to please themselves, knowing they were about to render a worthy service.

Let me say right here that ten smaller men might have thrown my letter into their wastebaskets. The really big men I have known were notable for their willingness to render service to others. That may be why they were really *big.*

Selling and auto-suggestion. You may not be in the business of selling—but you always sell *yourself.*

You may not believe you have any reason to persuade anybody else of anything—and yet, a good deal of your success and happiness depends upon achieving a reasonable acceptance of your ideas by others. Make a little analysis of your affairs and this will become evident.

You may not see any reason to persuade *yourself* of anything—but it is the very process of self-persuasion which brings on deep subconscious BELIEF and gives you command of life's Supreme Secret.

That is why I began this chapter by talking about enthusiasm. Enthusiasm is the great vehicle of persuasion, whether the persuasion is directed toward another or toward one's self.

Enthusiasm often amounts to automatic auto-suggestion.

Enthusiasm does not come from "nowhere," but once it arrives it seems absolutely to take hold of everything else.

For many years I did most of my writing at night. Naturally enough, I would grow tired after a few hours. One night I was engaged on a piece of work which filled me with enthusiasm. After a while I looked out the window, across Madison Square in New York City, and noticed the Metropolitan Life Insurance Company's tower. I saw a strange, silvery-gray reflection on the tower. The moon, I thought, but I had never seen the moon reflected in such an odd color. It was not a reflection of the moon, but of the sun! My enthusiasm had kept me working all night without fatigue. Moreover, the same enthusiasm kept me working all through the day and the next night as well, stopping only for some light food. After that, with my task completed, I felt normally tired.

Enthusiasm is a vital force that energizes all the forces of your mind and body. Make enthusiasm part of any auto-suggestion process; part of *you.*

Help other minds to vibrate in harmony with your own. We have spoken of "mind radio." I speak now of something which may be the same, or, if not, is surely akin. It is the contagiousness of enthusiasm; its almost magical power to "sell" ideas to others.

Anyone who has spoken to an audience has sensed, at times, that he is "getting over." For a few magical moments his enthusiasm catches every other mind in that room or hall, and what he says in those moments stays with his audience; they carry it home with them.

Enthusiasm, however carefully handled, is the indispensable tool of any salesman. It brings the two minds—the seller's mind and the buyer's mind—into *rapport,* or harmony. It allows the salesman to transmit to the buyer a feeling of need for the product, an appreciation of its worth, a willingness to part with money for the sake of making his life more full and happy—a service in which he sees what the product will do for him.

What you say is important, of course. No mere combination of words, however, can do the work it is supposed to do unless those words carry the spirit of conviction, belief, faith, *enthusiasm* which conveys all these.

In order to make this point clear, let us look at what happens when the opposite effect comes into play. Enthusiasm is perfectly positive; what happens when a negative thought is conveyed?

For instance: Once I went into an office of the Dictaphone Company to look at one of their dictating machines. Even their old model in those pre-plastic days looked useful, and I was inclined to agree with the salesman who pointed out how much it could help me in my work. I didn't buy, however. A stenographer at the salesman's side was transcribing one of his letters from an old-fashioned shorthand notebook! I was negatived right out the door.

Or, suppose you are selling anything at all; let's call it a widget. You sit down with a prospect and enthusiastically describe to him how happy the Joneses down the street are with your company's widget. The prospect demurs that he saw an advertisement for another company's widget and it looked like a better product.

At this point, you the salesman may be tempted to "pan" the other company's widget. Any salesman I have trained knows this is a mistake. You cause the prospect to *think negative*. You give him a sourness concerning the entire subject of widgets. The needing, wanting, buying mood is replaced by a fearful, let-me-alone mood; the mind-to-mind contact is lost.

Here is a principle to remember every time you talk to another person or write to him, and want to sway him your way. *When ideas reach us, either through suggestion or autosuggestion, they form themselves into two groups, negative and positive.* The negative impressions are stored all together in one memory-bank of the brain, and the positive impressions are stored in another memory-bank.

Now, suppose one of your words or expressions reaches another mind and is identified as *negative*. It opens the *negative* memory-bank and tends to stir up every negative memory of a similar nature, as though you had pulled on just one link of a chain but, inevitably, dragged all the other links along with it.

Suppose a stranger asks you to cash a check. If you never had a check "bounce" back at you, you may cash the check without worry. On the other hand, if you have lost money through cashing checks for strangers, another request will immediately bring up all the doubts and fears in your memory-bank.

That is why a small negative word, a small negative thought, even a small and not *logically* negative sight (maybe that girl with the notebook had only just been hired and had not had time to get used to the Dictaphone) is enough to set big negative gears in motion. That is why success of every kind depends on a positive point of view . . . within yourself and conveyed to others.

Enthusiasm is the one great emotion which automatically guarantees that your point of view will be positive!

Does that mean that you must never mention a negative matter, never admit you even know about illness, poverty, accidents, war? It does not mean this. We are well advised to keep negative trends out of our general conversation; to accentuate the positive, talk on the side we want to prevail. But reality is reality. Take it as it stands, when it is negative, and show a way out! Then your statement, to your own mind or to another's, carries *service,* points the way to a better life.

Perhaps the best illustration is one of the simplest. An old advertising slogan, still going strong, is: *Got a headache? Take X aspirin.* The negative condition is admitted; the positive, happy way out is immediately shown. It was not aspirin —of which I used to take plenty—but peace of mind which finally rid me of headaches, so I forbear to name the aspirin makers—but I cannot think of a better negative-into-positive transformation than is carried in those six words. Note the principle: *Is something wrong? Here's how to make it right.*

Good selling is honest selling.   I speak of selling in the sense of "selling" ideas which thereupon can be transmuted into reality.

I think back to that memorable moment when my new stepmother—whom I had been told to view with suspicion— took me under the chin and announced that Napoleon Hill was not a bad boy but a smart boy whose mind needed only to be guided. The honest conviction and tender enthusiasm of those words struck away all the falsehoods that had been fed into my young mind. From that moment on I looked for ways to improve myself; and when I looked, I found them.

Good selling is honest selling. *No person can afford to express, through thoughts or acts, that which is not in harmony with his own belief, for if he does he must pay by the loss of his ability to influence others.*

I know it is only when I speak from the heart that I can persuade an audience to accept my message.

At one time I might have reaped a considerable monetary advantage because I was known not to be allied with Big Business or with any political faction. I was approached by a representative of a Latin American government which the

United States at that time refused to recognize. He wanted me to visit his country, study its affairs, then write a series of articles recommending recognition.

I knew, however, I would not be able to write with enthusiasm and so with conviction. The reason was simple; I did not believe in the cause. I valued my integrity more than I valued the money I would have earned by dipping my pen into muddy ink.

Read this carefully: *If you compromise with your own conscience, you will weaken your conscience. Soon your conscience will fail to guide you and you never will have real wealth based on peace of mind.*

When I speak this way I give you full credit for being an adult, an intelligent person who uses his intelligence. You can see that such precepts, or the same precepts expressed better by Emerson or other great thinkers, are not merely "bright sayings." They are vital laws of life. They *work*.

Let me add one more precept to this very important matter of conveying ideas from your mind to another's:

You cannot afford to suggest to another person, by word of mouth or in writing, or through any act, that which you yourself do not believe.

Surely that is sufficiently straight-from-the-shoulder.

Where is your enthusiasm focused? When you train salesmen, you meet hundreds of men who may be described loosely as *salesman types*. They are first of all remarkable for their enthusiasm. Everything they say has punch behind it. Every action, even the action of sitting down, appears to proceed from some source of inward persuasive energy.

I have seen some of these men succeed splendidly—and I have seen others fail, and fail, and give up.

As Emerson said: "I learn the wisdom of St. Bernard, 'Nothing can work me damage except myself; the harm that I sustain I carry about with me, and never am a real sufferer but by my own fault.' "

The trouble with those enthusiastic men who failed was that they were all enthusiasm and not much else. The damage they sustained to their careers came from their fault in not backing their enthusiasm with plain, honest knowledge—with a willingness to go the extra mile—with a sincere interest in someone besides themselves.

Over and over I have seen such men sell a product because they simply overwhelmed the customer with the driving power of their personalities. They would come back to the office and boast about the money they had made that day. Then the orders would be canceled—or it would turn out the salesman had forced a purchase which simply could not be paid for, a fact which would have been apparent if the salesman had taken the trouble to listen and understand.

Enthusiasm needs a focus. The very existence of the focus makes you have something besides enthusiasm to offer.

In honest (and successful) selling of products or services, the focus is *the customer's best interests*. Do you wish the customer to accept, from your mind, the idea that he must own your product or service to make his life a better life? Very well:

Be prepared to answer his questions. Know your product or service inside-out. Know how he can apply the product to his own needs. (You can tell him enthusiastically; but enthusiasm is no substitute for information.)

If you make an appointment, be there on time. Recognize the customer as a man whose time is valuable. (Your enthusiastic story of why you were delayed is not an acceptable substitute.)

If you promise service, make sure the customer gets it. There is no customer like a repeat customer.

But this is not the course on salesmanship, so I forbear to give you a list which could cover a couple of pages. You see the principle: *Enthusiasm needs something solid behind it.*

How to focus your enthusiasm when you apply for a job. Any employer likes to talk to a man who applies enthusiastically for a position with his company. The employer knows that such enthusiasm can be carried over into the man's work, and this is a priceless ingredient.

But remember the law of negatives. By the time a man has given out a few dozen jobs, he has learned the inadvisability of letting anyone talk himself into a job when he has nothing to show but enthusiasm.

A large publishing company has found it advisable to test applicants' real willingness to work by showing them a time clock. It is explained that nothing is accepted as a substitute for starting work on time. This has a remarkable cooling-off effect on certain fast-talking applicants.

Enthusiasm does often put a man into a job, or get him bank credit, or make a sale when the person petitioned feels there is something behind the enthusiasm. The job-giver or the bank official may then be willing to forego some formal requirement. *Focused* enthusiasm, however, is truly irresistible. Let us see how to focus your enthusiasm when you apply for a job. We apply the process to getting a job, but you will see the many ways in which it can be applied to other situations.

Prepare a carefully written statement of reasons why you should have the job. You may not have been asked to prepare a resumé, but the written statement focuses the information in your own mind.

State your education. Name the schools you have attended, the courses you took. Tell, especially, of your education outside school, as in night courses. Enlarge on any kind of education which particularly prepared you to handle the job you seek.

State your experience. Give names of employers, dates of employment. Be sure to bring out experience which helps to qualify you in the eyes of the new, prospective employer.

Give references. Choose them with care. Choose them, if possible, in relation to what they can tell the prospective employer about you as *his* employee.

State the job you want. Sometimes, when applying for a job with a large company, you may not get the job you want because they are more interested in filling a vacancy somewhere else. Whether you take the other job is a matter of judgment. Nevertheless, focus your enthusiasm on a particular job when you are an applicant.

State your qualifications for that particular job. When you focus on the job you want, it may result in the company "finding" a vacancy where you want one to exist—or expanding the staff to include you.

Show you know a good deal about the prospective employer's business. Do not do this in a prying way, but show you know something about the market, sources of supply and customers, for instance, in his "trade." An hour or two with that trade's magazines—available in libraries—can teach you a great deal.

Offer to go to work on probation. Make it clear that this offer is based on your confidence in your ability to fill the needs of the job, your confidence that you will be permanently employed once you are given a chance to show you have what it takes. (Even this should be put into writing, whether required or not, to fix it in your mind.)

Now you are ready for your interview—ready to show enthusiasm that will carry over into your job. Let us see what you are ready to show in addition—or already have shown if you have presented a resumé.

You will show that the prospective employer will get a man with some kind of education. If you have taken night courses, he will see your education did not stop when you left school.

You will show you have "been around," and have learned from experience—the right kind of experience, from his point of view.

You will show you know what you want—which heavily implies you are focused enough to help him get what *he* wants.

You will show you can see a business as well as a job. This sets you up as a man who may be worth promoting.

You will show you want the job enough to risk being hired on probation—and, of course, you have faith in yourself.

Now, it is perfectly obvious that you want the job in order to earn money and further your other interests in life. But above and beyond this you have shown that it will be in the prospective employer's best interest to hire you. Don't forget that. You are selling yourself in terms of the other man's best interests. Look back on the several points we have mentioned and you will see that is what they add up to. Not primarily SEE WHAT A WONDERFUL PERSON I AM but SEE HOW MUCH I HAVE TO OFFER *YOU*.

The *plus* of enthusiasm lifts your words above the level of mere words and changes them into *belief* that you are the man for him!

Very well, you may say, but my written or spoken resumé does not add up to very much. My education ended in my early teens, I never took a night course in anything but playing the guitar . . . and so forth. You have latched onto the negative feeling that you have nothing to offer.

You have plenty to offer if you believe you have—and show it!

For example, take the matter of applying for a particular job. You may not be able to demonstrate that you already have the skills you need in order to hold that job—but you can show you know what the job requires. You can show you have oriented yourself to that job. This has a good effect on employers who are used to paying a man just for showing up every morning until he knows what he is doing. Also, where a company runs a training course, you can make it very clear that you are willing and eager to take the training course on your own time if necessary.

Take the matter of knowing something about the "line." You do not need education in order to read trade magazines. To be able to "talk a man's language" is surprisingly impressive. Any sensible interviewer takes school education with a grain of salt, anyway. With the exception of jobs which require the holding of particular degrees, he knows that many a high-grade job has been filled by a man without a high-grade education . . . that is, without a high-grade formal education.

Take the matter of offering to go to work on probation. Let the interviewer see *something* in you and this may swing the deal. Offer to put it in writing!

Have I left out such matters as wearing a clean shirt, a pressed suit and shined shoes? We are not all like a Barnes interviewing an Edison, so do not neglect such matters. I assure you, however, that a man's clothing often is not noticed when the *man* shines through.

Now step back for a broad look! Watch an artist painting a picture and you may see that every now and then he steps back to gain perspective on what he is doing. He needs a broad look.

I have told you how to apply for a job, in some detail, while reserving the "broad look." Take it now. Step back (not *backward*, which is something else!) and see yourself applying for a job and getting it. Fine. But why did you want that job?

There is the broad look which is highly essential—as essential as the composition an artist may sketch for his picture before he begins to paint.

As I said, it will be obvious to the prospective employer that you want the job in order to earn money and to further your other interests in life. To this end you will serve yourself by serving him. Very well; *will* that job further your other interests in life?

You can see the tie-in with that Chief Aim we spoke of a while ago. How will that job further your Chief Aim in life?

And more: How will that job help you fulfill yourself as a person who can work with joy, and so work with effectiveness, achievement and success? These questions are important.

Too many men are working in jobs they do not like. They will give you all kinds of reasons why they had to take such jobs, or why they are "stuck" in a job for family reasons and so forth. They may point to the money they make, and point to the various elaborate recreations this money makes possible. But they cannot point honestly to peace of mind and so they cannot point honestly to success.

Working hours grow shorter, but still any man who has a job spends a good portion of his life at that job. If that portion of your life is denatured and unhappy, it must have a degrading effect upon the rest of your hours and your days. In any event, why let any part of your life leave you unfulfilled when *it is not necessary?* Your work can be a grand fulfillment when you take perspective on it and see it is right before you plunge in.

Take these steps before you take a job. *Decide exactly what kind of job you want.* This in itself requires considerable self-analysis, and if you do not have a Chief Aim, you will have that fact drawn very strongly to your attention. Look back through this book. You are out to live your own life, to close the door on your past save as it may benefit you to live without fear, to win wealth of all kinds . . . all this through the power of your mind and, of course, through your own efforts. You are YOU and there is some kind of work that expresses YOU just as the writer expresses himself in writing, just as the craftsman expresses himself in the loving work of his hands. One of the things America does best is to offer a full range of occupations for its citizens' free choice. Everything in our economy helps you find the job you want; and if the particular job does not happen to exist, you can create it.

Choose the company or person for whom you wish to work. Again, there will be many to choose among. A company's record is generally public knowledge, worth a bit of trouble in finding out. An individual's record may also be public knowledge or may be judged in many ways, particularly by having known the individual. Find a company or person with whom you can co-operate. Find opportunity as well as a job.

If the person for whom you wish to work is yourself, give him the same kind of scrutiny!

Decide what you have to offer. Here a cold scrutiny may turn up empty spaces. You may first wish to fill them in, or you may, with perfect justice, find and be able to show ways you can compensate for anything that is lacking until experience fills it in. At this point, forget about a "job." Concentrate on what you can give that the other fellow wants. The Golden Rule will help you.

Present yourself and your qualifications to the person who can give you the job. And this is where we stood a moment ago, when we decided to step back and gain perspective. Knowing the job you want, preparing to get it and getting it are not separated processes—but they repay a broad, honest view, each in turn, and when they are backed by enthusiasm they overcome obstacles that stop other men.

Are you enthusiastic about yourself? Enthusiasm flows contagiously from one mind to another, and that is how we generally see it in action. Still—have you tried being enthusiastic about yourself? *With something behind it?*

It can be a good deal of fun, and very instructive, to take that step back from *yourself,* as though stepping out of your own skin, and then look at the person who bears your name.

When you can feel enthusiastic about that fellow—fine! Even if your enthusiasm is based only on his evident *promise,* his *belief,* his *willingness*—even if not much in the way of achievement has yet shown itself—fine! Tune in on his spirit. Weigh his qualities of *giving.* Observe how well he succeeds in doing justice to the powers God gave him. When you see he is a person you can appreciate—give him a cheer!

If you hear him making excuses for himself, shake your finger at him. Tell him that life reflects back the image we show to life. You cannot hold a mirror responsible for the image it reflects.

Does he understand? Does he see that *he* is the master of his fate?

Fine! Give him a cheer!

How about it?

Success requires no explanations. Failure permits no alibis.

CHECKING ON CHAPTER 15:

Enthusiasm and action
Enthusiasm transmits the impetus toward agreement and action, whether you sell a product, a service, or yourself. An enthusiastic letter caused big men to take time to do a favor, when the same words said without enthusiasm got no

results. Ask for a favor in the name of a third party, if possible, and in all events the person doing the favor should see a benefit to himself. Enthusiasm helps you do great amounts of work without fatigue.

Negative vs. positive

The mind has a memory-bank of negative memories and positive memories. When you offer a negative thought or action, you open the negative memory-bank and you may lose all your power to persuade. A negative can be effective when it is followed by a positive statement which does away with the negative feeling. Good selling is honest selling. If you compromise with your own conscience, you will weaken your conscience, it will cease to guide you and you cannot have peace of mind.

Enthusiasm needs a focus

Many an enthusiastic man loses out because there is not enough behind his enthusiasm. Honest and effective selling includes having knowledge with which to assist the customer—and a firm desire to be of service to him. The process of looking for a job is a good model for other "selling yourself" processes. It requires showing that you really want the job, a willingness to prepare yourself to handle the job, and, above all, concentration on the interests of your prospective employer.

The broad look

The affairs of life require a broad look to give you perspective. This includes evaluation of a job, before you take it, and relating it to your main goal. A good part of your life is spent in work, and you can, if you have the right job, be happy in your work and use your work to express yourself. Also you can take a broad look at yourself and see if you can feel enthusiastic about that person. See if he needs a warning—straighten him out if necessary—and encourage him with a hearty cheer.

1 6

It Is up to You to Live
the Life the Creator Gave You

*The Golden Rule can be applied all-out in a way that will
transform our economy for the better. When people are
helped to turn their ideas into the realities of business and
production, everyone in the United States will have more
wealth and happiness. Most of us believe in man-made gods
and man-made devils. Fear has no place in a well-lived life.
Put your faith, not in a Creator who bosses you but One
who makes it possible for you, as a human being, to win
success by your own efforts. Wealth now can be yours. Peace
of mind now can be yours at the same time, but remember,
this greatest of all wealth is known only to the person who
possesses it.*

"*HELP* me find peace of mind," the rich man said.

This was some years ago. A trip across the country was
not then a matter of six hours in a jet plane, but he had
come across the country to talk to me. "I have everything
money can buy," he said, "and I have lived long enough to
find out that money cannot buy peace of mind. Please help me
find it."

A good part of this chapter consists of what we discussed,
and which I shall give to you in a conversational manner.
First we went into everything this book has covered—I shall
omit that part—and then we branched out into what has been
for many years my most cherished project.

It is a business project—and a peace-of-mind project. It
could bring joy and prosperity to millions of men and
women, especially to those who need help in finding their
places in life. It would work hand in hand with our American
economy. It would not be a "make work" project, since it
would provide services whose need is proved. It would make
profit—that indispensable factor whose virtues have at length
been recognized even in the Soviet Union. It would be a business project that first of all would be a *human* project devoted to creating wealth through sharing wealth.

A job for a dedicated man. "Before I tell you about my project," I said to my visitor, "I want to make it clear that it will need a dedicated man to get it going. A man who has plenty of money, plenty of time, and plenty of executive know-how, for all these are needed to turn the idea into reality. He would have to be a man who would go to work with no thought of what *he* would get out of his efforts. I say he would have to have plenty of money because he might lose some of his money—and he would also have to be psychologically suited to accept this fact without losing the peace of mind the project would give him."

"Tell me more," said the man from California.

"Well then, what I have in mind is a nationwide organization to be called The Golden Rule Industries of America."

The visitor looked puzzled. "Where does the Golden Rule come in?"

"Suppose you had just about enough money to live on, or even less, but you had a sound business idea you wanted to develop. What would you like someone to do unto you?"

"I surely would like someone to come along and give me capital!"

"That's what I meant. The Golden Rule Industries of America would devote itself to finding people who have sound business ideas, capitalizing those ideas and helping those people get started in their businesses. Then it would follow up with business management advice, as might be necessary. It would take care of the two major factors which make businesses fail—lack of capital and unsound management. It would fill those needs for honest people who want to get ahead but cannot fill those needs for themselves."

My visitor looked thoughtful. "There must be thousands of such cases."

"I am sure there are. Let me tell you of a few I know to exist.

"There is a young woman who is clever at designing. She wants to design and manufacture women's garments for the retail trade. Golden Rule Industries could set her up in business, make sure she got started on the right foot, and watch her grow. Eventually she would give employment to hundreds of people. Bear in mind that she, and every other person whom Golden Rule Industries aids with capital and business advice, will be a person who applies the Golden Rule to others, employees in particular. Golden Rule means that too."

"I see."

"A mechanic has built a model of an automobile which can be manufactured and sold for one thousand dollars. It will travel fifty miles to the gallon, will carry three people—ideal for the small family—and is so simple of design that its upkeep will be very small. Golden Rule Industries could set up this man in a small shop and let him expand as his business justifies. Undoubtedly the entire automobile industry would respond with better cars at lower prices.

"A bright high school boy builds excellent model airplanes. He wants to develop his skill into a national business and employ other high school boys, after school, as his staff. Golden Rule Industries could help this youth and his friends start a business and develop it."

"That would be a wonderful head start toward a productive life!" my visitor exclaimed.

"It certainly would. I have in mind, too, a certain poor farmer. I have sympathy with poor farmers. This man wants to introduce the growing of a certain fiber plant now being developed in Africa, which can be grown in our southern states. There is an undoubted future in this, and Golden Rule Industries could provide this man with the land, machines and employees he needs.

"A young author has written a very creditable novel based on life in the mountains of Tennessee. He has not been able to get it published, but Golden Rule Industries could take it over for him and capitalize its publication if need be.

"A young lady stenographer has invented a chair so designed that it moves back and forth with the movement of the body and adjusts itself to fit the curvature of the back. This is a great idea. It will lessen fatigue, improve work, and should have a tremendous market. It would be a real pay deal for Golden Rule Industries."

"Where do these ideas come from?" my visitor wanted to know.

"Many of them represent cases I have handled for my clients. In my endeavors to help people stand on their own feet, I became aware of the many who have good ideas and plenty of ability, and need only capital and good management advice in order to get started. Now let me tell you of a rather special area in which Golden Rule Industries could do a world of good.

"In every prison there are many well-educated men capable of conducting business and educational courses for the benefit of the other inmates. This could result in these men being ready, willing and able to lead honest, useful lives when they are freed. A group of businessmen tried out this plan in the Ohio State Penitentiary, and it worked like a charm. The International Correspondence Schools contributed more than thirty-five thousand dollars worth of textbooks. The plan could be expanded greatly—and it is society that would profit. *I have personally appropriated this idea and it is creating miracles of rehabilitation in many prisons.*

"A mechanic has made a model of a prefabricated dwelling made of aluminum sections. Any able man with a couple of helpers can set up the walls and roof in a day's time and start living in the house with his family while he finishes the interior. There are similar houses on the market, but this one also can be taken down as easily as it is put up, and moved to another location, without damage to its components."

"There's profit in that idea," said the man from California.

"Yes, and I have a number of other ideas just as profitable. Many of them need only some way to get started despite the opposition of established interests who see only that their business would be affected, without seeing the benefit to the economy at large. Now let us digress from the business ideas themselves and look at Golden Rule Industries' general policy.

"Golden Rule Industries should be developed with the idea that it will pay a profit in itself as it goes along. I would, therefore, incorporate the idea of profit-sharing. Each enterprise would pay back to the Industries 10 per cent of its net earnings. Half of this amount would go to the Industries for the use of the capital and the business management. The other 5 per cent would be used as a payment on the original investment. When the investment was fully repaid, each enterprise would pay the Industries 5 per cent of its net earnings thereafter in return for management services and other services which might be necessary.

"You can see that this policy would create a revolving fund which could be used over and over to help more and more enterprises get started. But no enterprise would be bound forever to the Industries. After it paid back its capitalization, it could leave the Industries. We wouldn't want a monopoly. But I am quite sure that even if an enterprise left the Industries, it would continue on the Golden Rule basis of sharing the wealth it creates with its own employees, for it would be apparent by then that this is the way to make a business and its people prosper."

My visitor had arrived in my office with a woebegone face. Now he was vibrant and looked ten years younger. "That's great!" he exclaimed. "And I can see that one business after another would want to come in and join hands in such an undertaking. Why, it's the best way I ever heard of to prevent strikes and other labor troubles."

"I believe it would create harmony and peace of mind where those qualities are badly needed," I said. "And it would create all-important self-respect in giving people an opportunity to help themselves instead of feeding at the public trough at the expense of others. The plan would have a sweeping effect on our entire economy.

"Moreover, The Golden Rule Industries of America should operate its own radio and TV station. There would be no commercials. All the broadcasting time would be devoted to teaching people, in their own homes, all the essentials of personal achievement. People would find out at last that success is an inward matter which each of us must build within himself, rather than waiting for someone to hand him what he needs. We will have a nation that does not look for 'isms' to take care of it—a nation of people who will work hard to create wealth, in the happy confidence that they will receive a good share."

"Great heavens, man!" my visitor broke in. "You are talking about the millennium."

"No," I said, "I am presenting a practical plan to save this nation from destruction by the greedy who have not yet learned the necessity—and the virtue—of sharing riches.

"Golden Rule Industries would go beyond the transformation of industry in improving this land of ours. It would run a school for training men and women for public office—everything from dog-catcher to President. I hope this school eventually would attain such status as to make sure the voters may select public servants on the basis of their ability—instead of on their astuteness in swinging votes with the application of suitable amounts of money."

"Amen, amen!" said my visitor.

"Along with this school of political economy there would be a citizens' committee of men and women who are capable of examining and grading all candidates for public office. The people would once again come into full possession of their government."

"Great! But don't you think there would be a great deal of opposition to your plan—both industry-wise and government-wise? After all, you shut out a lot of nice, juicy opportunities for exploitation."

"I'd expect opposition," I replied. "Opposition is a healthy circumstance. It makes one either prove the soundness of his plan or discover its weaknesses. I'd expect to make adjustments as I went along.

"There are other features I have in mind for Golden Rule Industries which might provoke even more opposition. The power of the Industries' centralized buying would be such as to cause howls from those who think only of profit. When we helped our members buy homes of their own—as I believe should be done—there'd be screams of *socialism*—from other interests.

"When we helped Industries' members, including their employees, with such services as may be given by physicians, dentists, attorneys, even beauticians—and made sure they received the finest service at the lowest possible fees—the screams would rise to a crescendo. In the end, however, it would be recognized that the plan represents democracy operating on the highest possible scale of efficiency. All men who wish to live and let live will welcome this plan that adds so much to *living*. Our strength would lie in the fact that such people vastly outnumber the people who want to dominate and exploit others."

My visitor thought a moment. "And this would begin with finding people who have sound business ideas, and getting them into action."

"That is right. It would bring worthy beliefs of the human mind onto the plane of worthy achievement. The more we have in the world of this process, the better world we build."

My visitor sat a while. At last he arose and laid some large bills on my desk.

"I want you to have this honorarium in return for the help you have given me. I am going to swing into action with a new and better philosophy of life than any I ever have known in the past. I do not know if I am the man with the money, the time, the philosophy and the business experience to initiate Golden Rule Industries. But I see now what life can be when men co-operate in the production of goods and services for each other. I see why I made money but never found peace of mind. I see what has been lacking in my life, and I feel better, Dr. Hill. Yes, sir, I feel better than I have felt in years. You have done more for me than a number of doctors have been able to do."

My visitor never returned. Golden Rule Industries still re-mains a dream—yet, in part, it is a dream I see coming true. Our economy grows less and less the hunting ground of the industrial pirate. It is only here and there that I see the devel-opment of co-operation, but I do see that groundswell of *sharing the wealth,* and it is this philosophy, based on the Golden Rule, which will keep America great; not the practice of handing out government doles to people who have done nothing to deserve them.

Peace of mind vs. man-made gods and man-made devils.   We are approaching the end of this book. You see by now that the power of firm, free belief comes with an untrammeled mind: the power to turn what the human mind believes into what the human mind achieves rarely can be found by a man who is hemmed in with fear and misdirection.

There are some exceptions. You can see men in business still making money while they harm others in making it, but this type is nowhere nearly as prevalent as it was fifty years ago.

You can see exceptions elsewhere, too. Unfortunately, the human mind is capable of believing in man-made images which it sets up as Great Truths. This belief can lead to so-called achievement on its own plane; for instance, the achiev-ing of great societies known as religions which teach that you will fry in Hell if you do not believe certain things.

I write here for strong people—for people who realize that the most cherished beliefs nevertheless can be wrong in that they hinder the development of the human spirit. They claim to develop that spirit—but they develop it as much as a man's view of the world would be developed if he walked in a narrow alley between two high walls all his life.

Regardless of your emotions right now, surely you have been impressed by the fact that the Creator provided you with control over your own power of thought and made it impossible for any other person to rob you of this privilege —unless you let him.

In my decades of research into the roots of personal achieve-ment, I came across a book called *Catalogue of the Gods.* This book gave a brief description of each of the THIRTY THOUSAND man-made gods which men have worshiped since the beginning of civilization. Yes, THIRTY THOU-SAND.

These sacred objects ranged all the way from the common

angle-worm to the sun which warms our earth. They included almost every conceivable object between these two extremes, such as fish, snakes, tigers, cows, birds, rivers, oceans, and the genital organs of man.

Who made these objects into gods? Man himself. Which ones were authentic gods? Ask any worshiper and he would tell you, and eventually you would have a list of thirty thousand authentic gods, one just as authentic as another.

If I undertook to describe the miseries of mankind which can be laid at the feet (if they had feet) of those thirty thousand gods, and the fears and miseries and failures they have inspired in the minds of men, I would need more than one lifetime in which to do the job properly.

Man made a great step forward in his own behalf when he began to see a Creator, not gods, and removed this Creator from any connection with earthly objects. The ancient Hebrews performed this service for man. (One of the Egyptian kings appears to have come to the same conclusion some centuries before they did, but his priests saw to it that he died young.)

Yet what have we done with this belief? My own case is the one I know best. Until my father married the woman who saved me, the family in which I grew up was dominated by fear. It contributed to the support of an organization dedicated to maintaining that fear; it is known as the Hard-shell Baptists. A preacher could visit our community only once a month, but on those occasions I was forced to listen to four or five hours of preachment. We were thundered at with pictures of a Hell waiting to receive us with fire and brimstone, and at times I could smell the stuff burning.

One night when I was seven or eight I dreamed I was down there chained to an iron post. My body was almost covered with a great pile of fresh brimstone. Here came Satan, swishing his tail, and with an evil grin he set fire to the brimstone. I awoke screaming. One needs no formal knowledge of psychology to know this is not good for any child. But when I tried to stay away from the church that gave me dreadful nightmares, I was thrashed without mercy.

The Creator I know. One day I overheard my stepmother say to my father: "The only real devil that exists in this or any other world is the man whose business is that of making devils." I accepted this statement instantly and never have departed from it.

I have taken pains to put into this book the fact that my father's prayers seemed to have focused powers of healing beyond medicine, which saved my life when I had typhoid fever. That was his time of *faith*, not fear.

In denying that I have anything to fear, I also deny that anyone has knowledge enough to tell me anything definite about the spirit that rules the universe.

A theologian might say—although these days they are becoming wary of saying it: "Somewhere up there is Heaven, where God dwells, and all His *acceptable* children go there when they leave their earthly bodies, and gather around Him."

A scientist might say: "I have turned my telescope outward into space in all directions. I have looked into space for distances equivalent to millions of light-years, but nowhere do I see the slightest trace of anything resembling Heaven."

The Creator whom I know is not separated from me by light-years nor by any other distance. I see evidence of His existence in every blade of grass, every flower, every tree, every creature on this earth, in the order of the stars and the plants which float out there in space, in the electrons and protons of matter, and most especially in the marvelous working principles of the human mind and the body within which it operates.

If you would rather speak of a force or a presence or a limitless intelligence rather than a Creator, it is the same. It is there. Is it affected by our worship? I doubt it. Can we sometimes attune ourselves so that we receive help from universal vibrations? This, I believe, is almost certainly true.

I do not even attempt to guess the over-all purpose or plan behind the universe. So far as I can tell, there is no plan for man except to come into this world, live a little while, and go. While he lives he is given the opportunity to make himself and his fellow men better beings, perhaps a more advanced form of man, as Lecomte du Noüy suggests. But—his ultimate purpose? I do not think anyone knows more about that than I know, and I know nothing about it.

Your greatness is here and now. Your happiness is here and now. Here are some of the factors which create peace of mind. They are involved in creating money-wealth as well; but let us set that aside for the time being. Here are some peace-of-mind factors; read them carefully; note that you have met them in this book, in one form or another, and *note* *that you have heard about them from other sources as well.*

You must come to realize you have a conscience which will guide you, and stay on good terms with your conscience so it will guide you well.

You must take possession of your own mind, do your own thinking, live your own life.

You must keep yourself so busy living your own life that you will not be tempted to interfere in the lives of others.

You must learn to free your life of unnecessary encumbrances, both material and mental.

You must establish harmony in your own home and harmony with those among whom you work.

You must share your blessings with others, and do this wholeheartedly.

You must look at the realities of life as they are, not as you wish them to be, and properly evaluate them.

You must help others to find and develop their own powers to make themselves what they want to be.

Now, I did not invent these ways of winning peace of mind. They were known of old. They are the ways which have proved themselves right, strong and eternal. If I have made these ways more clear to you, and if I have given you practical ways in which to apply them, well and good; but the wisdom behind them is the gathered wisdom of mankind.

And so you have heard before of these peace-of-mind factors. Perhaps they were told to you as *ways to help yourself get to Heaven.* This belief leaves you up against a blank wall. I give them to you as representative of *the tried and true methods which help you live a healthier, wealthier, better life, here, on this earth, now.* Is this not sufficient?

The Creator in your life.   You have seen that I do not deny the concept of a Creator as an eternal and all-pervading intelligence, or cosmic force. But the Creator with whom I made my peace many years ago does not require me to be afraid of Him; nor does He offer Himself to me merely through the intervention of any particular religion.

My Creator gave me His greatest blessing when He made me human.

He gave me the power to choose between good and bad, and made my concept as wide as all the affairs of the world and all its people. He set me at large upon the world to learn that my good deeds are rewarded in kind, and my bad deeds are just as inexorably made to draw penalties according to their nature. He gave me a mind beyond the mind of any other of His creatures, and He made me free to use my mind as only a human being can use his mind-power.

I can pray, and in constructive prayer that does not amount to begging for special favors. I can find faith which vastly enlarges my powers. Yet always I know I am the master of my fate, I am the captain of my soul, for so my Creator made me, and so I need not call upon Him constantly for guidance. Have you ever noticed that *the one who does the praying very often has a large part in the answering of the prayer?* I allow for the prayer that goes Beyond; but I believe that many a prayer stays within the one who prays and strengthens him in his realization of his own human abilities.

The Creator's place in your life is to help you be more triumphantly your own master. The Creator made you a creature who can think for himself, be himself, believe in what he wishes to accomplish, and mightily achieve! Do less than this and you cannot possibly fulfill yourself in all your glorious humanity.

The mind of man is filled with powers to be used, not to be neglected. These powers, these blessings, either are used —and the benefits of their use shared with others—or you incur penalties for not using them.

If you needed a house, and knew how to build a house, and had all the materials you needed for building a house, and had a lot on which to build a house, and yet neglected to build a house—then you would understand your penalty as you sat exposed in the rain and the snow.

Too many of us do not use our power to gather in the wealth and peace of mind which is available all around us. Then we are penalized by poverty, by misery, by worry and ill health—and we blame everyone but ourselves.

Anything the human mind can believe, the human mind can achieve.

Believe in poverty and you will be poor.

Believe in wealth and you will be rich.

Believe in love and you will have love.

Believe in health and you will be healthy.

You have seen what lies behind these statements. It would be well to read this book again and refresh your understanding. No book can give you all its wealth at the first reading. Make friends with this book, read it again, put it away for a while, take it out and read it once more, and you will read much between the lines—and much that applies to *you.*

I have shared with you what may be merely words, or great wealth and contentment—depending on how you use them. I am glad I cannot force you to use the knowledge I have given you. I am glad it is up to you to improve your own life.

I leave you now with no great ceremony.

Remember: There is no good thing in the world that is not available to you if you sufficiently desire it.

And remember: No matter what others may see of your possessions after you make a great deal of money . . . no matter how they may respect your offices and influence and talents . . . no matter how much they may admire your generosity, your kindliness, your willingness to live and let live . . . you yourself are the only one who can hold and enjoy your greatest treasure, peace of mind.

Cherish your visions and your dreams. They are the children of your soul, the blueprints of your ultimate achievements.

Checking on GROW RICH!—WITH PEACE OF MIND:

Know your own mind—live your own life
You can make your life what you want it to be—but it must be your own life. We all have a great effect upon each other, but the dream you make into solid reality is *your* dream. Let your effect on others show itself in helping them realize their own powers in finding their own high destiny. Setting a time limit for a specific accomplishment is a vast aid in attaining your goal despite any obstacles. Go back and read how to set up spiritual defenses within your mind, so that your thoughts remain your own, attuned to great powers.

Close the doors on your past
Look to the past only for what it taught you. Many great men have histories of failure, but they never were held back by the spiritual chains of old mistakes. We need wealth for peace of mind, since the poverty-stricken also are stricken with insecurity and worry; but the trappings of wealth can rob you of peace when they become an end in themselves. The job that builds your future is the job to which you give the fullest measure. Where you start never matters so much

as where you are going. Start by going the extra mile. Go back and read what it means to go the extra mile.

The basic mental attitude that brings wealth and peace of mind

Make sure your mind says YES to life. A positive mental attitude keeps your mind on your goal and shows you the road to your goal. We are governed by nine basic motives, seven of which are connected strongly to peace of mind. When you rise above the temptation to be dishonest, you do more for your peace of mind than any money can, and you set up positive emotion-habits which take root in everything you do. A positive mental attitude often is the secret of "genius" mind-power. Go back and read how to set up ten Princes of Guidance to keep negative influences out of your mind.

When you are free of fear, you are free to live

Fear is like prayer in reverse; it appeals to negative forces which hurt us, instead of to positive forces which help and sustain us. The fear of poverty brings poverty; the fear of criticism cripples initiative. To free yourself of the fear of adversity, remember that every adversity carries the seed of an equivalent or greater benefit. Caution under dangerous circumstances is advisable, but search your fears and you will see that invariably they are self-made, a man-made devil. Self-confident faith in yourself is an indispensable ingredient for good living. Go back and check the complete list of fears which bring forth corresponding damaging reality—if your mind allows.

Will you master money—or will it master you?

You may lose peace of mind by pursuing money too anxiously. The man who makes a big splash may be the man who has gone overboard. "Enough" money is a relative sum. When you feel you will be satisfied with enough for solid comfort and security, and some luxuries, you often attain more. Work is a human necessity, and anyone who gets his money without work—as is the case with many rich men's sons—has been robbed of his birthright of self-reliance. Some of the money you make should stay with you, for thrift gives many benefits besides money in the bank. Go back and read the basic steps that can build your income and can be applied to almost any circumstances.

The blessed art of sharing your riches
Wealth that is shared creates more wealth. The helping hand
you give another can repay you many-fold. Millionaires today realize that when wealth is distributed it creates opportunities. Discontented workers become contented, ambitious
workers when they learn the Science of Personal Achievement. When you share the wealth in your own home, you
create peace of mind in a most important area of your life.
The three basic motives of love, sex and money are said to
rule the world. When you practice sharing you will never
have to ask: "What wealth have I to share?" Go back and
read the basic ways of sharing; they are a road to wealth.

How to develop your own healthy ego
Ego is the "self-assertive tendency of man." It can transcend
many an obstacle, even get a man a great job when he looks
like a tramp. Ask yourself certain questions concerning your
childhood, and you may find what is hurting your ego and
be able to overcome this long-ago influence. A healthy ego
makes you more receptive to the influences which guide you
from a region beyond the power of our five senses to know.
A salesman sells through his ego. When the ego is strong,
it attracts success. When the ego is weak, it can be strengthened. Go back and read how men found their own ego-
boosters, and learn how to find your own.

How to transmute sex emotion into achievement power
Unlike other mammals, man's sexual drive is always with
him. This drive can be wasted, or it can be transmuted into
sparkling energy which shows in everything a man does.
Like ego, sexual energy can help you rise above outward
appearances. Many a man uses his energy in the wrong
direction, but performs miracles of achievement when he
puts himself on the right path. You can make sure you are
the beneficiary of your sexual drive—not its victim. Sexual
energy can invigorate the subconscious mind's ability to form
new patterns out of known facts and thus come up with new
inventions and new opportunities. Go back and read about
the connection between experience and intuition. See what
intuition can do for you.

To succeed in life, succeed in being yourself
Let nothing be bigger in your life than being yourself. Many
a man has been bribed away from the job in which he ful-
filled himself and now has riches but no peace of mind.

You can help others without interfering with their possession of themselves; do not expect other people to meet your idea of "perfect." Practice self-control as a means of being your best self, and you will not suffer the results of anger and animosity. Your mind is your only master. Be sure to live your life exactly as you wish to live it; for a while every day do only what pleases you. Be patient in your search for peace of mind; that great quality is built out of many days of progress. Go back and read about the definite, forceful ways you can practice being yourself.

The Master Mind group; a power beyond science

A great deal of knowledge in other minds can be transferred to your own. You can get "in tune" with a mind sympathetic to yours and double your mind-power. Modern discoveries tie in with older theories as to why one mind should be able to communicate with another's, and one day we may be able to tune in one mind to another just as today we tune in radio stations. When you see your problems through other eyes, you often see the solution of your problems. Form a Master Mind group of friends who share your interests, and all can reap great benefit from the spoken and unspoken thoughts you exchange. Go back and read the rules to follow for a successful, profitable Master Mind group.

Win mighty aid from the eternal Law of Compensation

Emerson's essay on Compensation is *must* reading for people who want understanding and wealth. When you give of yourself, the Law of Compensation assures a reward will come back to you, although it may take a long time. You will be compensated by punishment for any wrong done. Unseen, silent forces influence us constantly. The tendency to envy others and take advantage of others will disappear when you understand the Law of Compensation. Philosophy sometimes is "out of this world," but it can be practical and positive. The true philosopher is proof against much that upsets and defeats other men. Go back and read everything quoted from Emerson.

You are very important—for a little while

Nobody builds his success through his own efforts alone. Self-importance hurts the conscience, but true perspective on yourself aids peace of mind. Ultimately, nothing matters. This world matters now, however, and accounts are balanced in this world before you leave it. In the Jungle of Life there are unseen watchers. A great reservoir of wisdom is kept for the benefit of mankind, and those who conquer the enemies of man come through the jungle unharmed and are ready to take the next step upward. Your life-experience can and should qualify you for wealth and peace of mind to enjoy for yourself and to share with others. Go back and read the list of the enemies of man; see how many you met today.

Not too much, not too little

Wealth comes to the man who sees and uses his potential for wealth. Potential all around you is not wealth till you bring wealth into being. Grabbing for wealth may cause you to lose that wealth. Do not limit what you give, only what you take. The Golden Rule, ancient in the time of Jesus, remains a true guide. Give the other fellow what he needs and you do justice to the Golden Rule. You can notice the effect on character when a person never has allowed the Golden Rule to enter his life. A man's services generally are worth what he is paid for them, and a man has a way of putting a price on himself. The Golden Rule cannot be cheated. Go back and read and remember the Golden Rule in the form that really makes it work.

The magic power of belief

Anything the human mind can believe, the human mind can achieve; this is the Supreme Secret. A wish occurs on the surface of the mind; a true belief becomes part of you. Decide on the belief you want, send it down into your subconscious mind, and your subconscious will thereafter see to it that you act on the belief. Nobody knows the limit of the power of belief. It even effects physical changes in the body. The human mind now is transforming humanity and the world in which man lives. You can take your part in this mighty process by using every bit of your human power. Go back and read how to implant belief in your subconscious mind through the art of auto-suggestion.

Enthusiasm—and something more

What you say without enthusiasm may get no results, while the same thing, said with enthusiasm, wins 100 per cent achievement. Enthusiasm helps in selling anything, but it cannot make up for lack of honesty and a true regard for the customer's best interests. Enthusiasm opens vast reserves of energy. Any negative thought or action interferes with the process of selling, but a negative can be transmuted into a positive. Focus your enthusiasms toward a goal, and know that if your goal is not honest you cannot feel and use the magic of enthusiasm. Take a broad look at yourself and see if you are a person who arouses enthusiasm in yourself. Go back and read the formula that can get you the job you want.

It is up to you to live the life the Creator gave you

A rich man who could not find peace of mind found out a way to run business that could give peace of mind to millions and wealth as well. It is the Golden Rule applied to our economy. Too many of us are reared according to rules which require us to live in fear, and believe in a Creator who must be placated. Man has made thirty thousand gods; can they all be authentic? A few of the rules for peace of mind may sound like rules you learned for going to Heaven, but they refer to happiness here and now—happiness you can attain for yourself. The mind of man is filled with powers to be used, not neglected.

Think awhile. See what part of this book comes most strongly to your memory. Go back and read that part very carefully. You have kept it in your subconscious; therefore it must have, somewhere in it, a message of special importance to YOU.